EDUCATION TRENDS IN PERSPECTIVE

ANALYSIS OF THE WORLD EDUCATION INDICATORS

2005 Edition

UNESCO INSTITUTE FOR STATISTICS

ORGANISATION FOR ECONOMIC CO-OPERATION AND DEVELOPMENT

WORLD EDUCATION INDICATORS PROGRAMME

UNESCO

The constitution of the United Nations Educational, Scientific and Cultural Organization (UNESCO) was adopted by 20 countries at the London Conference in November 1945 and entered into effect on November 4, 1946. The Organization currently has 191 Member States and six Associate Members.

The main objective of UNESCO is to contribute to peace and security in the world by promoting collaboration among nations through education, science, culture and communication in order to foster universal respect for justice, the rule of law, and the human rights and fundamental freedoms that are affirmed for the peoples of the world, without distinction of race, sex, language or religion, by the Charter of the United Nations.

To fulfill its mandate, UNESCO performs five principal functions: 1) prospective studies on education, science, culture and communication for tomorrow's world; 2) the advancement, transfer and sharing of knowledge through research, training and teaching activities; 3) standard-setting actions for the preparation and adoption of internal instruments and statutory recommendations; 4) expertise through technical co-operation to Member States for their development policies and projects; and 5) the exchange of specialized information.

UNESCO is headquartered in Paris, France.

The UNESCO Institute for Statistics

The UNESCO Institute for Statistics (UIS) is the statistical office of UNESCO and is the UN depository for global statistics in the fields of education, science and technology, culture and communication.

UIS was established in 1999. It was created to improve UNESCO's statistical programme and to develop and deliver the timely, accurate and policy-relevant statistics needed in today's increasingly complex and rapidly changing social, political and economic environments.

UIS is based in Montreal, Canada.

Organisation for Economic Co-operation and Development

The OECD is a unique forum where the governments of 30 democracies work together to address the economic, social and environmental challenges of globalisation. The OECD is also at the forefront of efforts to understand and to help governments respond to new developments and concerns, such as corporate governance, the information economy and the challenges of an ageing population. The Organisation provides a setting where governments can compare policy experiences, seek answers to common problems, identify good practice and work to co-ordinate domestic and international policies.

The OECD member countries are: Australia, Austria, Belgium, Canada, the Czech Republic, Denmark, Finland, France, Germany, Greece, Hungary, Iceland, Ireland, Italy, Japan, Korea, Luxembourg, Mexico, the Netherlands, New Zealand, Norway, Poland, Portugal, the Slovak Republic, Spain, Sweden, Switzerland, Turkey, the United Kingdom and the United States. The Commission of the European Communities takes part in the work of the OECD.

OECD Publishing disseminates widely the results of the Organisation's statistics gathering and research on economic, social and environmental issues, as well as the conventions, guidelines and standards agreed by its members.

Photo credit: Panos Publications Ltd.

TABLE OF CONTENTS

■ **Foreword**.. 5

■ **Reader's Guide** 7

■ **Chapter 1: TRENDS IN EDUCATION PARTICIPATION AND OUTPUTS** 11
Introduction... 12
  1. Educational attainment: levels and trends 13
  2. Patterns in school life expectancy.................................... 21
  3. Demographic contexts and education systems............................ 25
  4. Changing patterns of educational participation........................ 29
  References... 49

■ **Chapter 2: RESPONDING TO INCREASED PARTICIPATION: TRENDS
IN RESOURCES INVESTED IN EDUCATION** 51
Introduction 52
  1. Trends in public and private expenditure: the importance of economic
     and social developments... 55
  2. Responding to increased demand: trade-offs in infrastructure investments
     and human resources in education.................................... 84
  References.. 107

■ **Chapter 3: COUNTRY PROFILES** 109
Argentina.. 110
Brazil... 112
Chile 114
China.. 116
Egypt.. 118
India.. 120
Indonesia 122
Jamaica.. 124
Jordan... 126
Malaysia 128
Paraguay 130
Peru 132
Philippines.. 134
Russian Federation 136
Sri Lanka.. 138
Thailand 140
Tunisia.. 142
Uruguay.. 144
Zimbabwe... 146

■ **Annexes** 149
  A1.   General notes... 150
  A2.   Definitions, methods and technical notes............................ 154
  A3.   Cross-reference between data tables and technical notes 168
  A4.   Data tables 171
  A5a. International Standard Classification of Education (ISCED97)......... 205
  A5b. Allocation of national education programmes to ISCED97.............. 208

FOREWORD

The world has changed markedly in the eight years covered by this report, with greater global interdependence and competition and dramatic short-term changes in the economic fortunes of nations. At the same time there has been strong growth in the demand for learning opportunities, from early childhood programmes to advanced tertiary-level studies, as individuals and societies recognise the important long-term benefits of education.

In searching for effective approaches to promoting and managing growth in education systems, governments are increasingly looking internationally, using cross-nationally comparable indicators to benchmark national education systems and examining policy outcomes in other countries.

In many countries, this international perspective has been reflected by efforts to strengthen the collection and reporting of comparative statistics and indicators on education. Building on the OECD Indicators of Education Systems (INES) programme, 11 countries, together with UNESCO and the OECD and with the financial support of the World Bank, launched the World Education Indicators programme (WEI) in 1997. The original group of participants consisted of Argentina, Brazil, Chile, China, India, Indonesia, Jordan, Malaysia, the Philippines, the Russian Federation and Thailand. In addition to the original 11 countries, eight new countries, Egypt, Jamaica, Paraguay, Peru, Sri Lanka, Tunisia, Uruguay and Zimbabwe, subsequently joined the programme.

The objectives of the WEI programme are to: explore education indicator methodologies; reach consensus on a set of common policy concerns amenable to cross-national comparison and agree upon a set of key indicators that reflect these concerns; review methods and data collection instruments needed to develop these measures; and set the direction for further developmental work and analysis beyond this initial set of indicators.

This report marks the eighth year of this on-going collaborative effort. During this time, participating countries have advanced the conceptual and developmental work in many different ways. They have applied the WEI data collection instruments and methodology at the national level. In collaboration with the OECD and UNESCO, they have co-operated in national, regional and international meetings of experts, and worked jointly on the development of the indicators, in areas such as governance, teachers and financial investments in education.

This report is the fourth in a series that analyses indicators on key education policy issues, bringing together data from participating countries with comparable data from OECD countries. It focuses on trends in education between 1995 and 2003, identifying which countries have made progress and the contextual and policy factors that have contributed to the different educational outcomes.

It explores how school-age populations and participation and graduation rates in education, especially at secondary and tertiary levels, have changed since 1995 and it looks at the factors that act as constraints to growth. It links changes in demand for education with trends in investments of human and financial resources in education and how they relate to the quantity and quality of educational provision. It looks beyond public education systems and discusses change in terms of the range of public and private actors that are involved in the finance and governance of education.

Despite the considerable progress that has been achieved in the first eight years of the WEI programme, further progress will be needed. For example, while it has been possible to compare countries in terms of the inputs into education – students, teachers and spending patterns – comparative information on the quality of education in WEI countries is only beginning to emerge. The WEI Survey of Primary Schools (WEI-SPS) serves as an example of efforts to move from the use and interpretation of nationally-aggregated data to information at the school- and teacher-level to better understand what makes effective schools and educational systems. Thus participating WEI countries, together with UNESCO and the OECD, continue to build upon the past successes of the project and to set new directions in indicator development and robust statistical analyses that can assist governments in bringing about improved schooling and preparing young people to confidently enter a changing world.

Michael Millward
Director, a.i.
UNESCO Institute for Statistics

Barry McGaw
Director for Education
OECD

Ruth Kagia
Education Director
Human Development Network
The World Bank

READER'S GUIDE

Definitions and methods

The World Education Indicators programme (WEI) places great importance on the cross-national comparability of indicators presented in this report. To accomplish this, participating countries have sought to base the collection of data on a common set of definitions, instructions and methods that were derived from the OECD Indicators of Education Systems (INES) programme.

The annexes to this report provide the definitions and methods that are most important for the interpretation of the data presented in this publication, as well as notes pertaining to reference periods and data sources.

There are five annexes:

* *Annex A1* provides general notes pertaining to the coverage of the data, the reference periods and the main sources for the data.
* *Annex A2* provides definitions and technical notes that are important for the understanding of the indicators presented in this publication (the notes are organised alphabetically).
* *Annex A3* provides a cross-reference between data tables and technical notes.
* *Annex A4* provides the full set of data tables used in this publication.
* *Annex A5* documents the classification of the 19 WEI countries' educational programmes according to the 1997 International Standard Classification of Education (ISCED97).

The full documentation for national data sources and calculation methods is provided in the OECD 2005 edition of *Education at a Glance* and at *www.oecd.org/edu/eag2005*.

In order to enhance the comparability of the indicators, countries participating in the WEI programme have adopted the international standard for the classification of educational programmes – ISCED97, which was developed by UNESCO to enhance the comparability of education statistics.

Important notice to readers

While the comparability of data is a prerequisite for the validity of international comparisons, it often poses challenges for the interpretation of indicators within the national institutional context. This is because the implementation of internationally comparable standards and classifications requires countries to report data in a way that may not reflect national institutional structures.

For example, education that is classified as ISCED Level 1 (primary level of education) may differ from the national definition of primary education, *e.g.* in terms of the number of grades covered by the term.

For some countries, grades typically associated with primary or basic education according to their national systems are classified as lower secondary education in order to facilitate more accurate international comparisons.

Readers are thus invited to refer to the categorisation of national educational programmes according to ISCED97 provided in Annex A5 in order to better assess data from a national context.

Similarly, readers should be aware that the use of international definitions and methods for the coverage of education data and the calculation of indicators may yield different estimates from those obtained with national sources and methods.

Comparability over time

WEI data are the result of a continuous process of convergence towards an international framework that is itself evolving over time. As a result, the coverage of data has changed over time for many WEI countries. In light of this, in past reports, readers were discouraged from using WEI data to analyse trends over time. To address the need for trend data, WEI countries carried out a retrospective data collection using, for most countries, data for the school year beginning in 1995 based on the methodology and coverage of the 2002 school year to ensure comparability. All comparisons over time presented in this report are based on this special retrospective data collection.

The reference periods for comparison over time were not identical for all countries. The intended base year for comparison is the school year which had the greatest overlap with the calendar year 1995. This could be 1994/95, 1995 or 1995/96. Peru and Uruguay were able to provide data for 1993 and 1996, respectively. In order to compare countries with different time spans between reference school years, the use of annual growth rates is preferable. Yet, to facilitate the presentation of data, absolute change is presented in the report. Annual growth rates are presented in Annex A4, Table 1.10. Index of change, presented in other tables, can be converted to annual growth rates using the formula provided in Annex A2 or are readily available at *www.uis.unesco.org/wei2005*.

Reference period

The reference period for this report is the academic year ending in 2003 and the financial year 2002. Where the academic year is spread across two calendar years, the academic year 2002/03 is presented as 2003. For time comparisons the reference year is the academic year having the greatest overlap with the year 1995. This can be 1994/95, 1995 or 1995/96.

For Argentina, Brazil, Malaysia, Paraguay, Peru, Uruguay and Zimbabwe, data for the academic year 2003 were not yet available. For these countries data for the academic year 2002 are presented. For Thailand more recent data were available and are presented. For the trend data, the baseline year for Peru is 1993 and 1996 for Uruguay.

In the report all data are referred to as 1995 and 2003, despite the differences noted here. The tables in Annex A4 provide details on the reference period, indicating the beginning and end of the academic year for WEI countries. For OECD countries, 2003 is given as the reference year including countries where 2003 refers to the 2002/03 school year. Please refer to the 2005 edition of *Education at a Glance* for further details.

Please note that the convention of citing end of the academic year as the reference year is different from that currently used in other UNESCO publications, where the beginning of the academic year determines the reference year.

Coverage of the data

Although a lack of data still limits the scope of some indicators in WEI countries, the coverage extends, in principle, to the entire national education system regardless of the ownership or sponsorship of the institutions concerned and regardless of education delivery mechanisms.

With one exception described below, all types of students and all age groups are meant to be included: children (including those classified as exceptional), adults, nationals, foreigners, as well as students in open distance learning, special education programmes or educational programmes organised by ministries other than the Ministry of Education provided that the main goal of the programme is the educational development of the individual. However, vocational and technical training in the workplace, with the exception of combined school- and work-based programmes which are explicitly deemed to be part of the education system, is excluded from the education expenditure and enrolment data.

Educational activities classified as 'adult' or 'non-regular' are covered, provided that the activities involve studies or have subject-matter content similar to 'regular' education studies, or that the underlying programmes lead to qualifications similar to those gained through corresponding regular educational programmes. Courses for adults that are primarily for general interest, personal enrichment, leisure or recreation are excluded.

Population data

Population data are collected through the WEI data collection and are, for the most part, based on national census data. For 1995, where data are not available to present changes in population, United Nations Population Division (UNPD) population estimates, 2002 revision, are used.

Symbols for missing data

Five symbols are employed in the tables and graphs to denote missing data:

a   Data not applicable because the category does not apply.
n   Magnitude is either negligible or zero.
...   Data not available from countries.
—   Data not requested from countries.
x (y) Data included in another category/column (y) of the table.

Calculation of international means

The WEI and OECD country means, which are often provided as a benchmark, are calculated as the unweighted mean of the data values of WEI or OECD countries for which data are available or can be estimated. The country means, therefore, refer to an average of data values at the level of national systems and do not take into account the absolute size of the education system in each country.

Chapter 1

TRENDS IN EDUCATION PARTICIPATION AND OUTPUTS

Prepared by Michael Bruneforth and Albert Motivans
UNESCO Institute for Statistics

■ INTRODUCTION

Education brings a wide range of benefits for both individuals and societies, which is why it is recognised both as a human right and as instrumental to economic growth and social cohesion. The steady expansion of education systems in WEI countries between 1995 and 2003, the period under study in this report, reflects the increased demand for educational opportunities, especially at upper secondary and tertiary levels. The higher education and skill levels which are associated with these programmes can add further momentum to improvements in outcomes for both individuals and societies. But expanding the range and benefits of educational opportunity goes beyond simply promoting growth in student numbers, it must also ensure relevant content and effective learning.

The expansion of educational systems is a process that needs to be monitored carefully. Rapid growth can overcome existing infrastructures and negatively affect the quality of learning outcomes. The goal is not only to expand student numbers but to develop more efficient, effective and equitable systems.

It is also important to distinguish between the different educational levels where expansion takes place. Universal primary education has been nearly achieved in most WEI countries and there are a wide range of policy aims and cost differentials in expanding educational opportunities before or after basic schooling. Maintaining an even distribution of expansion across different education levels is considered important to sustainable improvements (World Bank, 2005), but can be difficult given changes in school-age population and variation in costs. For example, the annual public expenditure for one tertiary student is equal to that for 10 upper secondary students in Brazil and the total annual expenditure on 11 primary pupils in Indonesia is equivalent to 3.5 secondary students or 1 tertiary student.

With such large differences in costs the question thus arises, of who should play a role in financing the expansion of education. The provision and financing of basic or compulsory education for all children is traditionally seen as an important role of the state, while at other levels, more emphasis is placed on private governance and sources of funding.

The chapter touches upon these issues as it examines the change in demand for education in WEI countries since 1995. First, it compares changes in educational attainment among populations and subgroups between 1995 and 2003 and examines of the implications of educational attainment as a measure of human capital.

The chapter also assesses changes in the overall volume of educational provision as measured by the indicator school life expectancy, a measure which summarises participation across the educational system. The chapter also examines the demographic context in countries and the extent to which population growth contributes to demand for education and how it constrains expanding coverage of educational systems.

The chapter also looks at changes in participation and completion rates by education level since 1995 – or the proportion of children of the relevant age that are enrolled or graduate. Finally the chapter examines public and private roles in the provision of education and its expansion and addresses gender issues related to participation by educational level.

1 EDUCATIONAL ATTAINMENT: LEVELS AND TRENDS

Measures of educational attainment reflect the knowledge and skills, or human capital, of the population. Human capital plays an increasingly important role in the social and economic outcomes of individuals and societies. Recent research shows that the impact of human capital and education on economic growth in WEI countries may be even stronger than in OECD countries (UIS/OECD, 2003). The comparison of growth patterns in OECD and WEI countries suggests that while investment in capital is important at early stages of industrialization, the role of human capital increases with industrial development and eventually grows in relative importance. Overall, the WEI study results indicate that for every single year that the average level of schooling of the adult population is raised there is a corresponding increase of 3.7 per cent in long-term economic growth (ibid). Trends in WEI countries since 1995 reflect rapid improvements in the educational attainment not only for the youth population but for the working-age population as a whole.

Figure 1.1 displays the distribution of the adult population (hereafter defined as 25 to 64 years, with the lower limit just beyond the typical age of tertiary graduation) by the highest level of education attained. In almost all WEI countries more than 70 per cent of the adult population has completed primary schooling. In Malaysia, the Russian Federation and Uruguay primary completion is near universal, as it is achieved by more than 90 per cent of the adult population. Yet, almost half of the same population did not complete primary education in Thailand and more than one-third did not in Paraguay. The situation in Thailand is explained by low levels of educational attainment among the older population, *e.g.* just 15 per cent of the population aged 55 to 64 years had completed primary education (see also Annex A4, Table 1.2). The picture is different in Paraguay, where 27 per cent of 25 to 34-year-olds had not completed primary education.

Primary completion is almost universal in Malaysia, the Russian Federation and Uruguay, but more than one-third of the adult population in Thailand and Paraguay did not complete primary education.

In WEI countries, more women than men had not completed primary education, on average 23 per cent of women compared to 18 per cent of men in the same age group (see also web-resource complementing Annex A4, Table 1.2).

Figure 1.1
Educational attainment of the adult population, 2003
*Distribution of the population aged 25 to 64 years by highest level
of education completed*

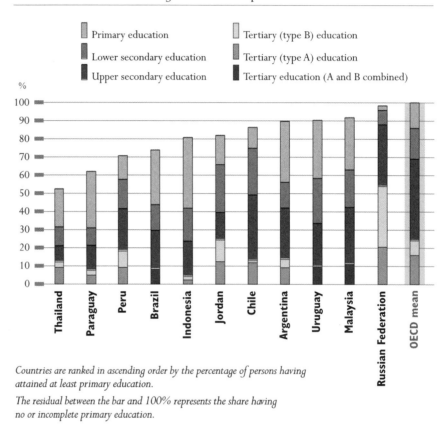

*Countries are ranked in ascending order by the percentage of persons having
attained at least primary education.*

*The residual between the bar and 100% represents the share having
no or incomplete primary education.*

How to read this chart: For the percentage of the population that has attained at least
upper secondary education, the segments for tertiary type A, B and upper secondary
must be added because persons who attained tertiary education also have attained upper
secondary education. Similarly, the segments for primary, lower and upper secondary
and tertiary education together give the total percentage of the population with at least
primary education. The segment on primary education alone indicates the percentage of
persons having attained primary education only.

Source: OECD / UNESCO WEI, Table 1.1 in Annex A4.

*Secondary educational
attainment is less
prevalent in WEI countries.*

The attainment of secondary education among the adult population is much
less common in WEI countries than in OECD countries. One exception is the
Russian Federation, where 96 per cent of the adult population has completed
lower secondary and most of them also have an upper secondary education.
The level of educational attainment in the Russian Federation exceeds the
OECD average. More than two-thirds of the population have attained secondary
education in Chile and Jordan, and almost half received an upper secondary

education in Chile. On the contrary, less than half of the working-age population has secondary education in Brazil and Indonesia and less than one-third in Thailand and Paraguay.

Finally, countries differ with respect to the prevalence of tertiary education attainment. Between 9 and 12 per cent of the adult population in almost all WEI countries have achieved tertiary (type A) education.

There is wide variation in terms of attainment of tertiary (type B) education. In Jordan an additional 12 per cent of the population has attained this level compared to only one per cent in Chile. More than half of the adult population in the Russian Federation has attained tertiary education when both type A and B are combined. In Jordan the combined total is 24 per cent, which is similar to the OECD average. Only a small proportion of the adult population has achieved tertiary education in Indonesia (4 per cent) and Paraguay (7 per cent).

Tertiary attainment in the Russian Federation and Jordan is above or equal to the OECD average.

Patterns of educational attainment among the adult population are the result of the output from education systems over several decades. While adult education is growing in importance, changes in levels of educational attainment are driven by the higher attainment levels of the youngest age cohorts.

Population age structures provide an important context to understand change in educational attainment over time. Figure 1.2 illustrates trends for two age groups – 15 to 19 and 20 to 24-year-olds – that have completed primary and upper secondary education in nine WEI countries. Because these age groups are close to the typical graduation age for primary or secondary education levels, they reflect the output of educational systems from the last ten or so years. Although in countries where there are many over-age students who are still enrolled, this may underestimate measures of completion.

The figure shows that a large share of the population has not completed primary education especially in the WEI countries in Latin America. For example, in Paraguay 19 per cent of 15 to 19-year-olds had not completed primary education in 2003 and in Brazil and Peru the proportion was about 10 per cent. Nevertheless, all three countries made substantial progress compared to levels in 1995. In Brazil and Peru the share without primary education was halved, although it should be noted that the result is not statistically significant in the case of Peru.

Since 1995, Brazil, Paraguay and Peru have successfully lowered the proportion of youth without primary education.

A number of countries made impressive gains in levels of upper secondary educational attainment (Figure 1.2). The share of 20 to 24-year-olds having completed upper secondary education doubled in Thailand in just eight years. Brazil, Chile, Malaysia and Paraguay also made considerable progress. At the same time, a number of countries did not achieve gains. Indonesia, which had a higher level of attainment than Thailand in 1995, fell behind in 2003. The

The share of the youth population having attained upper secondary education doubled in Thailand in just eight years.

Figure 1.2
Educational attainment of the youth population, 1995 and 2003
*Percentage of the population aged 15 to 19 years that completed primary education;
percentage of the population aged 20 to 24 years that completed
upper secondary education*

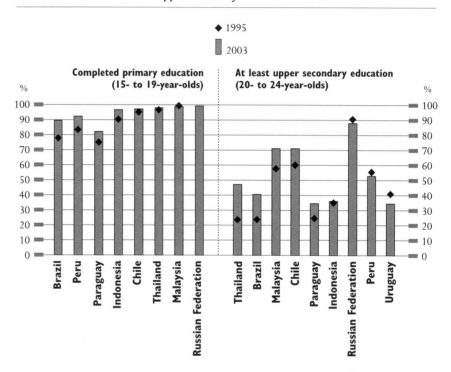

Countries are ranked in descending order by the percentage point difference between 1995 and 2003.
Source: OECD/UNESCO WEI, Table 1.2 in Annex A4.

relative share of persons with upper secondary education decreased slightly in the Russian Federation (although levels are very high) and Peru. In Uruguay the share of young adults having upper secondary attainment dropped from 40 to 36 per cent.

Figure 1.3 displays the age and educational attainment structure for WEI countries in 1995 and 2003. The pyramids provide a comparison by age group along the vertical axis, and between 1995 and 2003 on either side of the pyramid. By presenting the absolute size of the population by age and education, it is possible to assess how quickly change may occur in different countries. For example, in countries with small, less-educated and older populations, change will be much faster when larger and better-educated cohorts enter the adult ages. Levels of educational attainment will improve slowly in Uruguay, while the educational attainment profile of Malaysia and Thailand will improve in the relatively near future.

Figure 1.3
Educational attainment of the population by level and age group, 1995 and 2003

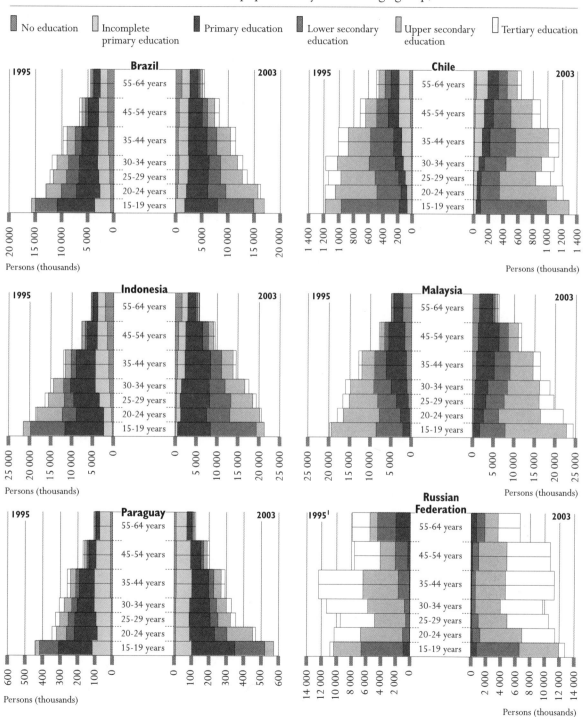

1. Those with no primary education are included in primary education.
Notes: Ten-year age groups, *i.e.* 35-44, 45-54, 55-64, are represented by double bars. The axis gives the number of persons per five-year age group. For ten-year age groups, the number must be multiplied by two.
Source: OECD/UNESCO WEI database (*www.uis.org/wei2005*), see also Table 1.2 in Annex A4.

Figure 1.3 *(continued)*
Educational attainment of the population by level and age group, 1995 and 2003

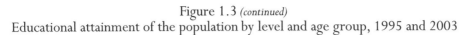

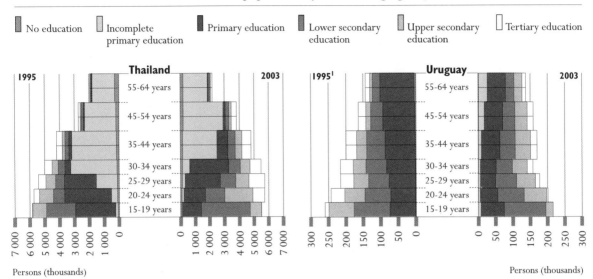

Persons (thousands)   Persons (thousands)

1. Those with some primary education are included in primary education.
Notes: Ten-year age groups, *i.e.* 35-44, 45-54, 55-64, are represented by double bars. The axis gives the number of persons per five-year age group. For ten-year age groups, the number must be multiplied by two.
Source: OECD/UNESCO WEI database (*www.uis.unesco.org/wei2005*), see also Table 1.2 in Annex A4.

There are sizeable differences in the educational attainment of the 55 to 64-year-old population as compared to the youth population. And the share of persons with no or little education decreases sharply from older to younger age groups. Nevertheless, in Brazil, and Paraguay, the absolute number of persons without any education remains high.

Thailand improved levels of educational attainment by expanding educational opportunities for both children and adults.

Thailand stands out in terms of overall progress. The educational attainment profile of the population in 2003 reflects substantial expansion of primary and secondary education. While 77 per cent of the 45 to 54-year-olds had not completed primary education, the level drops to 9 per cent for persons aged 25 to 34 years. Among the 15 to 19-year-old age group, just 2 per cent had not completed primary education. Progress was also evident at higher levels of education. For 20 to 24-year-olds the proportion of upper secondary and tertiary degree holders doubled. Compared to 1995, the share of 15 to 19-year-olds having completed at least lower secondary education increased from 50 to 75 per cent.

The overall change is partly due to better-educated young people, but also to older adults who have upgraded their qualifications through adult education programmes. The proportion of 35 to 44-year-olds with less than primary education decreased from three-quarters to about half in just eight years.

Tertiary educational attainment grew in many WEI countries. The share of 25 to 34-year-olds who attained tertiary education almost doubled in Malaysia and Thailand in 2003 compared to 1995. Brazil, Chile, the Russian Federation and Thailand also experienced substantial increases in tertiary attainment.

In Paraguay almost 20 per cent of 15 to 19-year-olds have not yet completed primary education, which falls well short of universal primary education. Furthermore, the decreasing number of tertiary degree holders aged 20 to 24 signals either declining participation in tertiary education or the tendency for students to extend the duration of university studies. One positive trend in Paraguay has been the strong increase in upper secondary education among the youth population.

Almost 20 per cent of 15 to 19-year-olds left school without completing the primary level in Paraguay.

Progress in educational attainment is the result of increasing investment in education by governments but also by individuals. With growth in the number of young well-trained individuals entering the labour market in WEI countries, does education pay off? Do individuals get returns from their investment?

There is widespread concern that with increasing numbers of secondary graduates, labour markets in middle-income countries will not be able to absorb school leavers. For OECD countries, indicators on labour market outcomes of education clearly show that higher levels of education are associated with higher labour market participation and employment rates. Similar indicators for WEI countries seem to contradict this finding for middle-income countries. Yet a recent study based on WEI data examines this issue more closely (see Box 1.1).

Box 1.1
Labour market outcomes of education: evidence from WEI countries

In OECD countries, better educated people face a lower risk of unemployment and their labour force participation rates tend to be higher. Does this also hold true for WEI countries? Based on national labour force survey data compiled as part of the WEI project, a study assessed labour market outcomes for seven WEI countries for 1998: Brazil, Chile, Indonesia, Malaysia, Peru, Thailand and Uruguay.

It shows a weak relationship between educational attainment and employment; with the exception of Uruguay, a higher level of educational attainment level does not reduce the risk of unemployment. In fact, in Indonesia, the unemployment rate is highest among the most highly educated.

Yet, unemployment, taken alone, does not sufficiently reflect the employment situation. Having worked for just one hour during the reference period is considered as employed. Despite being "employed", many people are looking and available for work. This phenomenon leads to the notion of underemployment. Figure 1.4 shows that underemployment is far more widespread than unemployment in several of the WEI countries.

Figure 1.4
Unemployment and underemployment rates, 1998

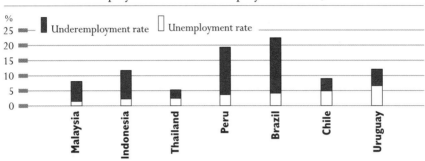

Countries are ranked in ascending order by the unemployment rate.

Taking underemployment into account, a positive relationship between educational attainment and labour market outcomes is more evident (see Figure 1.5). Notable exceptions are Peru and Indonesia where the combined unemployment and underemployment rates for tertiary graduates exceed 20 and 30 per cent respectively. The excess supply of skilled labour cannot be absorbed by the labour market which may lead to employment difficulties for those with high levels of educational attainment.

Figure 1.5
Combined unemployment and underemployment rates
by level of education, 1998

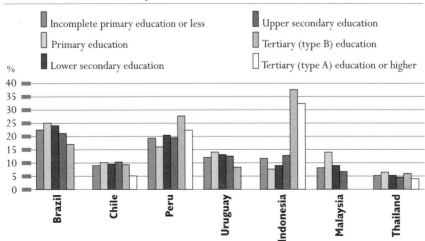

Source: Michaelowa and Waller, 2003; figures based on WEI 1998 data.

2 PATTERNS IN SCHOOL LIFE EXPECTANCY

This section examines changes in the overall output of education provided by education systems in WEI countries, as reflected by the school life expectancy measure. The indicator is based on a common scale – the number of school years provided – and thus, it is possible to compare the output across education systems with different programme types and durations from pre-primary to tertiary education levels.

School life expectancy is defined as the total number of years of schooling that a child at age 5 can expect to receive in the future, assuming current probabilities of enrolment in school by age. It indicates the average duration of schooling, and not the number of grades reached. Since school life expectancy is an average, there is variation in the number of years of schooling, *e.g.* there are those children who never go to school and those who spend more than 20 years in the system. As with any average, school life expectancy masks differences within the population. This is important in countries where not all children participate in school, and especially at secondary and tertiary education levels, where participation is much more limited.

Although school life expectancy does not directly forecast the educational attainment of the population, when adjusted for rates of repetition and drop-out, it provides a perspective on potential educational attainment of the adult population in the near future.

The average school life expectancy in WEI countries in 2003 is 13.5 years, almost four years less than the average in OECD countries. With the exception of India (9.8 years), the average school life expectancy exceeds 11 years in all WEI countries. The highest number of expected years of schooling is found in Argentina (17.6 years), Brazil (16.1) and Uruguay (16.4) (see Figure 1.6).

Children in WEI countries can expect to participate in school for 13.5 years, almost four years less than in OECD countries.

Argentina is the only WEI country where the number of expected years in education exceeds the OECD average. Most other WEI countries fall well short of levels in OECD countries. A few OECD countries – notably Austria and Luxembourg – fall below the school life expectancy of the WEI countries with the next highest results (Brazil and Uruguay).

However, levels in OECD countries also reflect relatively large proportions of part-time enrolments. Part-time education adds three or more years of schooling in Australia, Belgium, New Zealand, Sweden and the United Kingdom. Most WEI countries do not have substantial part-time programmes, with the exception of Argentina, Thailand and the Russian Federation (see Annex A4, Table 1.4).

In several WEI countries school life expectancy is inflated by high rates of grade repetition. In Brazil, one in five primary students repeats a grade, which

Figure 1.6
School life expectancy, 1995 and 2003
Expected years of schooling for a 5-year-old child

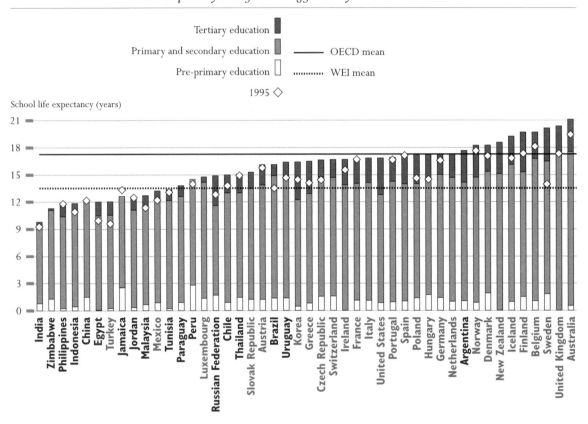

Countries are ranked in ascending order of school life expectancy in 2003.

Notes: School life expectancy for Jamaica excludes tertiary enrolment but includes pre-primary enrolment for children younger than 5 years.

Source: OECD/UNESCO WEI, Table 1.4 in Annex A4.

translates into two years of school life expectancy. In Peru, Tunisia and Uruguay one year of school life expectancy can be attributed to repeated school years (see Annex A4, Table 1.18).

In Brazil school life expectancy increased by more than two years since 1995.

Figure 1.6 shows substantial increases in the volume of education provided in both WEI and OECD countries between 1995 and 2003. Children in 2003 in Brazil could expect to stay 2.7 years longer in education than children in 1995, which represents an increase of over 20 per cent. An increase of 10 per cent or more was recorded in Chile, Indonesia, Malaysia, the Russian Federation and Uruguay. Yet, not all countries progressed in terms of participation. School life expectancy decreased by more than one year in Jamaica.

In the 21 OECD countries with comparable data for both years, Spain was the only country that did not increase school life expectancy since 1995. Half of the OECD countries increased school life expectancy by more than two years, and another quarter of countries added more than one year.

In WEI countries with comparable data, school life expectancy increased by 0.9 years. Yet, OECD countries extended the average school life expectancy by 1.9 years. Since 1995, the gap in educational provision widened between the two groups of countries by more than one year.

The average duration of schooling in WEI countries increased by almost one year, yet not enough to catch up to OECD countries.

What explains the difference, when absolute gains in the number of students in WEI countries are much higher? Education systems in countries with rapidly growing youth populations have to grow faster than the population in order to increase enrolment rates. On the contrary, in countries where youth populations are stable or declining, any increase in enrolment translates into improvements in coverage. In other words, some WEI countries have expanded rapidly but participation indicators have improved less than expected due to high rates of population growth.

Figure 1.7 shows that the absolute number of students in WEI countries grew faster than in OECD countries. On average, the number of students at all levels of education in WEI countries grew by 16 per cent since 1995. The number of enrolments grew at less than half this rate in OECD countries, on average 6 per cent. Education systems expanded by more than 20 per cent in Chile, China, India, Jordan, Malaysia and Paraguay among WEI countries and in Sweden, Turkey and the United Kingdom among OECD countries. Education systems contracted by 11 and 7 per cent, respectively, in Spain and Portugal and were practically unchanged in the Czech Republic, France, Germany, Ireland, Italy, Jamaica, the Russian Federation and Thailand, mostly in response to decreasing population size.

In WEI countries the absolute number of students typically grew faster than in OECD countries, but so did the school-age population.

Enrolling more children does not translate directly into higher enrolment rates and longer school life expectancy. The Philippines increased the total number of students by one-fifth since 1995, yet this did not lead to an increase in school life expectancy. A similar increase of enrolment, 20 per cent, in Sweden led to a large increase (46 per cent) in the expected duration of schooling. Another example is illustrated by trends in the Czech Republic and Malaysia where school life expectancy increased in both countries by about 15 per cent since 1995. Malaysia had to enrol 26 per cent more students in order to achieve this growth while the number of students in the Czech Republic actually declined.

Enrolling more children does not automatically translate into higher enrolment rates and longer school life expectancy.

By and large, education systems in WEI countries have expanded rapidly but have been constrained by demographic change to a greater extent than OECD countries. In the near future, the pace of population growth among primary school-age populations is projected to slow down in most WEI countries, which could potentially free up resources to catch up to OECD countries.

Figure 1.7
Change in enrolments and school life expectancy, 2003 (1995 = 100)
Absolute number of students at all education levels in 2003 as a percentage of students in 1995

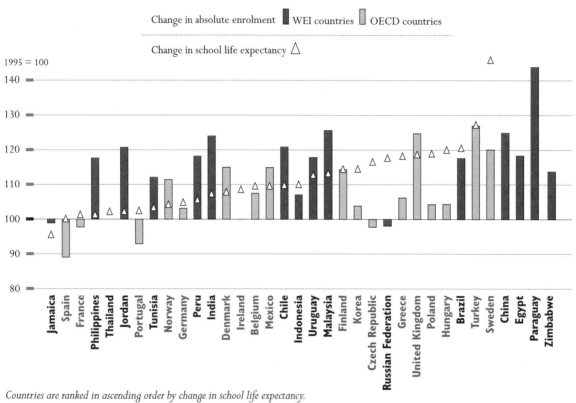

Countries are ranked in ascending order by change in school life expectancy.
Source: OECD/UNESCO WEI, Tables 1.4 and 1.9 in Annex A4.

WEI countries' efforts to expand educational opportunities are also influenced by economic factors. Figure 1.8 plots school life expectancy by level of national income, as measured by Gross Domestic Product (GDP) per capita. Not surprisingly, the expected number of years spent in primary and secondary education is positively related to the level of national income. This relationship is found in WEI countries as well as in other countries. In OECD countries this relationship is less clear since participation levels out among high-income countries.

Some WEI countries deliver higher school life expectancy than expected based on their national income.

Figure 1.8 also shows that there is considerable variation among countries. Some countries have achieved high levels of school life expectancy despite low levels of national income. And others have not kept children in school for as long as expected given their level of national income. There is little doubt that the level of national income influences absolute levels of investments in education. But countries at similar levels of national income also differ substantially with respect to overall levels of education participation.

Figure 1.8
School life expectancy and national wealth, 2003
School life expectancy, primary to tertiary and GDP per capita, US$ PPP converted

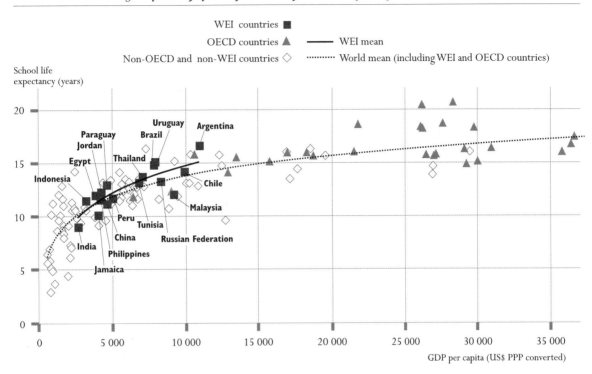

Notes: This figure excludes pre-primary education to allow for comparison with countries outside the WEI and OECD groups.
Sources: OECD/UNESCO WEI, Table 1.4 in Annex A4; UNESCO Institute for Statistics, 2005; World Bank, 2005a.

For example, China and Paraguay have similar levels of per capita income; however the average duration of schooling in China is two years less than in Paraguay. Malaysia has a substantially higher GDP per capita than Brazil or Uruguay, yet in the latter two countries, children can expect to spend more years in school. This difference is also partly explained by high levels of grade repetition.

3 DEMOGRAPHIC CONTEXTS AND EDUCATION SYSTEMS

Trends in access to education should be interpreted in light of population change. While efforts required to extend coverage in many OECD countries are relatively low (albeit more expensive), population growth remains an important constraint to expanding systems in WEI countries. Additional resources are required even in order to maintain current participation levels, and thus fewer resources remain to invest in broadening the coverage of schooling.

Education systems in OECD countries have faced more than four decades without population pressure.

Figure 1.9 presents the long-term growth of the school-age population since 1960. It shows that, on average, education systems in OECD countries have grown for decades without the pressure of additional demand due to population growth. The number of children in 1995 and 2003 in OECD countries has been the same as in 1960. In the near future, school-age populations are projected to decrease even further. Outside the OECD and WEI countries, the picture is quite different. The number of children has more than doubled from 1960 to 1995 and continues to grow at a slow rate.

Most WEI countries face a downturn in population growth.

Since the mid- to late-1990s, population growth slowed in most WEI countries. Before 1995, the primary school-age population continued to grow, but slower in comparison to other developing countries. Since 1995, the rate of growth has decreased further. While the demographic pressure on basic education systems has decreased or disappeared in WEI countries, secondary and tertiary school-age populations are still growing. For the basic school-age population, aged 5 to 14 years, populations were already stable in 7 out of 19 WEI countries since 1995 or earlier. In Argentina, Chile, China, Egypt and Zimbabwe, the size of basic school-age population has been stable since 1995. However, basic school-age populations will continue to grow in Jordan until 2012, in Malaysia until 2006 and in the Philippines until 2005. In Paraguay the youth population is projected to continue to grow even beyond 2015.

The fastest growing age groups in WEI countries are at the upper secondary and tertiary education levels. These populations will continue to grow in India, Jordan, Paraguay, Peru and Philippines until after 2010. Growing student numbers will therefore continue to drive demand, especially where participation is considered compulsory.

School-age populations grew fastest in Jordan, Paraguay and Zimbabwe.

In Jordan, Paraguay and Zimbabwe, the number of children aged 5 to 14 grew faster than the non-WEI average. In 2003, the number of 5 to 14-year-olds in Jordan was 5.5 times higher than in 1960, and the numbers continue to grow. In Zimbabwe, the high population growth rates in the past have been reversed, mainly due to the HIV/AIDS pandemic.

At the same time, the child population has decreased in China since 1998 and Sri Lanka since 1996. The Russian Federation showed little change until the mid-1990s, when falling birth rates started to have an impact on the 5 to 14-year-old population.

Projections suggest that by 2015 the number of children aged 5 to 14 years will be half of the levels of 1960 and 1995. Such a rapid decrease in population base also requires education systems to adjust. Chapter 2 provides more detail on how teaching forces and student to teacher ratios have changed in response to changes in the school-age population.

Figure 1.9
Patterns of population growth, 1960-2015
*Population aged 5 to 14 years expressed as a percentage
of population aged 5 to 14 years in 1960*

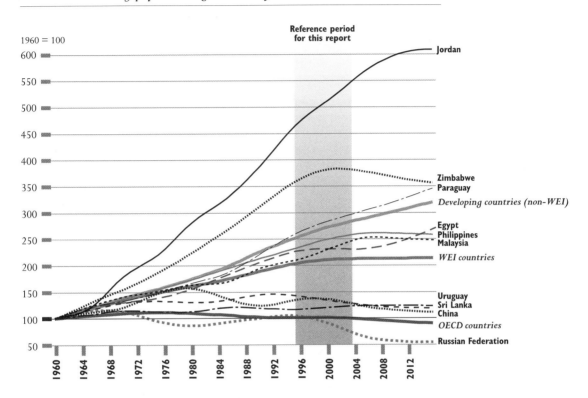

Note: Countries that joined the OECD after 1960 are included in OECD for all years.
Source: UN Population Division.

Another demographic factor that shapes demand for educational opportunities is the age distribution of the population. In countries where the size of the youth population is relatively small compared to the size of the working-age population, the working-age population has to generate resources needed for comparatively fewer children. In countries where the proportion of children relative to the working-age population is much higher, there is greater demand to generate resources for education.

The relative size of the school-age population is an important consideration in assessing the level of resources needed to expand educational opportunities. One way to assess the impact of population age structure is to calculate how many students need to be enrolled per 100 adults (age 20 and older) to increase participation rates. Figure 1.10 simulates the additional enrolment needed in order to increase school life expectancy by two years, the average increase in OECD countries from 1995 to 2003.

The youth population represents a greater proportion of the total in WEI countries compared to OECD countries.

The simulation reveals substantial differences in the burden that would be placed on the adult population due to higher enrolment. Just 2.8 more students per hundred adults in Italy need to be enrolled in order to increase school life expectancy by another two years. The figure is nearly three times higher in Zimbabwe, where 10 more students have to be enrolled per 100 adults in order to make similar progress in participation rates.

Figure 1.10 shows that the number of additional enrolment per 100 adult persons is below 5 in all OECD countries except Mexico and Turkey. Among WEI countries, the demographic situation is favourable in China, the Russian Federation, Thailand and Uruguay. In all other WEI countries, to increase school life expectancy by two years would place a much greater burden on the adult population.

Many WEI countries continue to face demographic challenges in expanding educational coverage. First, they must keep pace with population growth, while in OECD countries the participation rates have increased despite a decrease in student numbers. Second, the relative burden on the adult population is higher in WEI countries than in OECD countries.

Figure 1.10
Additional enrolment needed per 100 adults in order to increase
school life expectancy by two years, 2003

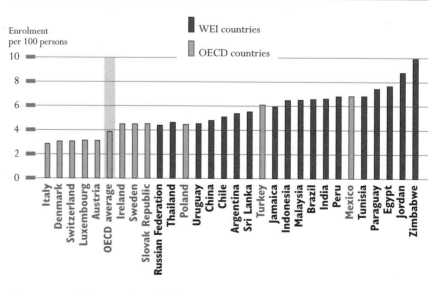

Countries are ranked in ascending order by additional enrolment needed.

Notes: Enrolment representing 20% of all 15 to 19-year-olds plus 10% of 20 to 29-year-olds is equivalent to two years of school life expectancy, close to the increase of 1.9 years OECD countries showed from 1995 to 2003. Accordingly, additional enrolment of this magnitude leads to an increase in SLE of 2 years. The enrolment increase needed is divided by the number of persons of working age, 20 years and older.

Source: OECD/UNESCO WEI, Table 1.3 in Annex A4.

4 CHANGING PATTERNS OF EDUCATIONAL PARTICIPATION

Trends by education level

The expansion of enrolment in many WEI countries has taken place across different levels of the education system. Historically, countries that experienced the most rapid and sustainable increases in educational attainment, as well as economic performance, have pursued expansion which is balanced across primary, secondary and tertiary levels of education (World Bank, 2005).

Figure 1.11 compares the average change in student numbers at each level of education for WEI and OECD countries from 1995 to 2003. Overall the total number of students in WEI countries grew by 16 per cent compared to 6 per cent in OECD countries. The average relative increase in WEI countries exceeds that in OECD countries at every level of education except primary, where both groups of countries showed very little change. In OECD countries, pre-primary enrolments grew by 9 per cent, and by 3 per cent at the primary level, while student numbers in lower secondary fell. However, tertiary enrolment skyrocketed, growing by 43 per cent since 1995.

On average, OECD student numbers increased substantially in tertiary education with little or no change at other levels.

In WEI countries, the largest increase in enrolments was at the tertiary level where, on average, WEI countries experienced 77 per cent growth in tertiary

Figure 1.11
Index of change in enrolment by level, 2003 (1995 = 100)

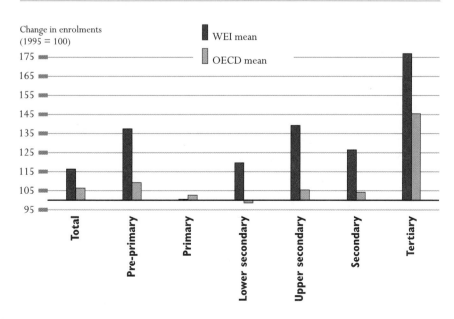

Notes: WEI and OECD means are calculated as the unweighted average of growth rates by country.
Source: OECD/UNESCO WEI, Table 1.9 in Annex A4.

student numbers over the period. The growth in pre-primary and upper secondary numbers exceeded 35 per cent in both cases.

It is important to use caution in interpreting growth rates because a small rise in absolute student numbers can translate into a high rate of change in relative terms. For example, in the Philippines, pre-primary enrolment in 2003 was 67 per cent higher than 1995 levels and primary enrolments were 12 per cent higher. However, the absolute increase in pre-primary enrolments was only 304 000 compared to an increase of primary enrolments of about 1.4 million.

Pre-primary education

Globally, early childhood care and education has received greater policy attention in the last decade. It is recognized that equitable access to quality early childhood care and education can strengthen the foundations of lifelong learning and support the broad social and educational needs of families (OECD, 2001). Thus, expanding and improving comprehensive early childhood care and education, especially for the most vulnerable and disadvantaged children, is the first of the six *Education for All* goals adopted by the World Education Forum (UNESCO, 2000).

On average, children in WEI countries can expect to receive 1.3 years of pre-primary education in 2003. Jamaica, the Russian Federation and Thailand have the highest participation rates, with an average of more than 2.5 years; while the average is less than half a year in Egypt, Indonesia and the Philippines (see Annex A4, Table 1.5).

Pre-primary education was one of the fastest-growing sectors of the WEI education systems in the period 1995 to 2003 as numbers grew, on average, by 37 per cent. In India and Paraguay enrolment more than doubled. In India the number of enrolments rose from 9.2 to 24.3 million. Enrolments grew in Egypt and the Philippines by more than 50 per cent. More specifically, the absolute number grew from 258 000 to 446 000 in Egypt. Pre-primary enrolment remained unchanged or decreased in Brazil, Chile, Jamaica, the Russian Federation and Thailand. Most of these countries already have high pre-primary participation rates, except for Chile. In the Russian Federation, the decline in enrolment was linked to more than 25 per cent decrease in the size of the population aged 5 and 6. Since enrolment fell proportionately less than the pre-primary school-age population, participation rates have actually improved (see Figure 1.12).

The expansion of pre-primary was generally slower, partly because participation rates are already high, with an average increase of 9 per cent among OECD countries. Exceptions are Denmark, Finland, Portugal, Sweden and Turkey, where pre-primary enrolments grew by more than 20 per cent.

Figure 1.12
Change in student numbers and population, pre-primary, primary
and lower secondary education, 2003 (1995 = 100)

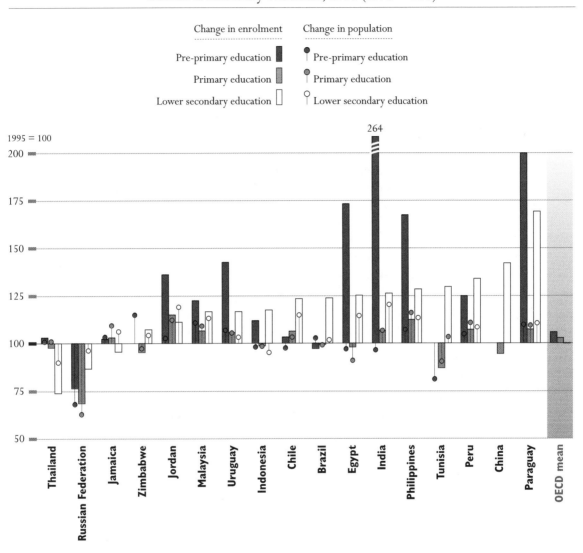

Countries are ranked in ascending order of change at the lower secondary level of education.

Notes: The change in population (circles) refers to the change in the approximate age group for that level of education: pre-primary, 5-6 years; primary, 6-11 years; lower secondary, 12-15 years.

Source: OECD/UNESCO WEI database (*www.uis.unesco.org/wei2005*), see also Table 1.9 in Annex A4.

Basic and compulsory education

The goal to reach universal primary education is at the centre of the commitments made by countries and the international community in Jomtien and Dakar (UNESCO, 2000) and is also reflected by the United Nations Millennium Declaration.

It is increasingly clear that "basic education" should extend beyond primary education.

Yet, it has become increasingly clear in all parts of the world that a "basic education" can no longer be limited to primary education. The 47th session of the UNESCO International Conference on Education in 2004 concluded that promoting quality education and training for all young people between ages 12 and 18 is essential to securing a better future and constitutes an essential mechanism for combating social exclusion at the local, national and global levels (UNESCO-IBE, 2004). This understanding is also reflected in national policies, especially in middle-income countries. National *Education for All* policies typically consider lower secondary as part of basic and compulsory education (World Bank, 2005). Compulsory schooling policies also reflect that most countries interpret basic education as including the lower secondary level. With the exception of Jamaica, Malaysia and the Philippines, WEI countries include lower secondary education as part of their system of compulsory education.

Although high levels of primary enrolment may suggest that universal primary education has been achieved, other indicators suggest that large numbers of children still leave school without completing primary education. Projections based on household survey data suggest that several countries in Latin America, among them WEI countries, do not currently meet the goal of universal primary education and will face difficulties in achieving the goal by 2015, the target set by the international community (see Box 1.2).

Box 1.2
Universal primary completion in Latin America: are we really so near the goal?

There is a widely-held notion in the region that universal completion of primary education is an aspiration that has largely been fulfilled. A recent report by the UNESCO Regional Bureau of Education for Latin America and the Caribbean shows that the guarantee of universal completion of primary education is not yet a reality. In 2002, nearly 6 million 15 to 19-year-olds had not completed primary education across 18 countries in Latin America.

Given historical trends of educational attainment, it is predicted that six per cent of the children who are currently under five years of age (and who will be between 15 and 19 years in 2015) will not complete primary school – representing 3.5 million children by the year 2015.

Among the WEI countries in Latin America, the projected likelihood of completing primary education in 2015 is 95 per cent or above in Argentina, Chile, Peru and Uruguay, between 90 and 95 per cent in Brazil and between 80 and 90 per cent in Paraguay. These figures underscore the need for additional efforts in order to reach all children and to achieve the goal of universal completion of primary education.

Source: UNESCO-OREALC, 2004.

The change in primary school enrolment in WEI countries ranges from an increase of 15 per cent in Jordan to a dramatic drop of 31 per cent in the Russian Federation. However, as noted, this is the result of a sharp drop in the school-age population in the Russian Federation. Enrolment in Jamaica, Malaysia, Paraguay and the Philippines grew more slowly than the school-age population (which rose by about 10 per cent) (see Figure 1.12).

The primary school-age population grew faster than enrolment in some WEI countries, which may indicate that more children are excluded.

Increases in enrolment rates at the lower secondary level can reflect changes in the structure of the educational system. For example, Paraguay extended compulsory education to include lower secondary education in 1994. The system was implemented with primary grade 1 students, who finished compulsory education at grade 9 in 2002. This had the effect of increasing lower secondary enrolment by 69 per cent from 1995 to 2003. In China, India, Peru, the Philippines and Tunisia, the number of students grew by more than one-quarter. Yet, most WEI countries with high growth rates at this level succeeded in meeting demand and even further increasing participation rates.

The rapid increase in lower secondary enrolment in Paraguay reflects the success of policy reform that extended compulsory education.

Current rates of entry to lower secondary education as well as enrolment rates indicate that most WEI countries, despite rapid growth, still need further expansion in order to universalise compulsory education. Gross entry rates to lower secondary education are 85 per cent or less in India, Indonesia,

Most countries need to further increase participation to meet their own national standards.

Figure 1.13
Net enrolment rates for 5 to 14-year-olds, 1995 and 2003

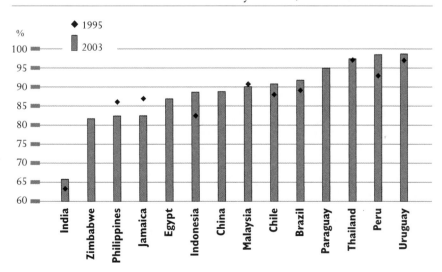

Countries are ranked in ascending order of net enrolment rates in 2003.
Source: OECD/UNESCO WEI, Table 1.6 in Annex A4.

Jordan, Paraguay, Thailand and Zimbabwe. In all of these countries, education is compulsory until the end of lower secondary education, yet entry rates show that less than 85 per cent of children enter lower secondary education. On the other hand, entry rates are close to or more than 100 per cent in Argentina, Brazil, Chile, Egypt and Uruguay, indicating that virtually every child begins lower secondary education (see Annex A4, Table 1.15).

In Jamaica and the Philippines, school participation by 5 to 14-year-olds has dropped since 1995.

Another way to judge the coverage of the education system is by using net enrolment rates. Figure 1.13 presents the net enrolment rate for a fixed age group from 5 to 14 years (which may not correspond to national definitions of the compulsory school-age population). The data reflect gaps in the coverage of the 5 to 14-year-old population, *e.g.* in India, one out of three children in this age group is not enrolled in school. In Jamaica, the Philippines and Zimbabwe, less than 85 per cent of the age group is in school. In Jamaica and the Philippines rates are lower in 2003 than in 1995. On the contrary, in Thailand and Uruguay virtually all children of this age group are in school. Peru has reached this level of enrolment as a result of an increase since 1995. Participation rates also increased in Indonesia (7 percentage points), Brazil and Chile.

Nearly every child is enrolled 10 years in Argentina, and 9 years in Chile, Peru and Uruguay.

Figure 1.14 indicates the age ranges for which most children are in school. The age span over which virtually all children (90 per cent or higher) are enrolled in school is longest in Argentina (10 years), followed by Chile, Peru and Uruguay (9 years). In Brazil, where the average school life expectancy is 2.5 years higher than in Peru, education is virtually universal for only 7 years. At the same time, enrolment rates exceed 90 per cent for only 2 years in India, and 5 years in China and Egypt.

The age span in which nearly all children are enrolled was extended in four WEI countries and shortened in one since 1995. In Jamaica, enrolment rates for a number of ages are lower in 2003 than in 1995.

Despite growing education participation on average in most WEI countries, only four extended the time span during which virtually all children are enrolled. In Uruguay, enrolment rates for 14 and 15-year-olds exceeded the 90 per cent threshold by 2003. In three countries the span of universal education has been extended by one year. In Peru the enrolment of 14-year-olds rose above 90 per cent. However, in Jamaica, the duration of near universal participation decreased by one year. It is important to note that enrolment rates by single year of age should be interpreted with caution, as the decline is eventually not statistically significant.

With the introduction of compulsory education in Malaysia in 2003, all WEI countries have set standards concerning the legal or official minimum duration of formal schooling which define the age range for compulsory school attendance. Constitutional pledges which guarantee the right to education may or may not mention compulsory schooling, but this often takes the form of an aspiration. Without implementing legislation, this aspiration rarely translates into reality. Yet, these aspirations indicate an intended national policy standard to which countries should be held accountable.

Figure 1.14
Age range of universal primary to secondary education, 1995 and 2003
Age range where over 90% of children are enrolled in school and ending age of compulsory education

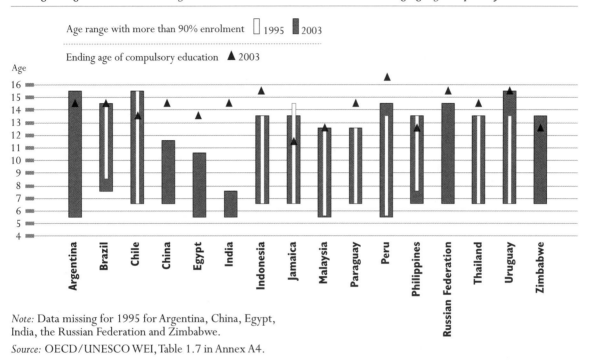

Note: Data missing for 1995 for Argentina, China, Egypt, India, the Russian Federation and Zimbabwe.
Source: OECD/UNESCO WEI, Table 1.7 in Annex A4.

With the exception of Jamaica, Malaysia and the Philippines, all WEI countries include lower secondary education in compulsory education. Given these national standards, one should expect all children to be enrolled in school until the end of lower secondary education. Yet, almost every other WEI country fails to meet its own standards. In China, Egypt and India, more than 10 per cent of children are excluded from schooling for the last three or more years of compulsory education. National standards are met in Argentina, Brazil, Chile and Uruguay, where compulsory education includes lower secondary education, as well as in those WEI countries where compulsory education stops after primary education or at ages 12 to 13. Peru and Uruguay are the only countries that showed progress towards reaching universal coverage in compulsory education between 1995 and 2003.

With the exception of Jamaica, Malaysia and the Philippines, WEI countries include lower secondary as part of compulsory education.

Figure 1.13 and Figure 1.14 use enrolment rates by single year of age to examine the issue related to the share of children excluded from education. Yet, these statistics can be vulnerable to data quality problems. Population and enrolment data, the basis for enrolment rates, not only come from different sources but are both subject to error. Therefore, caution is needed when interpreting these data, especially when assessing patterns over time.

Trends in enrolment rates by single year of age should be interpreted cautiously.

Figure 1.15
Enrolment rates by single year of age, 5 to 14 years, Indonesia and Jamaica, 2003

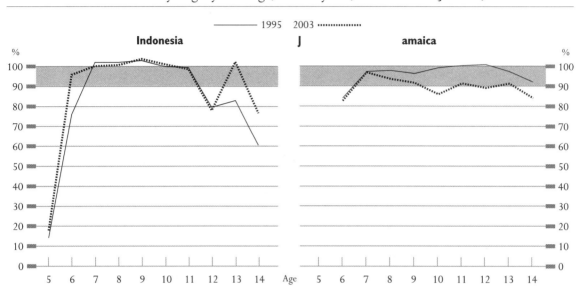

1995   2003

Source: UIS/OECD WEI database (*www.uis.unesco.org/wei2005*).

For example, where countries are near the benchmark of 90 per cent set as "near-universal" participation, results should be viewed with care.

In Jamaica, the share of out-of-school children is rising. Keeping these limitations in mind, enrolment rates by single year of age provide important information for understanding the underlying dynamics of enrolment patterns. Figure 1.15 presents enrolment rates by single year age groups for the 5 to 14-year-old population in Indonesia and Jamaica.

Since 1995, overall enrolment rates in Indonesia for the age group 5 to 14 years increased from 82 to 89 per cent. The main reasons appear to be, as shown in Figure 1.15, increases in enrolment rates for 6, 13 and 14 year-olds. In the case of 6 year-olds, the increase (20 percentage points) reflects primarily a widened access to primary education for under-age children as the official starting age in primary is 7 years. As for the 13 and 14 year-olds, with respective increases of 19 and 16 percentage points since 1995, it is safe to say that government implementation of the nine-year universal basic education programme in the mid-1990s was an important catalyst towards improving access to lower secondary education.

In Jamaica, overall enrolment rates fell for the age group 5 to 14 years. Although more than 90 per cent of children aged 7 to 13 are in school, the share of out-of-school children in 2003 appears to be higher than in 1995, often reaching 10 per cent of children aged 9 and older.

Upper secondary education

Upper secondary education typically serves different aims than basic education, *i.e.* it provides a bridge between school and university or prepares students to enter the labour market directly. Therefore, it requires more qualified and specialized staff and more varied curricula as reflected in the diversity of programmes. The diversity and thus complexity of upper secondary provision becomes more pronounced as education systems expand and upper secondary programmes become more widespread.

Entry rates to upper secondary education indicate that participation at this level is becoming more widespread in WEI countries (see Annex A4, Table 1.15). In 11 out of 13 WEI countries, at least every second child enters upper secondary education, and in Chile, Thailand and Uruguay the share increases to 90 per cent. The WEI average of 65 per cent indicates that in many WEI countries participation in upper secondary education has become the norm rather than the exception. Although one notable exception to this pattern is Zimbabwe, where only 6 per cent of children enter upper secondary school (see Annex A4, Table 1.15).

Upper secondary education is increasingly the norm in WEI countries. On average 2 out of 3 children enter upper secondary education.

There are considerable differences between WEI and OECD countries in terms of enrolment in upper secondary education. For example, in OECD countries, children stay on average 3.8 years in upper secondary education. With the exception of Chile and Uruguay, WEI countries fall at least one year short of this mark. And the WEI average, at 1.9 years, is only half that of the OECD average. Apart from Chile and Uruguay's strong showing, school life expectancy exceeds 2 years in Argentina, Brazil, Egypt, Thailand and Tunisia. Upper secondary school life expectancy is shortest in the Philippines (0.6 years) followed by China, Indonesia, Jordan and Zimbabwe, from 1.1 to 1.4 years (see Annex A4, Table 1.4).

In Chile, children can expect to be enrolled almost four years in upper secondary education, or as long as in OECD countries.

Compared to 1995, upper secondary enrolment increased in WEI countries. This is reflected by growth in upper secondary school life expectancy of 0.4 years. The increase was highest in Brazil and Paraguay at one year. However, not all countries were able to expand upper secondary education. School life expectancy at this level did not grow in Jordan, the Philippines and the Russian Federation.

The additional demand on upper secondary institutions due to increases in student numbers since 1995 was great. Figure 1.16 shows that upper secondary schools also faced a growing upper secondary school-age population. The population aged 15 to 19 grew by more than 10 per cent in 9 out of 15 WEI countries. In Egypt and Zimbabwe, countries with high rates of population growth, enrolment did not grow fast enough. Participation rates in these countries fell despite an increase in enrolment of more than 20 per cent since 1995. Other WEI countries were able to both meet the additional demand of growing upper secondary school-age populations and the expansion of the coverage of upper secondary education.

In Egypt and Zimbabwe, enrolment did not keep up with population growth.

Figure 1.16

Change in student numbers and population, upper secondary and tertiary education, 2003 (1995 = 100)

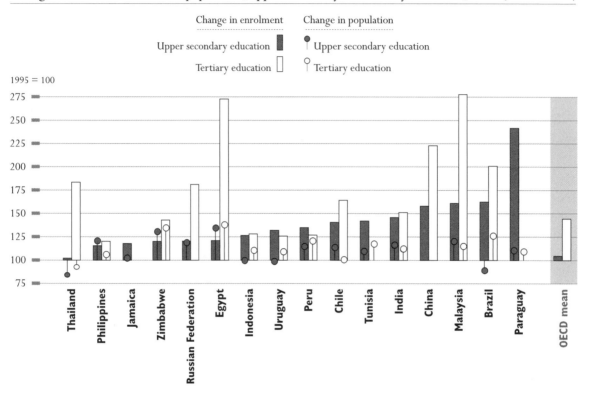

Countries are ranked in ascending order by the change in upper secondary enrolment.

Notes: The duration of the reference period for the change differs by country. This may affect comparability. See Table 1.10 for annual change rates.

Source: OECD/UNESCO WEI, Table 1.9 in Annex A4.

On average, upper secondary enrolment grew by 39 per cent in WEI countries from 1995 to 2003, compared to 5 per cent in OECD countries. Some countries saw millions of new students enter upper secondary programmes, *e.g.* Brazil (from 5.9 to 9.6 million) and China (from 18.0 to 28.5 million). In Paraguay, enrolment more than doubled from 105 000 to 211 000 students. In remaining WEI countries, enrolment increased by more than 20 per cent, except for Jamaica, the Philippines and Thailand.

The rapid expansion of educational systems, especially in a short timeframe can place the quality of education at risk. Chapter 2 looks at monitoring change in human and financial resources that accompany the changes in enrolment. Internationally comparable studies of learning achievement provide other insights, especially in that the expansion of quantity is not sufficient without attention to quality. Evidence from international student achievement studies underscore that access to school alone does not ensure good learning outcomes (see Box 1.3).

Box 1.3
Enrolment and learning outcomes: evidence from PISA 2003

Participation in schooling is a necessary but not sufficient condition for good learning outcomes. The skill levels or learning outcomes of students help to reveal some of the gaps which may not be evident from a focus solely on the number of enrolments.

Figure 1.17 illustrates the extent to which young people lack basic mathematical literacy knowledge and skills for six WEI countries participating in the OECD Programme for International Student Assessment (PISA) in 2003. For comparison purposes, the figure also includes the top three and bottom three OECD countries and focuses on 15-year-olds, who were the target of the PISA study.

It presents two groups of youths who may be at risk because of low basic literacy knowledge and skills. The first group includes the 15-year-olds who had either dropped out of school or had never been enrolled in school. It may be thus assumed that they had not acquired the basic knowledge and skills that PISA attempted to assess. Out of the six WEI countries, these youths made up five per cent of the 15-year-old population in the Russian Federation, 16 per cent in Thailand,

Figure 1.17
Percentage of 15-year-olds not in school or enrolled and achieving low levels of mathematics literacy

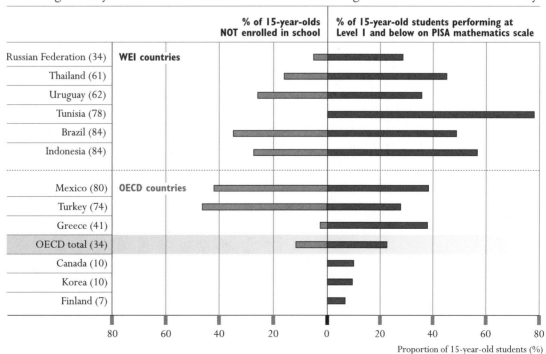

Note: The numbers in parentheses give the total percentage of 15-year-olds not in school or who performed poorly on the PISA assessment of mathematics literacy.
Source: OECD, 2004.

26 per cent in Uruguay, 27 per cent in Indonesia and 35 per cent in Brazil. Tunisia reported all individuals of this age to be in school. Of the OECD countries participating in PISA 2003, almost 12 per cent of the 15-year-old youths were reported to be out of school, which were primarily due to high rates of non-participation in Mexico and Turkey.

The second group reflects the share of 15-year-olds who performed at Level 1 and below on the mathematical literacy scale in PISA 2003, generalised to the national population. These students did not demonstrate basic mathematical skills in the assessment. They represented 29 per cent of the 15-year-old population in the Russian Federation, 36 per cent in Uruguay, 45 per cent in Thailand, 49 per cent in Brazil, 57 per cent in Indonesia and 78 per cent in Tunisia. In contrast, for OECD countries participating in the PISA study, about one out of four 15-year-old students was a low performer. The number varied between one in fourteen students in Finland and one in 2.6 students in Greece and Mexico.

In WEI countries, 22 per cent of upper secondary students are enrolled in technical and vocational education.

As upper secondary education expands, it diversifies so that general education develops both the academic and the vocational and technical streams. Figure 1.18 presents the share of upper secondary enrolment in technical and vocational education. In WEI countries, on average, 22 per cent of upper secondary students, or one in five, are enrolled in technical and vocational education, which is about half of the OECD average.

Figure 1.18
Technical and vocational education, 1995 and 2003
*Enrolment in upper secondary technical and vocational education
as a percentage of total upper secondary enrolment*

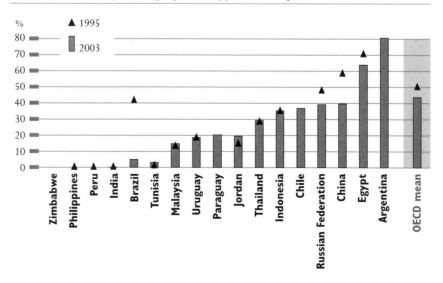

Countries are ranked in ascending order by the percentage of enrolments in 2003.
Source: OECD / UNESCO WEI, Table 1.12 in Annex A4.

Growth in upper secondary enrolment varies across the different types of programmes. Overall, general education, which is designed to lead to tertiary education, grew faster than other programmes. The trend is similar in OECD countries where vocational enrolment decreased by more than 5 percentage points since 1995. In China, enrolment in general education doubled while vocational education has not grown since 1995. Thus, the share of vocational enrolment among total secondary students fell from 58 per cent to 40 per cent. In Brazil, enrolment in vocational education decreased by 2 million students while numbers in general education grew by more than 5 million. This is related to a change in the structure of upper secondary programmes. Students enrolled in the newly introduced *Educação Profissional de Nível Técnico* (starting in 1996) must enrol in and complete general education and obtain a labour-market relevant vocational qualification in addition to the general education certificate.

While general secondary enrolments have grown, student numbers in vocational programmes have remained stable or fallen.

Improved access to higher levels of education is only part of the picture. Ensuring the benefits of greater access to education is critically dependent upon the actual completion of education programmes. Graduation rates provide a measure of attainment (see Figure 1.19).

The expansion of upper secondary education is reflected by graduation rates which range from 21 and 31 per cent in India and China, respectively, to 87 and 84 per cent in the Russian Federation and Malaysia, respectively. More than half of the youth population graduates with an upper secondary qualification in most (10 out of 15) WEI countries. In Argentina, less than half of the population obtains an upper secondary qualification, despite having the longest overall number of expected years of schooling.

In two out of three WEI countries, upper secondary graduation rates exceed 50 per cent.

International comparisons of educational outcomes account for a variety of educational programmes and the International Standard Classification of Education (ISCED) helps to distinguish upper secondary programmes. It defines three types of programmes: those (called 3A) designed to provide access to tertiary type A programmes; those (3B) designed to provide access to tertiary type B education; and finally those (3C) which prepare for direct entry into the labour market or other follow-up education.

In most countries, these programmes represent different streams of education from which students follow. In these cases, graduation rates for 3A, 3B and 3C programmes add up to an estimate of the total share of the population obtaining an upper secondary degree. Yet, in Jamaica and Malaysia, upper secondary graduation rates are not easily combined. Students first obtain an O-level certificate, which does not provide access to tertiary education but frequently marks the end of initial education. Some students continue their education and obtain a second certificate, the A-level, entitling them to tertiary studies (see Annex 5B for more details on the structure of upper secondary programmes).

Jamaica and Malaysia have the highest share of upper secondary graduates, but the lowest number of graduates who are eligible to continue to tertiary studies.

By and large, countries that offer a wider variety of upper secondary programmes have high graduation rates. The promise of graduating after a relatively short first-stage upper secondary programme (O-level) attracts many students in Jamaica and Malaysia to upper secondary education. In fact, these countries have the highest share (more than 70 per cent) of upper secondary graduates. However, at the same time, Jamaica and Malaysia have the lowest share of graduates who are eligible to directly enter tertiary education, 4 per cent and 16 per cent respectively.

Latin American countries only offer upper secondary programmes that lead to university.

In Latin American countries, such as Argentina, Chile, Paraguay and Peru, upper secondary programmes are designed to prepare participants for tertiary education. With the exception of Argentina and Paraguay, they have the highest share of youth eligible to enter university education. Entry rates indicate that a majority of all young persons take up tertiary studies. Still, countries must consider whether their education systems offer appropriate options for secondary education for all young people. Further extension of access may need to be complemented by more diverse curricula.

Figure 1.19
Upper secondary graduation rates, 1995 and 2003
Graduates as a percentage of population at the typical age of graduation by programme destination

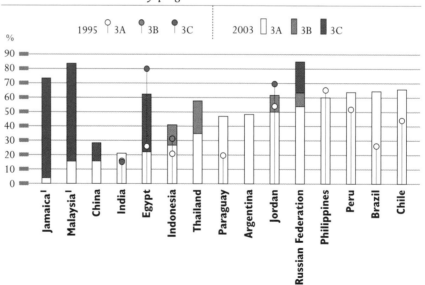

Countries are ranked in ascending order by upper secondary (3A) graduation rates in 2003.

1. Malaysia and Jamaica: Graduates who obtained ISCED 3A degrees also obtained ISCED 3C degrees before. The 3A and the 3C segment together indicate the total number of ISCED 3C degrees.

Note: Jamaica ISCED 3C refers to national O-level programmes, ISCED 3A refers to national A-level programmes. The classification used here differs from other publications and is adjusted to allow for improved international comparability.

Source: OECD/UNESCO WEI, Table 1.16 in Annex A4.

Tertiary education

Tertiary programmes were the fastest growing education sector in most WEI and OECD countries. The number of tertiary students increased in WEI countries, on average, by 77 per cent and by 43 per cent in OECD countries since 1995 (see Figure 1.16 and Annex A4, Table 1.9). In Brazil, China, Egypt and Malaysia, the number of students more than doubled. With the exception of the Philippines, student numbers grew by more than 25 per cent in all WEI countries.

Enrolment in tertiary grew by 77 per cent in just 8 years in WEI countries.

Tertiary education can be classified into two types of educational programmes. The ISCED distinguishes between type A and type B programmes. Tertiary type A programmes are largely theoretically-based and are designed to provide qualifications for entry into advanced research programmes and professions with high skill requirements. These programmes lead to the equivalent of bachelor, master or diploma degrees. Tertiary type B programmes are more occupationally-oriented and prepare for direct entry into the labour market. The programmes are typically of shorter duration than type A programmes (usually two to three years) and do not lead to advanced research programmes.

Enrolment in type A programmes tripled in China and Malaysia since 1995.

In countries that have both types of programmes, enrolment in type A programmes grew more rapidly than enrolment in type B programmes. The increase in tertiary type A enrolment in China and Malaysia in 2003 was three times higher than in 1995. In other words, enrolment grew yearly by 20 per cent in China and 17 per cent in Malaysia (see Annex 4A, Table 1.10). Enrolment in type A programmes doubled in Brazil, Egypt, the Russian Federation and Zimbabwe.

The increase in enrolment is due to the high entry rates to tertiary education in 2003. Here, a number of WEI countries have better results than OECD countries. In OECD countries every second young person enters tertiary type A programmes. In Argentina, Chile, and the Russian Federation, this is between 53 and 62 per cent, and in Thailand at 50 per cent. Rates are also high in Malaysia and Uruguay, where every third person enters tertiary type A education.

In Argentina, Chile, and the Russian Federation, more than half of the youth population enters tertiary type A education.

Entry into type B programmes is also widespread. In Argentina, Malaysia and the Russian Federation, between 30 and 40 per cent take up studies in type B programmes. However, these entry rates can not be added, since many students enrol in type B programmes first and continue studies in type A programmes later.

Zimbabwe has the lowest entry rates to tertiary education. New entrants to tertiary type A and type B programmes represent just 2 and 4 per cent, repectively, of the population at the typical starting age.

The Russian Federation and Thailand have the highest tertiary graduation rates in WEI countries.

Tertiary type A graduation rates in WEI countries range from 5 per cent in China to 33 per cent in the Russian Federation (the only WEI country exceeding the OECD average of 32 per cent) (see Figure 1.20). Egypt, Jordan, the Philippines and Thailand also have comparably high graduation rates, at over 20 per cent. Surprisingly, when considering the high entry rates to tertiary education, graduation rates in Argentina and Uruguay are the second lowest among reporting WEI countries, at 8 and 9 per cent, respectively.

Tertiary graduation in Malaysia increased fourfold compared to 1995.

Six WEI countries reported graduation data for both 1995 and 2003. During this period graduation rates grew fourfold for tertiary type A and type B programmes in Malaysia. In Chile and Thailand graduation rates for type A programmes doubled. In Thailand rates for type B programmes also increased. The smallest increase in tertiary type A programmes was observed in Indonesia, from 7.5 to 9.4 per cent. In the Philippines, tertiary type B graduation rates decreased substantially compared to 1995, but this was more than counterbalanced by a shift towards higher graduation rates in type A programmes. China had the lowest graduation rates in 2003, though given the large increase in entry and participation rates, these will likely increase in the near future.

Figure 1.20
Tertiary education graduation rates, 1995 and 2003
Graduates as a percentage of population at the typical age of graduation by type of programme

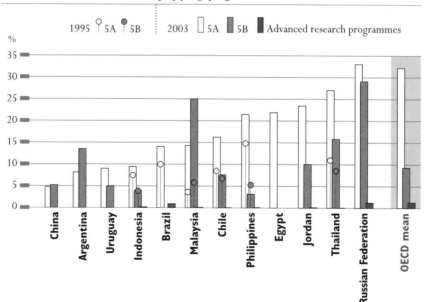

Countries are ranked in ascending order by tertiary (type A) graduation rates in 2003.

Note: Adding graduation rates for different types of tertiary education substantially overestimates the total graduation rate.

Source: OECD/UNESCO WEI, Table 1.17 in Annex A4.

Public and private provision of education

How was the rapid expansion of education facilitated in WEI countries? Was it mainly public schools that absorbed the growing number of new students or did private education providers play a significant role in meeting demand, especially at higher levels of education?

Education statistics classify an educational institution as private if it is controlled and managed by a non-governmental organization (*e.g.* religious group, association, enterprise) or if its governing board consists mainly of members not selected by a public agency. The classification is based on its governance rather than its funding sources. In terms of funding, educational institutions are classified as government-dependent (receives more than 50 per cent of its budget from the state) or independent (receives less than 50 per cent of its budget from the state). The majority of private educational institutions in WEI countries are government-dependent.

In WEI countries, there are a wide variety of private education providers, including religious-based schools, "second-chance" schools for drop-outs and elite schools. The scope of private provision is greatest at the pre-primary and post-secondary education levels.

Figure 1.21 presents the share of private education in WEI countries for the different levels of education. On average across WEI countries the share of private enrolment is higher than in OECD countries. In ten out of 16 WEI countries, the share of primary students enrolled in private education exceeds 10 per cent, which is the average share in OECD countries. In Zimbabwe, community schools cater to 87 per cent of all primary students, and almost half in Chile. Private education is almost entirely dependent upon government financing in both countries.

The share of private educational provision grew in Chile. In Jordan, Paraguay, Peru and Thailand, there were slight increases in the private share of enrolment, while in Brazil and Uruguay private primary education decreased from 12 to 8 per cent and 16 to 13 per cent, respectively.

At the secondary level of education, the share of students enrolled in private institutions remained stable or declined in most WEI countries. The private share fell sharply for upper secondary in the Philippines (from 35 to 24 per cent), Brazil (from 23 to 14 per cent) and Tunisia (from 14 to 7 per cent) between 1995 and 2003.

At the tertiary level, there are WEI countries where there is very little private provision (*e.g.* Egypt, India, Russian Federation, Thailand and Uruguay) and those where private institutions provide for a majority of tertiary students (*e.g.* Brazil, Chile, Indonesia, Paraguay and the Philippines). In terms of change since 1995, there was a clear shift towards a greater share of private provision, especially in Peru and Brazil.

Figure 1.21
Enrolment in private educational institutions, 2003
*Enrolment in government dependent and independent private educational institutions
as a percentage of total enrolment*

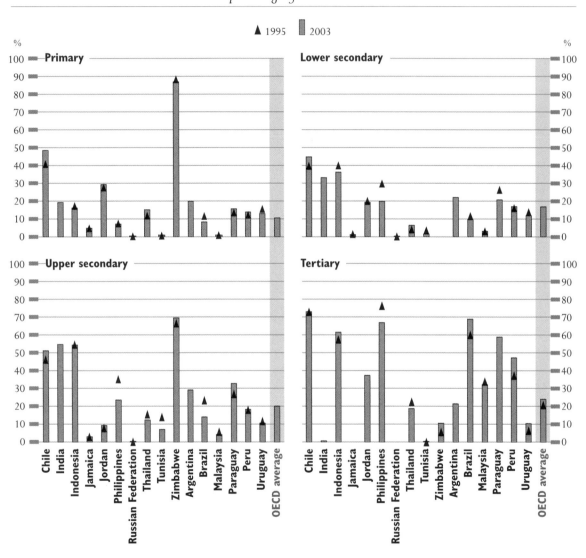

Source: OECD/UNESCO WEI, Table 1.13 in Annex A4.

Gender

Countries committed to the *Education for All* process and the UN Millennium Development Goals have agreed to eliminate gender disparities in primary and secondary education by 2005 and to achieve gender equality in education by 2015. However, today still less than half of the world's children live in countries where girls have equal access to primary education. When considering the upper secondary and tertiary levels of education, gender equity has not yet been achieved in most countries (UIS, 2005). While in many developing countries girls are disadvantaged and excluded from education to a greater extent than boys, in OECD countries, the opposite is often true. In two-thirds of the OECD countries, women can expect to stay on average more than half a year longer in education than men. In Iceland, New Zealand, Sweden and the United Kingdom, the difference exceeds two years.

Figure 1.22
Female share of enrolment, 1995 and 2003
*Percentage share of female students and percentage point change,
1995 to 2003, by level of education*

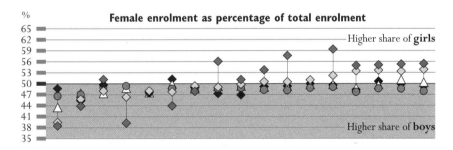

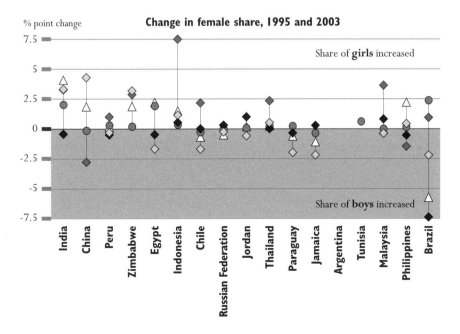

Countries are ranked in ascending order by the female share of upper secondary enrolment.
Source: OECD/UNESCO WEI, Table 1.11 in Annex A4.

Most WEI countries have not reached gender equality in education. Jamaica, Paraguay and Peru are the only countries with no substantial difference in school life expectancy between boys and girls. In the other 14 countries with available data participation in education is not equal by gender. In four countries girls stay, on average, substantially shorter in education than boys, *e.g.* for one year in India and Zimbabwe and about 0.4 years in Chile and Egypt. On the contrary, girls receive over one year more education than boys in Argentina, the Russian Federation and Uruguay and more than half a year in Brazil, Jordan, Malaysia and the Philippines.

Figure 1.22 presents the share of female students by level of education and how it has changed since 1995. Enrolment at the primary and lower secondary levels of education is generally well balanced by gender. The share of girls increased by two percentage points or more in Brazil, Egypt and India at the primary level and in China, India, Egypt and the Philippines at the lower secondary level compared to 1995. In Brazil the share of boys at the lower secondary level increased by over 7 percentage points.

At higher levels of education, participation by gender is less balanced. Girls account for less than 40 per cent of upper secondary enrolment in India. Women are under-represented at the tertiary level in China, Indonesia, India and Zimbabwe. At the same time, substantially higher participation by women at the tertiary level is the main reason for differences in school life expectancy by gender in Argentina, the Russian Federation and Uruguay. In Uruguay, two out of three tertiary students are women (see also Annex A4, Table 1.11).

Overall women have benefited more from the expansion of tertiary education than men. In all but three WEI countries, women's enrolment grew faster than men's and the relative share of female students increased. Indonesia and India reduced the difference in female and male participation from 37 to 44 per cent and from 35 to 38 per cent, respectively. The exception to this pattern is China, where the difference in participation increased by more than 2.5 percentage points since 1995, indicating that men benefited more from the tremendous growth in tertiary enrolment.

REFERENCES

Michaelowa, Katharina and **Marie Waller** (2003), *HWWA-Report 226:* "Labour Market Outcomes of Education: Evidence for Selected Non-OECD Countries", HWWA, Hamburg. Accessed at *http://www.hwwa.de/Forschung/Publikationen/Report/2003/Report226.pdf*

OECD (2001), *Starting strong – Early Education and Care,* OECD, Paris.

OECD (2004), *Learning for Tomorrow's World – First Results from PISA 2003,* OECD, Paris.

UNESCO Institute for Statistics/OECD (2003), *Financing Education – Investments and Returns*, UNESCO Institute for Statistics, Montreal.

UNESCO Institute for Statistics (2005), *Global Education Digest 2005*, UNESCO Institute for Statistics, Montreal.

UNESCO (2000), *The Dakar Framework for Action – Education for All: Meeting our Collective Commitments*, UNESCO, Paris.

UNESCO Regional Bureau of Education for Latin America and the Caribbean (2004), *Universal primary completion in Latin America: Are we really so near the goal?*, UNESCO, Santiago. Accessed at *http://www.unesco.cl/ing/biblio/ediciones/101.act*

UNESCO International Bureau of Education (2004), *Final report - International Conference on Education 47th session*, UNESCO IBE, Geneva. Accessed at *http://www.ibe.unesco.org/International/ICE47/English/FinalRep/Finrep_eng.pdf*

World Bank (2005), *Expanding Opportunities and Building Competencies for Young People – A New Agenda for Secondary Education,* World Bank, Washington, D.C.

World Bank (2005a), *World Development Indicators,* World Bank, Washington, D.C.

Chapter 2

RESPONDING TO INCREASED PARTICIPATION: TRENDS IN RESOURCES INVESTED IN EDUCATION

Prepared by Karine Tremblay
OECD

■ INTRODUCTION

There is increasing evidence that education matters, not only for the personal development, health status, social inclusion and labour market prospects of individual learners (see Box 1.1), but also for the broader economic performance of their countries (OECD/UIS, 2003). As the world has entered the age of the knowledge economy, education and human capital play a critical role in driving economic growth. This is true for the world's most advanced economies, but also in those emerging economies that are currently experiencing profound transformations and periods of rapid growth and development.

Education systems expanded rapidly in WEI countries between 1995 and 2003, both in absolute terms and in education participation rates.

In this context, education systems expanded rapidly in WEI countries between 1995 and 2003, in terms of coverage and rates of education participation, but also in absolute terms due to demographic dynamics. The latter resulted in a growing client base of youth populations that needed to be accommodated for, irrespective of changes in participation rates.

Overall, the demographic pressure at primary and lower secondary school ages levelled off for Brazil, China, Egypt, Indonesia, Jamaica, the Russian Federation, Sri Lanka, Thailand and Tunisia over the period, but remained a strong constraint in upper secondary and tertiary education.

In this latter respect, the demographic pressure caused by the growing amount of children of primary and lower secondary school age already levelled off over the period for Brazil, China, Egypt, Indonesia, Jamaica, the Russian Federation, Sri Lanka, Thailand and Tunisia. For the population of upper secondary school age, however, demographic pressure was still a strong constraint for WEI education systems, with the exception of Argentina, Indonesia, Malaysia, Sri Lanka and Thailand. At the tertiary level of education, the demographic burden was even stronger since only Chile, China and Thailand have been free of demographic pressure over the period (see Chapter 1).

As far as participation rates are concerned, most WEI countries managed to increase the coverage of participation in primary and lower secondary education between 1995 and 2003 (see Figure 1.12).

However, primary enrolments failed to keep pace with the comparatively large growth in the population of primary school-age in Jamaica, Malaysia, Paraguay, Peru and the Philippines. This resulted in a decrease in enrolment rates at the primary level of education. At the lower secondary level, only Jamaica failed to increase enrolments as fast as its population growth of 12 to 15-year-olds, resulting in a relative decrease in lower secondary enrolment rate and education coverage. All other WEI countries improved their participation rates in lower secondary education, most significantly Brazil, Paraguay, Peru, Tunisia and Uruguay, and to a lesser extent, Chile, Egypt, India and the Philippines (see Figures 1.12 and 1.16, as well as the web-resource complementing Annex A4 at *www.uis.unesco.org/wei2005*).

Most WEI countries improved participation rates in primary and lower secondary education.

When considering rates of enrolment for all basic education combined, net enrolment rates for the population 5 to 14 years of age improved in all WEI countries except in Jamaica and the Philippines and – marginally – in Malaysia, although it should be recognised that these countries started the period with a high base (see Figure 1.13).

Similarly most WEI countries saw upper secondary and tertiary education participation rates improve significantly between 1995 and 2003 (see Figure 1.16).

Despite increases of 16 to 24 per cent in the number of students enrolled in upper secondary education, only Egypt, the Philippines and Zimbabwe did not manage to increase enrolments as fast as population growth between 1995 and 2003, but rather experienced a decrease in education coverage in relative terms over the period. They faced an increase of one-fifth to one-third in their 15 to 19-year-old population between 1995 and 2003, making it already challenging just to maintain participation rates at their 1995 levels. At the tertiary level, however, all WEI countries for which data were available saw faster increases in enrolments than in growth of the corresponding 20 to 29-year-old population. This translated into improved enrolment rates. In this respect, progress in tertiary education participation rates was most notable in Brazil, Chile, Egypt, Indonesia, Malaysia and the Philippines.

Participation rates in upper secondary education increased everywhere except Egypt, the Philippines and Zimbabwe, where enrolments failed to keep pace with population growth.

The two parallel trends of increased education participation rates and demographic dynamics for the populations of school age – especially at the upper secondary and tertiary levels of education – resulted in a dramatic rise in absolute enrolments in all WEI countries (except for Jamaica and the Russian Federation) between 1995 and 2003. On average the number of students enrolled across all levels of education increased by 16 per cent. In the case of the Russian Federation, the decrease in absolute enrolments resulted from a decrease in the populations of primary and lower secondary school age while participation rates improved. In Chile, China, India, Malaysia and Paraguay, enrolments increased by more than 20 per cent across all levels of education (see Figure 1.7).

Participation in tertiary education increased in all WEI countries, but most impressively in Brazil, Chile, Egypt, Indonesia, Malaysia and the Philippines.

In primary education, absolute enrolment increased most in Jordan and the Philippines, by 15 and 12 per cent, respectively. At the lower secondary level of education, seven WEI countries saw their enrolments increase by more than 25 per cent: China, Egypt, India, Paraguay, Peru, the Philippines and Tunisia. At the upper secondary level of education, 10 WEI countries increased their enrolments by more than 25 per cent, and by 50 per cent or more in the case of Brazil, China, Malaysia and Paraguay. Tertiary enrolments more than doubled in Brazil, China, Egypt and Malaysia, while they increased by 50 to 80 per cent in Chile, India, Jordan, the Russian Federation and Thailand (see Figures 1.12 and 1.16).

The combination of demographic pressure and increased participation rates resulted in upper secondary enrolment increases of more than 50 per cent in Brazil, China, Malaysia and Paraguay. Tertiary enrolments more than doubled in Brazil, China, Egypt and Malaysia.

This dramatic growth in enrolments – most significantly at the upper secondary and tertiary levels of education – was accompanied by changes in participation patterns towards greater enrolments in general programmes (see Figure 1.18), but most importantly, by shifts between public and private providers of education in some countries (see Figure 1.21).

The increased level of upper secondary enrolments were disproportionately accommodated by private institutions in Chile and Paraguay, and by public institutions in Brazil, the Philippines and Tunisia. In tertiary education, the reliance upon private institutions increased everywhere except in the Philippines and Thailand.

While the reliance upon private institutions to deliver education at the primary and lower secondary levels increased in Chile, Peru and Thailand, and to a lesser extent in Jordan, Paraguay (primary level) and Zimbabwe (lower secondary level), the proportion of students accommodated in public institutions increased in Brazil and Uruguay, as well as in Indonesia, Paraguay and the Philippines at the lower secondary level of education.

In upper secondary education, Chile and Paraguay called upon private institutions to accommodate the growing number of students, while in Brazil, the Philippines and Tunisia, public schools welcomed a disproportionate number of additional students. The picture was less distinct at the tertiary level, where, with the exception of the Philippines and to a lesser extent Thailand, most countries have accommodated the growth in student numbers by relying increasingly upon private providers of tertiary education. This trend was especially strong in Brazil, one of the countries with the fastest growth in enrolments, and Peru (see Figure 1.21).

Changes in absolute enrolments have an impact on levels of education expenditure and require additional human resources.

In order to examine the WEI countries' responses to changing demands for education, it is important to consider both changes in absolute enrolments and in participation rates.

Irrespective of their origin – demographic dynamics or expanded coverage of education – changes in absolute numbers of students enrolled and their distribution between levels of education pose great challenges for education systems and policy-makers. This is because of their impact on overall levels of education expenditure and implications for the deployment of human resources. In a drive to ensure that the expansion of education systems does not take place at the cost of quality, large numbers of new teachers have to be recruited to teach the growing school client-bases. This implies difficult trade-offs for policy-makers between teachers' characteristics, working conditions, incentives and teacher exposure (student to teaching staff ratios and class sizes) if education budgets are to be maintained at sustainable levels,

Changes in participation rates have implications for the sharing of education costs between the public and private sectors.

By contrast, changes in participation rates have implications for the sharing of education costs between the public and private sectors at different levels of education. Improvements in education participation rates between 1995 and 2003 suggest that a higher proportion of households had children enrolled in education in 2003 than in 1995 – in particular at the upper secondary and tertiary levels where participation rates have increased most – and had to pay for their education. Besides, improvements in school expectancy similarly suggest that families and educational authorities had to pay for education on average for longer compared to 1995 (see Figure 1.6). This raises the question of whether participation in education has remained affordable for all, and government authorities need to allocate financial resources in a way that ensures that virtually all children have access to basic primary and lower secondary education. At the same time, governments must aim to not discourage increased participation rates at the upper secondary and tertiary levels of education where education matters most for the long-term economic performance of countries.

Therefore, this second chapter explores the way financial and human resources devoted to education have evolved in WEI countries between 1995 and 2003 in order to respond to the increased demands on education systems. Yet, trends in the allocation of human and financial resources to education cannot be interpreted in isolation from the economic and social contexts in which education developments took place. This is especially true given that the period under scrutiny – 1995 to 2003 – was a period of economic turmoil and volatile social trends for many WEI countries.

Policy-makers face difficult trade-offs to expand participation in education while maintaining education budgets at sustainable levels.

The rest of this chapter reviews major trends in educational expenditure. It examines trends in public and private spending in relation to the key economic and social developments that shape them, in order to assess to what extent trends in education finance can be explained by broader economic and social trends. It also examines trends in education finance in relation to trends in enrolments at different levels of education and in relation to changes in participation patterns and the role of private providers of education.

The trade-offs made by WEI education systems in responding to increased demand for education are also analysed. This chapter explores trends in the allocation of funds between capital investments and current expenditure, then examines the deployment of human resources and the ways in which WEI countries have recruited education staff to serve growing client-bases while struggling to maintain education budgets within sustainable levels. Finally, it considers student to teaching staff ratios, teachers' age structures and qualifications, teaching conditions and salary incentives as key policy levers in explaining trends in expenditure per student at different levels of education.

◼ TRENDS IN PUBLIC AND PRIVATE EXPENDITURE: THE IMPORTANCE OF ECONOMIC AND SOCIAL DEVELOPMENTS

Looking at the overall financial burden of education for WEI countries and changes in education expenditure between 1995 and 2002 gives a first indication of the impact of growing participation and enrolment in education.

In 2002, WEI countries spent 3.9 per cent of their GDP on primary and secondary education and an additional 1.3 per cent on tertiary education – similar to OECD countries.

In this respect, overall spending on WEI educational institutions in 2002 was similar to the relative levels of education expenditure found in OECD countries, with WEI countries spending on average 3.9 per cent of their GDP on primary, secondary and post-secondary non-tertiary education and an additional 1.3 per cent on tertiary education, compared with 3.8 and 1.4 per cent respectively for OECD countries (see Figure 2.1).

Figure 2.1
Expenditure on educational institutions as a percentage of GDP, 1995 and 2002
By level of education, source of funds and year

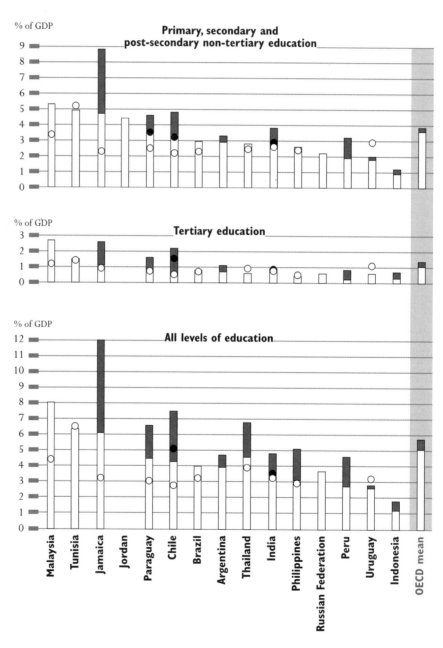

Countries are ranked in descending order of expenditure from public sources on educational institutions in 2002 in primary, secondary and post-secondary non-tertiary education.

Source: OECD / UNESCO WEI, Table 2.2 in Annex A4.

However, expenditure on primary, secondary and post-secondary non-tertiary education in Chile, Jamaica, Jordan, Malaysia, Paraguay and Tunisia was significantly higher than in OECD countries, highlighting the strong financial constraints and commitment resulting from current education participation rates. Similarly, Chile, Jamaica and Malaysia spent significantly more than OECD countries at the tertiary level of education relative to their level of wealth. These high levels of expenditure relative to GDP can be explained by comparatively larger school-age populations (Jordan and Malaysia at the primary level, Paraguay and Tunisia at the upper secondary level) and/or high rates of education participation (Chile, Malaysia and Paraguay).

However, expenditure relative to GDP was significantly higher in Chile, Jamaica, Jordan, Malaysia, Paraguay and Tunisia than in OECD countries.

Compared to 1995, expenditure on educational institutions increased significantly at the primary, secondary and post-secondary non-tertiary levels of education, on average from 3.1 to 3.9 per cent of GDP across WEI countries. The increase in expenditure relative to GDP at these levels of education was especially large in Chile, India, Jamaica, Malaysia and Paraguay, but was more moderate in Brazil. By contrast, the expenditure relative to GDP decreased in Uruguay and to a lesser extent in Tunisia. At the tertiary level, the dramatic rise in public expenditure in Malaysia resulted in expenditure more than doubling relative to GDP. Private expenditure increased – albeit less – in Chile. These trends need to be related to the dramatic growth in absolute enrolments in lower and upper secondary education that took place over the period in Paraguay, and in Chile, India and Malaysia at the upper secondary and tertiary levels of education (see Figures 1.12 and 1.16). In the case of Chile, these trends also result from an educational reform aimed at expanding public resources invested in education.

Following trends in enrolments, expenditure on primary and secondary education increased significantly relative to GDP in Chile, India, Jamaica, Malaysia and Paraguay compared to 1995. By contrast, it decreased in Tunisia and Uruguay.

Plotting changes in enrolments and expenditure at constant prices can further refine the links existing between growth in enrolments at different levels of education and trends in levels of education expenditure (see Figure 2.2).

WEI enrolments expanded most at the upper secondary and tertiary levels of education, where curricula were more varied, staff more specialised and therefore expenditure per student has traditionally been higher than in primary and lower secondary education (see Annex A4, Table 2.13). An increased proportion of students enrolled in upper secondary and tertiary education has translated into more than proportional increases in expenditure. The discrepancy between change in primary, secondary and post-secondary non-tertiary enrolments on the one hand, and change in expenditure at constant prices on the other hand, was greatest in countries that had experienced the strongest relative increase in upper secondary enrolments, namely Chile, India, Malaysia and Paraguay (see Figure 2.2).

In primary and secondary education, expenditure increased faster than enrolments since the growth in enrolments was stronger in secondary education where expenditure per student was higher.

Figure 2.2
Change in enrolment and in expenditure on educational institutions, 2003
*Index change in public and private expenditure on educational institutions
and in enrolment aligned to finance data (1995 = 100)*

Change in public expenditure ◆   ◆ Change in private expenditure

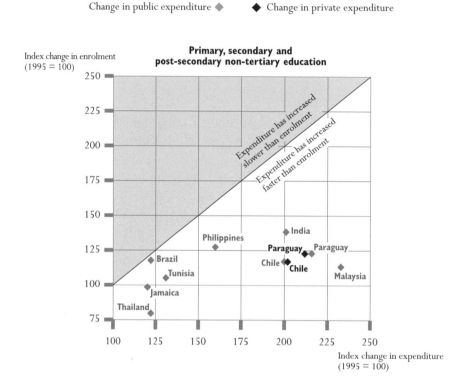

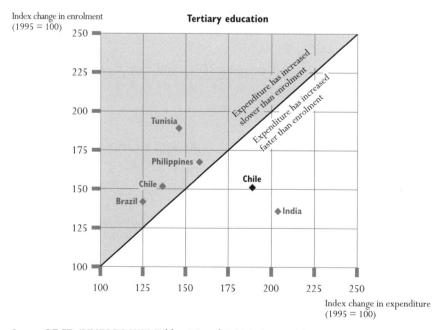

Source: OECD/UNESCO WEI, Tables 2.3 and 2.14 in Annex A4.

At the tertiary level of education, changes in enrolments and in expenditure were more balanced. In Brazil, Chile and the Philippines (where public and private trends balanced each other), expenditure increased at the same pace as enrolments. By contrast, Indian expenditure on tertiary education increased more than enrolments between 1995 and 2003, suggesting improvements in expenditure per student. The opposite pattern could be observed for Tunisia over the same period, highlighting the difficulty for its public authorities to cope with an 89 per cent increase in tertiary enrolments over a rather short period (see Annex A4, Table 2.14).

In tertiary education, expenditure increased faster than enrolments in India, at the same pace in Brazil, Chile and the Philippines, and slower than enrolments in Tunisia.

Overall, trends in education expenditure as a percentage of GDP for all levels of education underline the strong effort undertaken by WEI public authorities to finance the increased demands placed on education systems. This public effort was very strong in the case of Chile, Jamaica, Malaysia and Paraguay, and somewhat less so in Brazil and Thailand. But this massive public effort was matched by an equally important private effort in Chile and India where private expenditure on education increased by more than one percentage point of GDP for all levels of education between 1995 and 2002 (see Figure 2.1).

In Chile, Jamaica, Malaysia and Paraguay, the public sector undertook a strong effort to finance the expansion of the education system.

However, the driving forces of expenditure on education are not limited to trends in enrolment numbers and their breakdown by level of education. Cross-country comparisons and research evidence suggest that, everything else being equal, countries and/or constituencies with higher levels of income per capita spend more on education. Other factors that are positively correlated with education expenditure are female labour force participation and the existence of strong teacher unions (see Falch, 2004, for a review). By contrast, unfavourable dependency ratios and large proportions of elderly people in the population are associated with less spending on education per capita, highlighting trade-offs between social spending on education and other age-related expenditure by governments and private entities alike.

The driving forces underlying trends in public and private expenditure on education are nonetheless different. Trends in public and private spending have therefore been examined separately.

Trends in public expenditure on education depend on numbers enrolled and macroeconomic and fiscal trends

From the perspective of public authorities, the provision of education services competes not only with expenditure on security and defence, and on infrastructures, or with support to the economy, but it also competes within social spending with other expenditures such as health and social protection. Public authorities operate under budgetary constraints, and therefore, fiscal discipline and the need to maintain public accounts at sustainable levels often

The need to maintain public accounts at sustainable levels compels governments to make difficult choices regarding the allocation of limited resources.

compel governments to make difficult trade-offs and choices regarding the allocation of limited resources.

Evidence shows that government spending on education tends to be pro-cyclical.

In this respect, empirical evidence from Latin America and the Caribbean, based on 1970-1996 panel data, indicated that government spending on education in this region tended to increase in times of economic prosperity and fall in times of economic contraction, although less so for expenditure on primary and secondary education compared with tertiary spending (Snyder and Yackovlev, 2000). Panel analysis of Russian regional public expenditure on education in 1999 and 2000 similarly showed that regions with higher income per capita spent more on education (Verbina and Chowdhury, 2004).

Nevertheless public authorities are also constrained by commitments to provide basic education for all.

Public authorities are also constrained by legislation on compulsory education and commitments to provide basic education for all (see Chapter 1). As a result, trends in public spending on education also depend on trends in absolute enrolments at different levels of education – given different unit costs – irrespective of countries' fiscal resources.

Trends in public expenditure on education therefore need to be examined in relation to both trends in enrolments at different levels of education and the broader macroeconomic growth context that determines the amount of fiscal resources available to the public sector.

In Malaysia and Thailand, the increase in public expenditure on education was mainly driven by expenditure on tertiary education, while in Chile, Jamaica and Paraguay public expenditure increased most in primary and secondary education.

The amount that public authorities spent on educational institutions increased dramatically in Jamaica and Malaysia between 1995 and 2002, with additional expenditure amounting to three percentage points of GDP or more (see Figure 2.3). In Malaysia this increase was mainly driven by expenditure on tertiary education, which more than doubled as a result of the rocketing tertiary enrolments (see Figure 1.16), while in Jamaica, the increase in public expenditure was strongest in primary, secondary and post-secondary non-tertiary education. Public expenditure also increased relative to GDP – albeit to a lesser extent – in Brazil, Chile, Paraguay and Thailand. In the case of Chile and Paraguay, public expenditure increased more in primary, secondary and post-secondary non-tertiary education, reflecting in part the strong growth in secondary enrolments in these countries. The increase in public expenditure was more balanced between levels of education in Brazil, and public expenditure increased more in tertiary education than at lower levels in Thailand, again consistently with the dramatic increase in enrolments at that level while upper secondary enrolments hardly increased over the period (see Figure 1.16).

Public expenditure on education remained stable relative to GDP in India, the Philippines and Tunisia but decreased in Uruguay.

In India, the Philippines and Tunisia, public expenditure on education remained roughly unchanged relative to GDP between 1995 and 2002. However these countries experienced a robust growth of 30 to 45 per

Figure 2.3
Public expenditure as a percentage of GDP, 1995 and 2002
Public expenditure on educational institutions plus public subsidies to households
(which include subsidies for living costs and other private entities)
as a percentage of GDP (%) and index change in GDP at constant prices,
by level of education and year (1995 = 100)

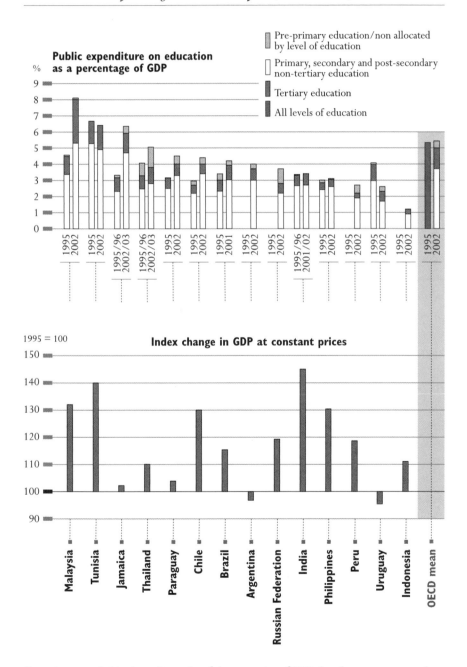

Countries are ranked in descending order of the proportion of GDP that the government spends on education in 2002.

Source: OECD/UNESCO WEI, Table 2.5 in Annex A4.

cent of their GDP over the period. This apparent stagnation therefore hid an increase in public expenditure in real terms. Uruguay was the only WEI country to experience a significant decrease in education expenditure relative to GDP between 1995 and 2002, by about 1.5 percentage points of GDP. At the same time, Uruguay's GDP contracted by about 5 per cent compared with its 1995 level, indicating that the decrease in expenditure was even stronger.

The Uruguayan situation underlines the need to take broader economic trends into account when analysing trends in public expenditure relative to GDP. Indeed, WEI countries have gone through markedly different growth patterns between 1995 and 2002: while Chile, India, Malaysia, the Philippines and Tunisia saw their economy expand by more than 30 per cent over the period, GDP grew by less than 5 per cent in Jamaica and Paraguay, and even contracted in the cases of Argentina and Uruguay.

Trends in macroeconomic growth are important to understand the fiscal stance of countries and the background context for public spending on education.

Trends in macroeconomic growth are important to better understand the fiscal stance of WEI countries in 1995 and in 2002, the two reference points between which comparisons have been made. A closer examination of WEI economic trends over the period is all the more important as the 1995 to 2002 period was characterised by strong economic instability for a number of WEI countries. Indeed, while the first part of the 1990s seemed favourable for the development of many WEI countries, the second part of the 1990s and the turn of the millennium were unstable for a number of WEI economies that faced unprecedented shocks and/or internal social turmoil. Financial crises spread over the developing world at the turn of the millennium and affected the majority of WEI countries directly or indirectly. As a result, the economic and fiscal conditions under which WEI governments had to operate and the increasing demand for education with which they had to cope were fairly constraining in a number of countries.

WEI economies differ in terms of structural economic specialisations. In 1995, agriculture employed large numbers in India, Indonesia, Paraguay, the Philippines and Thailand, but much less so in Argentina, Chile, Peru, the Russian Federation and Uruguay.

Before examining macroeconomic trends, it is worth recalling that WEI economies differ widely in terms of structural economic specialisations. While in 1995 agriculture employed a marginal proportion of the labour force in Argentina, Peru and Uruguay, and to a lesser extent in Chile and the Russian Federation, this sector provided employment to 40 per cent or more of the labour force in India, Indonesia, Paraguay, the Philippines and Thailand. Between 1995 and 2002, most WEI economies had shifted towards more industrialised and service-oriented specialisations. The proportion of employment in agriculture has decreased to the benefit of the services sector in Brazil, Egypt, Paraguay and the Philippines, but less so in Indonesia, Malaysia and Thailand. In more industrialised WEI economies, such as Argentina, Chile, the Russian Federation and Uruguay, structural reallocations of employment took place from industry to services (see Figure 2.4).

Figure 2.4
Employment by sector, 1995 and 2002
Employment in agriculture, industry and services as a percentage of total employment

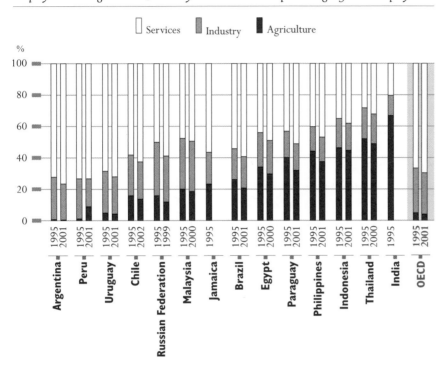

Countries are ranked in ascending order of the proportion of employees working in the agriculture sector in 1995.

Note: Wherever data for 2002 were not available, the most recent available data were used.

Source: World Bank, World Development Indicators 2004 edition.

Economic developments in WEI countries between 1995 and 2002

Foreign direct investments boomed in many emerging countries in the first half of the 1990s as democratisation and economic reforms, including large-scale privatisation, were underway and economic prospects were extremely encouraging; meanwhile pension funds from many industrialised countries were searching for high returns and a diversification of their investments.

The *Tequila* crisis that hit Mexico in December 1994 heightened the awareness of investors towards macroeconomic fundamentals in other emerging markets and contributed to the contagion throughout Latin America in 1995. In June and July 1997, Thailand was the first East Asian WEI country to be hit directly by a financial crisis. A series of similar shocks spread over emerging economies and directly hit Argentina, Brazil and the Russian Federation in the late 1990s, as well as indirectly affected a number of other WEI economies.

The second part of the 1990s and the turn of the Millennium were unstable for a number of WEI economies that were affected by unprecedented financial crises directly or indirectly.

All of these financial crises had commonalities. Before the crisis, all these economies were characterised by comparatively high deficits of current accounts in the context of fixed exchange rates that were maintained for too long, thereby leading to over-evaluated currencies. In addition, financial systems were insufficiently developed (in terms of risk management and supervision) to avoid an excessive reliance of the economy upon short-term – highly volatile – portfolio capital inflows, which exposed domestic businesses to currency risk (IMF, 1998). As foreign investors lost confidence in the long-term sustainability of the fixed exchange rate and reassessed the risk of their investments, capital was repatriated towards safer markets in expectation of devaluation. To counteract this speculative attack against the exchange rate and a massive outflow of capital, countries had to purchase their currency on the international markets – meanwhile drying up their exchange reserves – or alternatively, increase their leading interest rates to preserve the attractiveness of their country to foreign capital. However, this defensive policy had the double backlash effect of drying up international exchange reserves and slowing down domestic investment and consumption, thereby making the economy more vulnerable to subsequent speculative attacks and self-fulfilling speculators' prophecies of unsustainable exchange rates.

Thailand was the first WEI country to face a financial crisis in 1997.

International investors reassessed the risk of their investments in Thailand during spring 1997 in light of the growing deficits of the current account. The short-term nature of their investments translated into a sudden and massive capital flight that sparked the devaluation of the *baht* in July, hence generating further capital outflows. Since many Thai companies were indebted in USD, the devaluation prompted bankruptcies and the transmission of the financial crisis to the real economy. The GDP contracted in 1997 and, in particular, in 1998. However, despite its magnitude, the crisis was short-lived and the Thai economy recovered in 1999, boosted by strong domestic public consumption and international demand (see Figure 2.5).

The crisis spread to Indonesia, Malaysia and the Philippines.

The Thai crisis immediately spread to Indonesia, Malaysia and the Philippines. Due to its high level of debt labelled in USD, Indonesia was most severely affected with a record recession of 14 per cent in 1998, while the impact was less severe in Malaysia (-8 per cent) and the Philippines (-0.6 per cent). Malaysia actually managed to exit the crisis without support from the International Monetary Fund. All three countries resumed growth in 1999, although GDP growth slowed down again in 2001 in Malaysia and the Philippines as a result of lower international demand.

In contrast to the other Asian WEI countries, China and India were unaffected by the regional crises and maintained strong GDP growth.

In contrast to the Southeast Asian WEI countries, China was unaffected by the regional crises and maintained strong GDP growth between 1997 and 2002. The economic expansion was led by manufacturing exports and the implementation of a number of export-oriented reforms in the 1990s. In India and Sri Lanka, GDP growth was also quite robust throughout the period,

Figure 2.5
Key economic and social trends, 1993 to 2002
Annual growth rate of GDP, GDP per capita, consumer prices (%) and percentage of the labour force unemployed (%)

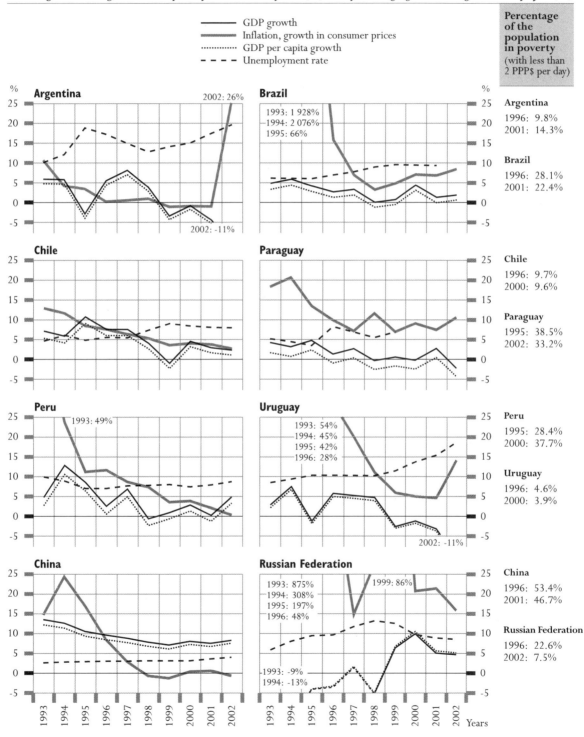

Source: World Bank, World Development Indicators 2004 edition.

Figure 2.5 (continued-1)
Key economic and social trends, 1993 to 2002
Annual growth rate of GDP, GDP per capita, consumer prices (%) and percentage of the labour force unemployed (%)

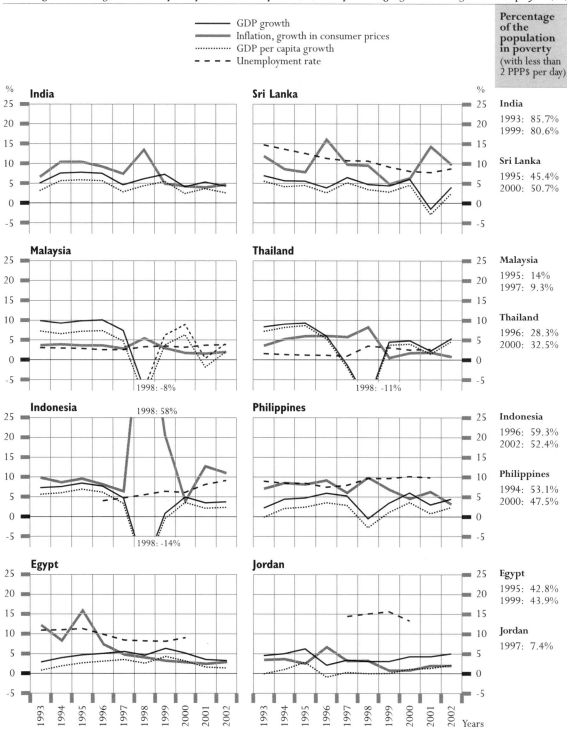

Source: World Bank, World Development Indicators 2004 edition.

Figure 2.5 (*continued-2*)
Key economic and social trends, 1993 to 2002
Annual growth rate of GDP, GDP per capita, consumer prices (%) and percentage of the labour force unemployed (%)

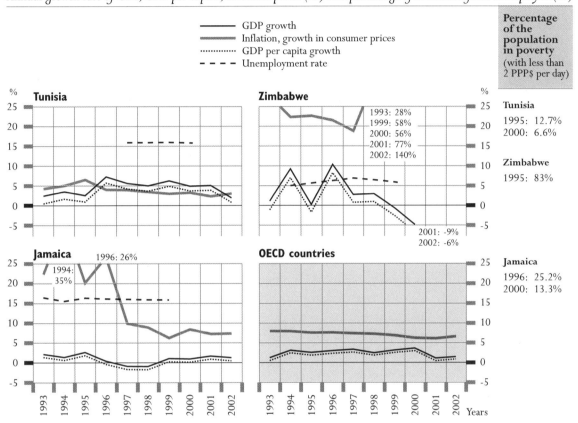

Source: World Bank, World Development Indicators 2004 edition.

with annual GDP growth rates of 4 per cent or more. In Sri Lanka, GDP growth slowed down in 1996, as a result of a drought and deteriorating security situation, and again in 2001, when the country experienced a 1.5 per cent recession due to continued civil strife combined with a slowdown in global demand and severe power shortages. Overall, the strong growth recorded in China and India between 1995 and 2002 has helped the recovery throughout the Asian region, and it counterbalanced the impact of the external shocks that hit Southeast Asian WEI countries.

In the aftermath of the Asian crisis, other emerging economies' fundamentals were carefully screened. This was the case for the Russian Federation in 1998. When the country embarked on its transition towards the market economy in 1992, the option of a 'big bang' economic transformation was chosen, with a rapid implementation of price and trade liberalisation and large-scale privatisation (OECD, 2005). This rollercoaster stabilisation of 1992-1994 prompted a large contraction of GDP in 1992 that carried on until 1997.

Following the Asian crisis, international investors reassessed the risk of other emerging markets, and the Russian Federation also faced a financial crisis in 1998.

The Russian economy then resumed growth in 1997 but remained highly dependant on foreign capital since it had inherited in 1992 the entire Soviet debt which plagued public budgets. When oil exports collapsed in the aftermath of the Asian crisis in 1997 and resulted in a deterioration of the external balance and expected fiscal accounts, capital started to flow out of the country. Interest rates skyrocketed to support the *rouble* but that did not prevent its devaluation in August 1998. The devaluation, however, improved the competitiveness of the Russian economy and GDP bounced back in 1999, initially driven by comparatively cheaper labour and energy inputs, and then by increasing oil prices from 2001.

Brazil also suffered from a similar external shock and a deterioration of its economy in 1998 and 1999.

In Brazil, the crisis was also sparked by concerns with large public deficits and public debt in the context of a USD-pegged exchange rate regime. Foreign capital was repatriated towards safer markets in mid-1998, leading to increases in interest rates, greater budgetary discipline and an economic recession. Despite the intervention and support of the International Monetary Fund, a new wave of capital outflow led to the abandon of the USD anchoring in January 1999. The subsequent depreciation of the *real,* associated with higher interest rates, halted capital outflow and boosted Brazilian exports' competitiveness relative to neighbouring Argentina, whose currency remained pegged to the USD until 2002. Brazil therefore resumed a 4.4 per cent GDP growth rate in 2000, which was only slowed down in 2001 by the lower demand of its trading partners as a consequence of the economic crises in Argentina and Uruguay and by unfavourable weather and energy conditions domestically. Overall, Brazil managed to maintain positive GDP growth rates throughout the 1995-2002 period, despite the financial crisis.

Argentina was the last WEI country to face a financial crisis and experienced a severe economic recession between 1998 and 2002.

Argentina was hit by a financial crisis between 1998 and 2002. In the early 1990s, liberalisation and structural adjustment policies, combined with the adoption of a currency board (based upon a fixed one to one parity of the *peso* with the USD), permitted a boom of the Argentine exports and economy and massive inflows of foreign investment. However, Argentina was hit by a series of external shocks during the second half of the 1990s. The GDP contracted in 1995 with the contagion of the Mexican crisis. Then in 1998, GDP growth slowed down as interest rates had to be raised to restore investors' confidence after the series of crises in Thailand, Brazil and Russia. And in early 1999, Argentina faced a speculative attack against the *peso* after Brazil abandoned its fixed exchange rate with the USD, in expectation of a similar move. The authorities decided to maintain the convertibility which proved costly for the economy given that the appreciation of the USD and devaluations in Brazil and Chile resulted in a deterioration of Argentina's competitiveness and external trade balance. The GDP contracted in 1999, 2000 and 2001. Public deficits increased and record interest rates to prevent capital flight inflated the external debt service and public deficits, making the external situation less and less sustainable. The situation collapsed when bank restrictions to capital mobility were imposed in late 2001, sparking riots and leading to the resignation of the government. The fixed convertibility was finally abandoned in January 2002.

The Argentine crisis spread towards other Latin American WEI countries, most notably Uruguay due to its close trade relations with Argentina. While GDP growth had been sustained during the early 1990s (except 1995), Uruguay entered into recession in 1999 and plunged together with Argentina in 2002. In Chile, growth in GDP was also robust until 1997 but slowed down in 1998 in the aftermath of the Asian crisis as a result of lower export earnings and tighter monetary policies. A severe drought exacerbated economic difficulties in 1999, with a slight recession. Yet, careful macroeconomic management and the abandonment of the USD-tied exchange rate in 1999 restored investors' confidence and the economy resumed growth in 2000, albeit at a slower pace given lower exports to Argentina. Similarly, Paraguay's GDP grew steadily in the early 1990s with the exception of a slowdown in 1996. But the expansion of the economy was halted in 1998-2000 with near-zero growth and a contraction of GDP in 2002, in response to regional contagion. By contrast, Peru's economic trends appear less connected with those of other WEI Latin American economies, most likely as a result of its lower level of trade interactions with Argentina and Brazil. Overall, the Peruvian economy displayed robust growth from 1993 to 1997, with a record 12.8 per cent in 1994. Peru's economic performance was, however, more disappointing from 1998 to 2001, with near-zero growth before taking off again in 2002.

The Argentine crisis spread towards Chile, Paraguay, Peru and – most importantly – Uruguay.

Other WEI countries in Africa, the Caribbean and the Middle East were less exposed to large scale financial crises. In North Africa and the Middle East, Egypt, Jordan and Tunisia all experienced moderate but sustained GDP growth in the range of 3 to 6 per cent per year between 1993 and 2002, with a slowdown in 1996 for Jordan as the Middle East peace talks came to a stall and generated scepticism over the region's future. By contrast, Jamaica registered sluggish economic growth throughout the period and a recession in 1997-1998, which sparked civil unrest in 1999. In Zimbabwe, economic trends were highly volatile between 1993 and 1998, before entering into a deep recession from 1999 onwards as a result of severe political and governance uncertainties.

In North Africa and the Middle East, Egypt, Jordan and Tunisia all experienced moderate but sustained GDP growth between 1995 and 2002.

Overall, most WEI economies that had experienced shocks between 1995 and 2002 showed signs of economic recovery in 2002, with the exceptions of Argentina, Paraguay, Uruguay and Zimbabwe, which were in economic recession in 2002. Yet despite recovery in 2002, the previous economic trends put a serious strain on fiscal accounts and prevented a number of WEI governments from finding resources to meet additional demand in education between 1995 and 2002. This difficulty is illustrated by trends in government finance (see Figure 2.6).

Most WEI economies showed signs of economic recovery in 2002, except for Argentina, Paraguay, Uruguay and Zimbabwe.

Figure 2.6
Government finance surplus/deficit, 1995 to 2002
Government finance surplus/deficit relative to GDP (%)

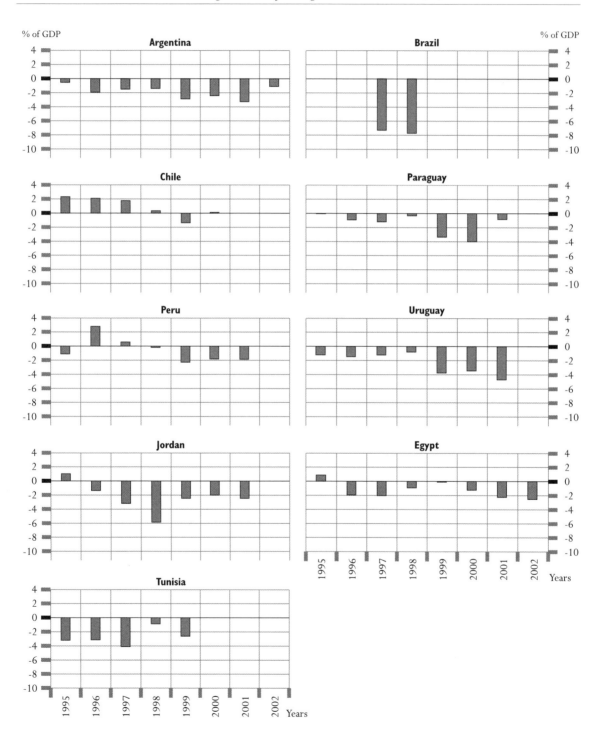

Source: International Monetary Fund, International Financial Statistics.

Figure 2.6 *(continued)*
Government finance surplus/deficit, 1995 to 2002
Government finance surplus/deficit relative to GDP (%)

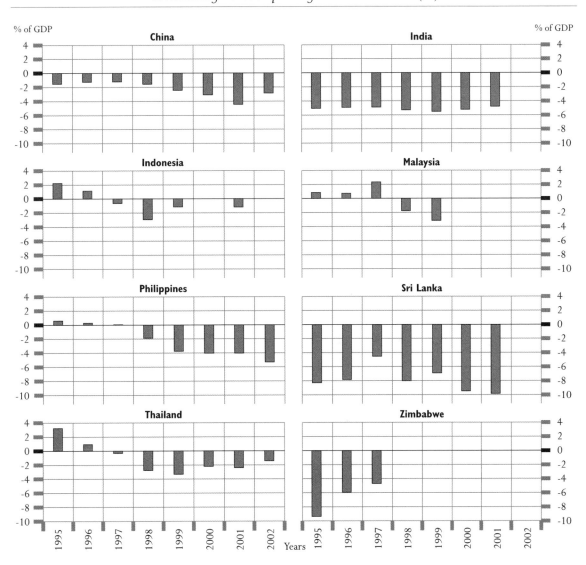

Source: International Monetary Fund, International Financial Statistics.

While a number of WEI governments enjoyed fiscal surpluses in 1995, subsequent trends indicate the apparition of public deficits in all WEI countries over the period – especially so in countries that were affected by major economic crises. In 1995, Indonesia and Thailand registered surpluses of more than 2 per cent of GDP, while surpluses were smaller in Malaysia and the Philippines. All four countries saw their fiscal accounts deteriorate from 1998, but differed in their ability to revert the trend. While Indonesia and Thailand

The volatile economic trends translated into growing fiscal deficits. Indonesia and Thailand then reversed the trend, but deficits widened in Malaysia and the Philippines.

had improved their fiscal accounts by 2002, deficits widened in Malaysia (up to 1999) and most significantly in the Philippines. These differing patterns can be examined in the light of education expenditure trends over the same period (see Figure 2.3). The traditionally low public expenditure on education in Indonesia and its moderate increase in Thailand between 1995 and 2002 did not result in a strong drain on fiscal accounts. By contrast, the dramatic increase in Malaysia's public expenditure on education over the same period was undoubtedly one of the factors underlying its budget deficit trends.

In Argentina, Paraguay, Peru and Uruguay, public accounts also showed signs of improvements at the end of the period, while public deficits remained large in Brazil, India, Sri Lanka and Zimbabwe.

Chile also experienced a brief budget deficit in 1999 as its economy went into recession, but then returned to fiscal surpluses, a noteworthy achievement given that in the meantime public expenditure on education had increased by about 1.5 percentage points relative to GDP. In North Africa and the Middle East, Jordan faced a temporary deterioration of its fiscal accounts in 1997 and most significantly 1998, but then managed to reduce its public deficit to about 2 per cent of GDP. Similar levels were recorded in Egypt at the end of the period, possibly reflecting the drain on public budget from large school-age populations (see Annex A4, Table 1.3).

In Argentina, Paraguay, Peru and Uruguay, public accounts deteriorated from 1999, but showed signs of improvements at the end of the period. By contrast, public education authorities in Brazil, India, Sri Lanka and Zimbabwe operated within the context of large public deficits, making it difficult to expand public expenditure dramatically (see Figure 2.3).

Shifting priorities of WEI governments in terms of public spending on education

These overall budgetary constraints of the public sector have implications for public spending on education insofar as public authorities need to make choices and trade-offs between different types of public interventions. Trends in public expenditure on education relative to total public expenditure therefore indicate whether reallocations of public funds between different sectors of public intervention have taken place between 1995 and 2002 (see Figure 2.7).

The share of WEI governments' expenditure devoted to education relative to other sectors increased in all countries – albeit marginally in Brazil, India and the Philippines.

It is noteworthy that the share of WEI governments' expenditure devoted to education relative to other sectors of public intervention increased in all countries for which trends were available, although this increase was fairly marginal in the case of Brazil, India and the Philippines. In the meantime, all WEI countries except Uruguay saw their total public expenditure increase compared to 1995, by more than 40 per cent in India, Jamaica and Malaysia, and by 20 to 40 per cent in Brazil, Chile, Peru, Thailand and Tunisia. Public expenditure on education increased in real terms for most countries, but also gained in relative importance among different types of public expenditures (see Figure 2.7).

Figure 2.7
Public expenditure on education as a percentage
of total public expenditure, 1995 and 2002

Public expenditure on educational institutions plus public subsidies to households
(which include subsidies for living costs and other private entities) as a percentage
of total public expenditure, by level of education and year (%) and index change
in total public expenditure on education (1995=100)

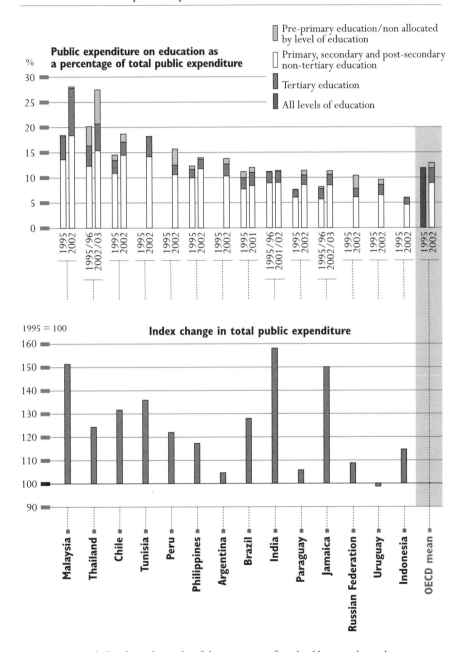

Countries are ranked in descending order of the proportion of total public expenditure that is spent on education in 2002.

Source: OECD/UNESCO WEI, Tables 2.1 and 2.5 in Annex A4.

The shift in public priorities was most significant in Chile, Jamaica, Malaysia, Paraguay and Thailand, where the share of total public expenditure spent on education increased by 30 per cent or more. Interestingly, these shifts in public priorities affected different levels of education in different countries. While in Chile, Jamaica and Paraguay, the extra public effort on education benefited mostly primary, secondary and post-secondary non-tertiary education, in Malaysia tertiary education grew in importance in the public budget from 4.6 to 9.4 per cent of total public expenditure – three times the level of spending of OECD countries (see Annex A4, Table 2.5).

Brazil, Indonesia, Malaysia, Tunisia and Uruguay devoted a large share of their public education budgets to tertiary education in 2002, while Chile, Peru and the Philippines put more emphasis at lower levels of education.

WEI countries also had interesting differences in their relative emphasis of public expenditure on tertiary education relative to lower levels. While Brazil, Indonesia, Malaysia, Tunisia and Uruguay devoted one-fifth or more of their public education budgets to tertiary education in 2002, Chile, Peru and the Philippines had opposite patterns with less than one-sixth of public expenditure on education directed towards the tertiary level. These patterns suggest different conceptions of tertiary education among WEI countries, with the first group of countries perceiving tertiary education as a public good requiring public intervention, while in the latter group, the private returns to tertiary education are perceived to justify comparatively less public financing compared to lower levels of education.

Another interesting aspect of public spending on education relates to the interactions existing between public authorities and private providers for financing education. WEI countries differed widely in the extent of private provision of education. While primary, secondary and post-secondary non-tertiary education was mainly delivered by public institutions in Brazil, Malaysia, the Philippines, Thailand, Tunisia and Uruguay in 2003, private institutions accommodated 20 to 50 per cent of students in Argentina, Chile, India, Indonesia and Jordan. When looking at trends in private enrolments, it is interesting to note that the expansion of education participation translated into increased recourse to private providers of education in Chile and most significantly in India (see Figure 2.8). By contrast the expansion of education participation in Brazil was accompanied by an increase in the proportion of students enrolled in public schools, highlighting the impact of the FUNDEF programme on public education participation (see Box 2.1 and OECD, 2005b).

In countries where 20 per cent or more of primary and secondary students were enrolled in private institutions, public authorities supported the cost of education of these students, with the exception of Jordan.

In countries in which 20 per cent or more of primary, secondary and post-secondary non-tertiary students were enrolled in private institutions, public authorities supported the cost of education of these students through transfers to private institutions or households (education vouchers), although the amounts transferred remained below what their share in enrolments would suggest. Jordan was an exception: public authorities did not provide any financial support for the 23 per cent of students enrolled in private institutions.

Figure 2.8
Enrolment in private institutions and public transfers to private institutions
and the private sector, 1995 and 2002
*Percentage of students enrolled in private institutions and percentage of public funds
transferred to private institutions and the private sector, by level of education and year*

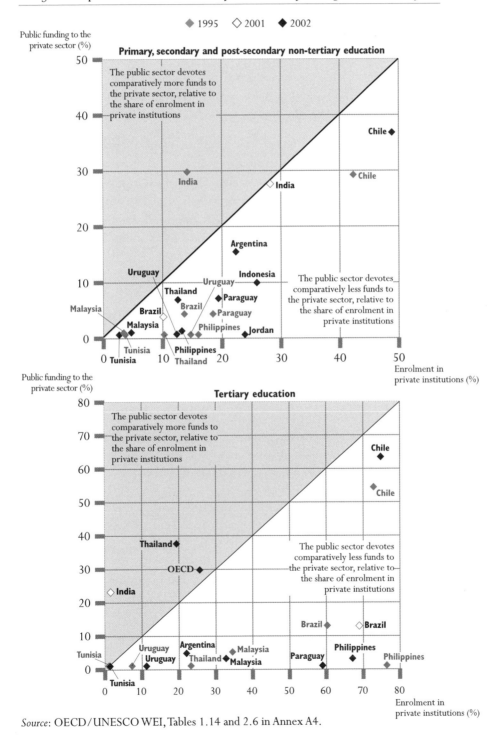

In India, the increase in the proportion of students enrolled in private institutions between 1995 and 2002 was accompanied by a stagnation of public funds going to the private sector. Yet in 2002 India balanced its public education expenditure equitably between the public and private sectors, according to their respective shares of enrolments. Similarly, the increase in the share of private enrolments over the same period in Chile was accompanied by a proportional increase in expenditure directed to the private sector, suggesting that the Chilean voucher system was well established. Indeed, most private institutions in Chile receive financial support from the government, and less than 10 per cent of primary and secondary enrolments are in independent private institutions that do not receive any funding from the government (see Table 1.13).

At the tertiary level of education, patterns of participation in private institutions differed markedly from lower levels. The proportion of students enrolled in private institutions was much higher than in primary, secondary and post-secondary non-tertiary education in Brazil, Chile, Malaysia, Paraguay, the Philippines and Thailand. In Brazil, Chile and the Philippines, the majority of tertiary students were enrolled in private institutions, while in India,

---

Box 2.1

Brazil's FUNDEF programme to improve access and equity

FUNDEF (the Fund for maintenance and development of elementary education and enhancement of the teaching profession) was established in January 1998 in Brazil to improve enrolment rates, with a particular emphasis on regional disparities, through improvements in the distribution of public funds for basic education.

Through the fund, a national spending floor for primary and lower secondary levels of education was set on a per student basis for all levels of government combined. Where states and municipalities could not afford this nationally-set level of expenditure per student, the federal government was required to top up the spending. As a result, FUNDEF has been most successful in increasing enrolment in poorer regions. For instance, primary school enrolment increased by 23 per cent and lower secondary school enrolment by 68 per cent in Brazil's Northeast region between 1995 and 2000, compared with nationwide average increases of 9 and 52 per cent respectively.

This extra funding has been particularly successful at the municipal level: enrolment in public municipally-funded primary schools increased from 32 per cent in 1995 to 47 per cent in 2000. Correspondingly, enrolment slightly decreased in all other primary schools, whether federal, state or private (the latter from 11 to 9 per cent of total primary enrolment over the same period).

Given the success of FUNDEF in improving enrolment in basic education and in making enrolment in basic levels of education now almost universal, recent policy discussions have focused on improving quality in basic education provision and extending FUNDEF to upper secondary education.

Tunisia and Uruguay, nearly all students attended public universities and tertiary institutions. Interestingly, the expansion of participation in tertiary education in Brazil led to a shift towards a larger recourse to private providers of education in relative terms, a trend opposite to that observed in primary, secondary and post-secondary non-tertiary education. These reverse trends suggest that in recent years Brazilian public authorities skewed their efforts towards expanding public education provision at lower levels of education (see Box 2.1).

Despite displaying a comparatively large share of enrolments in private tertiary institutions relative to OECD countries, public authorities in WEI countries hardly contributed to the cost of education of students enrolled in private institutions, with the exceptions of Chile, India and Thailand. Interestingly, India and Thailand stood out for spending more public funds on tertiary institutions than their shares of enrolments would suggest.

Despite widespread enrolments in private tertiary institutions in WEI countries, public authorities hardly contributed to the cost of education of these students except in Chile, India and Thailand.

Overall, these trends suggest that WEI countries varied both in the extent to which the public sector accommodated students and, wherever a significant proportion of students was enrolled in private schools, in the extent to which public authorities subsidised participation in private education or left the burden of private education financing to households.

Trends in private expenditure on education depend on participation patterns and social developments

Yet, the private sector does not only contribute to the financing of education through payments to private institutions. In some countries, students and families are also required to pay tuition in public institutions, although this is generally the case only in upper secondary and tertiary education (*e.g.* Chile and Paraguay). In Uruguay, public education is entirely free at all levels of education and tuition fees only apply in private institutions.

In any case, private financing of education – be it provided by public or private institutions – needs to be interpreted in light of trends in participation rates and broader social outcomes. Indeed, improvements in education participation rates between 1995 and 2003 suggest that a higher proportion of households had children enrolled in education in 2003 than in 1995 – especially at the upper secondary and tertiary levels where participation rates increased most – and had to pay for their education in countries where it was not provided free of charge. Furthermore, improvements in school expectancy similarly suggest that in 2003 families and educational authorities had to pay for education on average for longer than they did in 1995 (see Figure 1.6). This raises the question of whether participation in education remained affordable for all, especially given the volatile economic and social trends that several WEI countries experienced between 1995 and 2002.

A higher proportion of households had children enrolled in education in 2003 than in 1995 and had to pay for their education when it was not provided free.

The ability of families to pay for education depends on trends in GDP per capita, unemployment and other social outcomes.

While trends in public expenditure on education depend to a large extent on GDP growth and trends in fiscal accounts, the ability of households and families to pay for the portion of education costs that accrues to them depend more on trends in GDP per capita as an indication of average levels of income and unemployment and poverty rates as a proxy for the proportion of households facing difficult social conditions.

While GDP per capita trends typically follow those of overall trends in GDP over a comparatively short period of time, the gap between GDP and GDP per capita growth depends on population growth. Overall, the 1990s were characterised by easing demographic pressure in WEI countries, with slowdowns in population growth in all countries but Jamaica and Sri Lanka. Nevertheless, annual population growth rates were still around or above 2 per cent in Egypt, Jordan, Malaysia, Paraguay and the Philippines in 2002, thereby explaining slower progress in levels of income per capita in these countries than their overall GDP trends suggest (see Figure 2.9).

Brazil and Chile saw levels of income per capita improve steadily between 1995 and 2002, but trends were less favourable in Argentina, Paraguay, Peru and Uruguay.

In Latin America, while Brazil and Chile saw levels of income per capita improve steadily between 1995 and 2002 (with the exception of crises episodes), trends were less favourable in Argentina, Paraguay, Uruguay and to a lesser extent Peru. GDP per capita decreased from year to year since 1997 in Paraguay and since 1999 in Argentina and Uruguay. Besides, high unemployment rates in Argentina and Uruguay at the end of the period underlined the difficulties encountered by some families in paying for education. The incidence of poverty decreased noticeably in Brazil and Paraguay over the period, but in Argentina the crisis translated into increased poverty at its peak in 2002. Overall more than one-third of the population in Paraguay and Peru were considered to be living in poverty in 2002 and 2000, respectively, making it difficult to meet private costs of education. Similarly, in Jamaica the stagnation of levels of income per capita and high levels of unemployment suggest similar difficulties in that country for some households (see Figure 2.5).

Despite improvements in GDP per capita, the incidence of poverty in China, India, Indonesia, the Philippines and Thailand made it difficult for some households to meet the private costs of education.

Although levels of GDP per capita plunged in Asia in 1998 – especially in Indonesia, Malaysia and Thailand – they have been recovering in the region ever since. Unemployment remained fairly low between 1993 and 2002 in Malaysia and Thailand. But one-third to one-half of the population was considered to be living in poverty in Indonesia, the Philippines and Thailand at the end of the period, making it difficult for households to meet the private costs of education. Given the large incidence of poverty in China and India, a similar conclusion holds for these countries despite continuous growth in their GDP per capita between 1995 and 2002.

Given the volatile trends in GDP per capita growth experienced by some WEI economies, it is also important to look at changes in levels of GDP per capita in order to assess how income levels fared in 2002 compared to 1995. In this

Figure 2.9
Population growth, 1993 to 2002
Annual population growth rate (%)

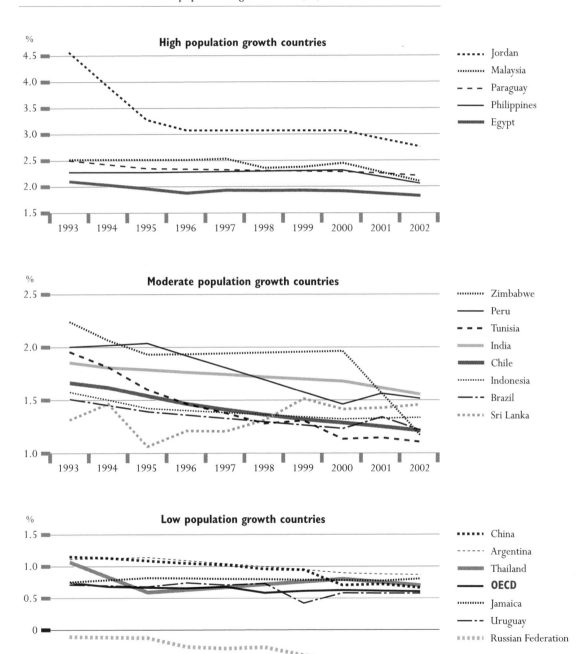

Source: World Bank, World Development Indicators 2004 edition, Table 2.1 in Annex A4.

© UNESCO-UIS/OECD 2005 Education Trends in Perspective – Analysis of the World Education Indicators

Figure 2.10
GDP per capita and unemployment, 1995 and 2002
GDP per capita in purchasing power parities and rate of unemployment (Constant US$ PPP converted)

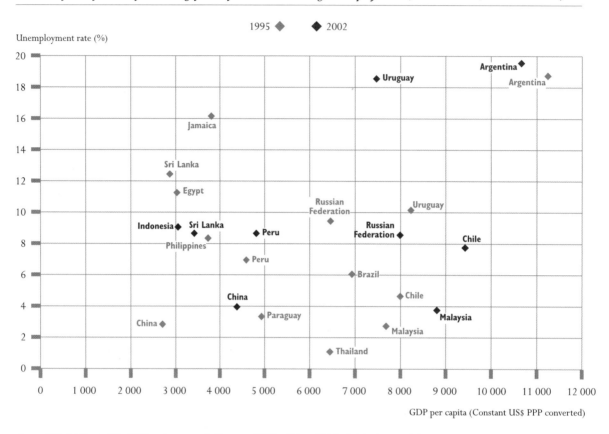

Source: World Bank, World Development Indicators 2004 edition, Table 2.1 in Annex A4.

respect, levels of income per capita increased in all countries where trends were available, with the exceptions of Argentina and Uruguay where unemployment also increased over the same period. This suggests that there were improvements in the living conditions of most WEI populations and in their ability to contribute financially to the expansion of WEI education systems. Progress in levels of income per capita was strongest in Chile, China and the Russian Federation, and to a lesser extent in Malaysia (see Figure 2.10).

With these social trends in mind, patterns of private funding at different levels of education in 2002 underlined the strategies adopted by WEI countries in providing education for all in light of their country-specific social constraints (see Figure 2.11).

Interestingly, Malaysia and Tunisia did not require households to contribute to the costs of primary to tertiary education in 2003 (see Annex A4, Table 2.4). By contrast, the situation appeared to be less favourable in India, Indonesia,

Paraguay and Peru, where households contributed on average 20 to 40 per cent of the cost of their primary, secondary and post-secondary non-tertiary education despite widespread poverty (see Figure 2.5). In interpreting these data, it should be remembered, however, that these indicators represent country averages, and education is actually provided free in public institutions in Paraguay and Peru (including textbooks at the primary level of education) and is often accompanied by social programmes in poorer areas (provision of school kits, breakfast and/or lunch programmes). Besides, the private expenditure considered in Figure 2.11 includes subsidies received from public sources, which can be important in some countries (*e.g.* Chile).

In 2002, students in Malaysia and Tunisia were not expected to pay for their education, whereas they had to contribute 20 to 40 per cent of the primary and secondary education costs in India, Indonesia, Paraguay and Peru.

Overall, the contribution of the private sector to total expenditure on education remains below 30 per cent at the primary, secondary and post-secondary non-tertiary levels of education for all WEI countries, except for Jamaica, where households contribute about one-half of the cost of education. This pattern underlines the emphasis of WEI public authorities on subsidising a large part of the cost of basic compulsory education.

In general, private contributions to primary and secondary education remained below 30 per cent except in Jamaica.

Figure 2.11
Patterns of private funding, 2002
Private sources (including subsidies received from public sources) as a percentage of total expenditure on educational institutions, by level of education (%)

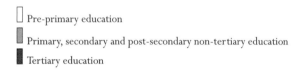

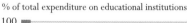

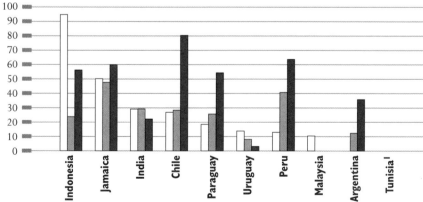

Countries are ranked in descending order of the proportion of private sources in total expenditure on educational institutions at the pre-primary level of education

1. Data not applicable because the category does not apply.

Source: OECD/UNESCO WEI, Table 2.4 in Annex A4.

At the tertiary level, education is far less subsidised by the public sector in Argentina, Chile, Indonesia, Paraguay and Peru, while the opposite is seen in India and Uruguay.

At the tertiary level of education, the proportion of the cost of education borne by households increased drastically in most WEI countries compared to primary, secondary and post-secondary non-tertiary education. This was significantly the case in Argentina, Chile, Indonesia, Paraguay and Peru. But in India and Uruguay, the portion of education cost accruing to households decreased at the tertiary level. This latter pattern suggests that public authorities subsidised more participation in tertiary education – which traditionally benefits the most affluent – rather than participation at lower levels of education which is more universal. However, the private contribution to education expenditure remained remarkably low in Uruguay (see Figure 2.11).

Lastly, changes in the relative proportion of public and private expenditure on education between 1995 and 2002 underline the strategies adopted by WEI countries in financing the expansion of their education systems over the period (see Figure 2.12).

Patterns of public-private shares of primary and secondary education costs remained stable between 1995 and 2002, except in India, Jamaica and Uruguay.

Interestingly, patterns of public-private shares of education expenditure remained fairly stable over time at the primary, secondary and post-secondary levels of education, with the exception of slight increases in the share of private expenditure in Jamaica and Uruguay, and a much more important increase in the relative share of private expenditure in India, from 5 to 29 per cent of the total (see Annex A4, Table 2.4). One possible factor behind this trend may lie in the large public deficits of India and the limits to further growth in public spending (see Figures 2.6 and 2.7).

But the massive expansion of tertiary education translated into higher contributions from the private sector in Chile, India, Jamaica, Paraguay and Uruguay.

By contrast, the massive expansion of WEI tertiary education systems in some countries occurred along with dramatic shifts in the way tertiary education was financed. In Jamaica and Paraguay, the private share of expenditure on tertiary education rose sharply, from less than 10 per cent to more than one-half of the total (see Annex A4, Table 2.4). The private share of the cost also increased, although less dramatically, in Chile, India and Uruguay. These trends might well have reflected the increase in the proportion of tertiary students enrolled in private institutions between 1995 and 2002 in the case of Uruguay, and to a lesser extent in Chile.

Overall, the growth in education participation between 1995 and 2003 translated into increased expenditure on education relative to GDP from both public and private sources in WEI countries. Relative to total public expenditure, public expenditure on education increased by 2 percentage points across WEI countries on average, while in the meantime total public expenditure increased in all countries but one. As far as private sources are concerned, the relative contributions of the private sector remained fairly stable at the primary, secondary and post-secondary non-tertiary levels of education, with the exceptions of India, Jamaica and Uruguay where large public deficits or severe macroeconomic constraints limited the margin

Figure 2.12
Relative proportions of public and private expenditure, 1995 and 2002
*Distribution of public and private sources of funds for educational institutions
after transfer from public sources, by level of education and year (%)*

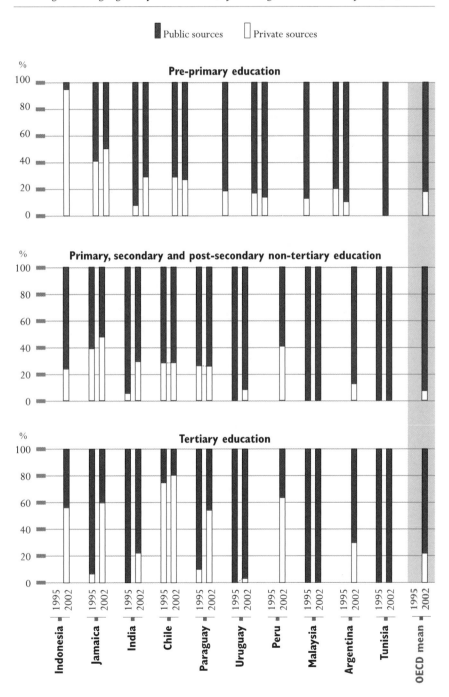

*Countries are ranked in descending order of the proportion of private sources in total expenditure on
educational institutions at the pre-primary level of education.*

Source: OECD/UNESCO WEI, Table 2.4 in Annex A4.

of the public sector to contribute further to education expenditure. At the tertiary level of education, the limitations placed on public funding appeared even stronger, and the expansion of education participation was made possible due to significant increases in the financial contributions of the private sector.

2 RESPONDING TO INCREASED DEMAND: TRADE-OFFS IN INFRASTRUCTURE INVESTMENTS AND HUMAN RESOURCES IN EDUCATION

In the context of large increases in both public and private expenditure on education and acute budgetary constraints for public authorities (see Figures 2.1 and 2.6), WEI education authorities had to make difficult trade-offs and decisions to allocate limited resources to different levels of education, types of institutions and alternative uses of funds in the best way.

Capital investments in the context of growing pressures on education budgets

Responding to increased demand for education implies balancing out different variables in order to preserve quality and maintain levels of expenditure at sustainable levels.

The expansion of education systems implies the construction of new education buildings and infrastructures, and therefore massive capital investments to meet the needs of growing student populations. Yet the bulk of education expenditure on education traditionally consists of current expenditure related to education personnel salary costs – a budgetary component that is deemed to increase proportionally with enrolments if student to teaching staff ratios and class sizes are kept unchanged. Funding large investments in education infrastructures would therefore imply large increases in education expenditure, which countries and public authorities cannot always afford. Responding to increased demand for education therefore implies the need to balance out different variables and policy levers in order to maintain levels of expenditure at sustainable levels, while not expanding education participation at the cost of quality.

In this section, how WEI countries have dealt with this difficult equation between 1995 and 2002 has been reviewed by looking first at trends and trade-offs made in the allocation of funds to current or capital expenditures and trends in the size and financial burden of the WEI teaching forces in relation with changes in student to teaching staff ratios. In most WEI countries, the massive expansion of secondary and tertiary education systems required the recruitment of large numbers of new teachers. Trends in the working conditions, as well as salary incentives, offered to teachers have been examined in order to assess the attractiveness of the profession to newcomers over time. All of these variables impact on overall expenditure per student. This section therefore concludes with trends of the policy trade-offs made by WEI countries in dealing with and responding to increased demand for education.

Figure 2.13
Expenditure by resource category, 1995 and 2002
Distribution of total expenditure by public educational institutions between current and capital, and distribution of current expenditure between compensation of all staff and other current expenditure, by level of education (%)

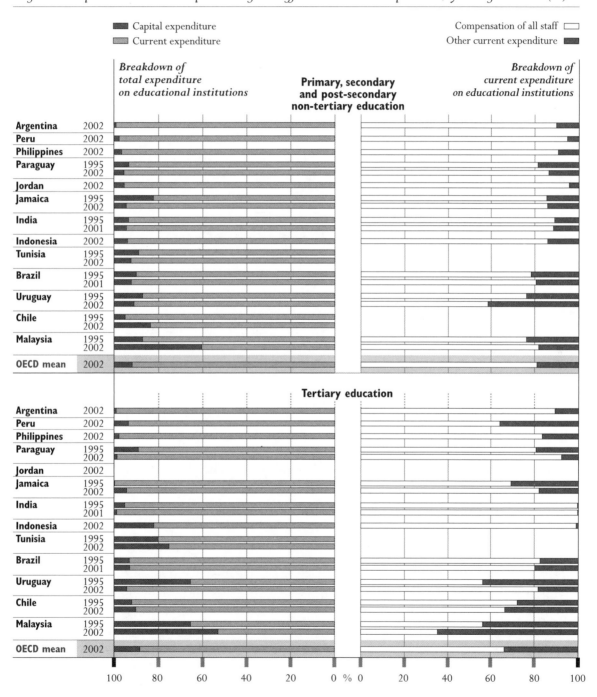

Countries are ranked in ascending order of the 2002 percentage of capital expenditure in total expenditure at the primary, secondary and post-secondary non-tertiary level of education.

Source: OECD / UNESCO WEI, Table 2.7 in Annex A4.

The impact of the expansion of education systems on school infrastructure investments may provide a first indication of the financial implications of the expansion of education systems. As far as uses of funds are concerned, the breakdown of total expenditure on education between capital investments and current expenditure highlighted diverse trends within WEI countries (see Figure 2.13).

The expansion of participation in primary and secondary education was accompanied by a decrease in the share of expenditure spent on capital, with the exception of Chile and Malaysia.

In primary, secondary and post-secondary non-tertiary education, the expansion of education participation was accompanied by a decrease in the share of expenditure spent on capital by public institutions in Brazil, India, Paraguay, Tunisia, Uruguay and most significantly in Jamaica. These trends may suggest that, at times of strong pressures on education budgets due to expanding enrolments and/or economic difficulties, public authorities slowed down capital investments relative to current expenditure. In the case of India, however, this trend may also reflect the growing importance of private institutions in education provision between 1995 and 2003, and hence the lesser emphasis of public institutions on capital investments over the period (see Figure 2.8). By contrast, Chile and Malaysia were the only WEI countries where massive capital investments took place, as illustrated by the more than twofold increases in the share of capital in total expenditure in these two countries. In 2002, Malaysian public institutions spent nearly 40 per cent of their expenditure on education infrastructure and capital investment. The very high level of public expenditure on education relative to GDP in Malaysia may have reflected a temporary process of large investments in education infrastructures. In the case of Chile, the high level of capital investment was the result of an education reform in 1996 that aimed at progressively abandoning the practice of double shifts in schools and therefore required the construction of new buildings in double shift schools.

In tertiary education, only Chile, Jamaica, Malaysia and Tunisia responded to growing enrolments with growing expenditure on capital.

At the tertiary level of education, the share of education expenditure spent on capital investments decreased in India, Paraguay and, most significantly, Uruguay – where some capital investments may have been postponed or cancelled due to the severe budget constraints in 2002. By contrast, a growing share of education expenditure was directed towards capital investments in Chile, Jamaica, Malaysia and Tunisia.

In Brazil, Malaysia and Paraguay, where primary and secondary enrolments increased significantly, the compensation of education personnel grew in relative importance in the budgets of public institutions.

Within current expenditure on education, the compensation of all education personnel grew in importance in the budgets of public institutions at the primary, secondary and post-secondary non-tertiary levels of education in Brazil, Malaysia and Paraguay. In Uruguay by contrast, other current expenditure represented about 40 per cent of total current expenditure in 2002, significantly up from 1995. The growth in other current expenditure in Uruguay reflects investments made during the period to improve classroom equipment and didactic materials. A similar trend of increasing non-staff expenditure could be observed at the tertiary level in Brazil, Chile and Malaysia, while the burden of staff costs grew in relative importance in Jamaica, Paraguay and Uruguay.

Figure 2.14
Change in student to teaching staff ratio and underlying factors, 2003
Index change in student to teaching staff ratio (STR), in enrolment aligned to personnel data and in teaching staff based on full-time equivalents, by level of education and year (1995=100)

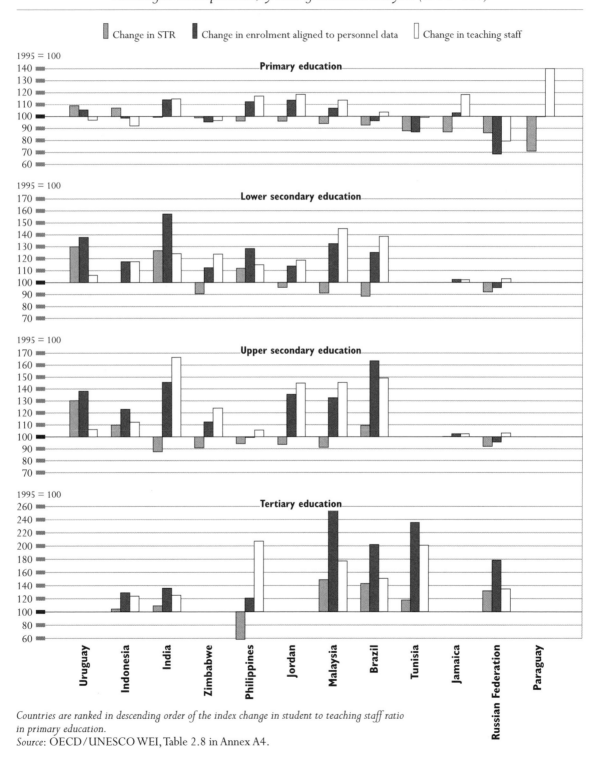

Countries are ranked in descending order of the index change in student to teaching staff ratio
in primary education.
Source: OECD/UNESCO WEI, Table 2.8 in Annex A4.

Teacher supply in upper secondary and tertiary education

These trends in the allocation of public institutions' current expenditure between staff costs and other uses need to be interpreted in light of trends in teachers' deployment, most significantly changes in teachers' numbers and their growth relative to changes in enrolments (see Figure 2.14).

The number of primary teachers decreased in Indonesia, the Russian Federation, Tunisia, Uruguay and Zimbabwe. However, primary student to teaching staff ratios decreased overall, except in Uruguay.

In this respect, the number of teachers working in primary education decreased between 1995 and 2003 in Indonesia, the Russian Federation, Tunisia, Uruguay and Zimbabwe, despite increases in enrolments at that level in Uruguay. The increase in the student to teaching staff ratio in Uruguay may therefore explain part of the decrease in the burden of staff costs relative to other current expenditure in primary, secondary and post-secondary non-tertiary education. By contrast, student to teaching staff ratios decreased between 1995 and 2003 at the primary and secondary levels of education in Brazil and Malaysia, and at the primary level in Paraguay. This trend alone could explain the higher burden of staff costs relative to other current expenditures in 2002 compared to 1995 in these three countries.

Overall, the increase in education participation at the primary level of education has generally been accompanied with a decrease in the student to teaching staff ratio, as illustrated by trends in India, Jamaica, Jordan, Malaysia and the Philippines. Uruguay is the only WEI country where the increase in primary enrolments translated in a slight increase in the primary student to teaching staff ratio.

In upper secondary education, teachers' numbers did not keep pace with increases in enrolments in Brazil, Indonesia and Uruguay, while India, Jordan, Malaysia, the Philippines and Zimbabwe managed to accommodate growing numbers and lower student to teaching staff ratios.

In upper secondary education, by contrast, trends were more uneven. In Brazil, Indonesia and Uruguay, the student to teaching staff ratios increased as a result of teachers' numbers not keeping pace with increases in enrolments. By contrast, India, Jordan, Malaysia, the Philippines and Zimbabwe succeeded in accommodating growing numbers of upper secondary students while lowering student to teaching staff ratios at the same time (see Figure 2.14).

At the tertiary level of education, teachers' numbers increased in all WEI countries for which data were available, although not as fast as enrolments did. The Philippines were an exception, with a doubling of tertiary teaching staff while enrolments only increased by 20 per cent, resulting in a dramatic drop in the tertiary student to teaching staff ratio from 38 to 22 over the period (see Annex A4, Table 2.8). In all other WEI countries for which data were available, the increase in tertiary participation was dealt with by increasing student to teaching staff ratios, by more than 15 per cent in the case of Brazil, Malaysia, the Russian Federation and Tunisia.

Large numbers of new teachers were recruited in WEI countries between 1995 and 2003, mostly in upper secondary and tertiary education.

These increases in student to teaching staff ratios in some countries should not hide the fact that the period 1995 to 2003 was characterised by recruitments of large numbers of new teachers in WEI countries, with the exceptions of

Indonesia, the Russian Federation, Tunisia, Uruguay and Zimbabwe at the primary level of education (see Figure 2.15). On average, the WEI countries' teaching forces increased most in upper secondary education (by 26 per cent) and tertiary education (by 59 per cent), while teacher numbers remained more stable in primary and lower secondary education (see Annex A4, Table 2.8). It is therefore interesting to see to what extent these recruitments affected the age and skill structures of WEI teaching forces.

Figure 2.15
Change in teaching staff, 2003
*Index change in teaching staff based on full-time equivalents,
by level of education and year (1995=100)*

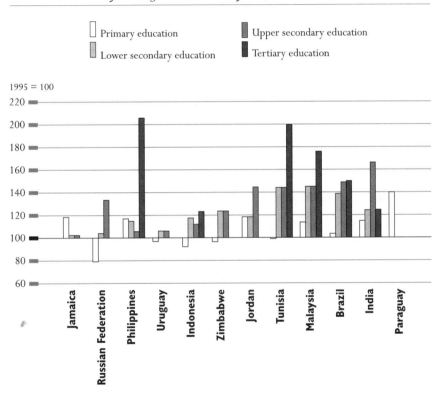

Countries are ranked in ascending order of index change in teaching staff at upper secondary level of education.
Source: OECD/UNESCO WEI, Table 2.8 in Annex A4.

Unfortunately, trend data on the age structures of WEI teaching forces were only available for Brazil, Indonesia and Malaysia, making it difficult to identify clear patterns. Overall, the structure of the Indonesian and Malaysian teaching forces by age group remained unchanged at both the primary and upper secondary levels of education between 1995 and 2003. In Brazil by contrast, the increase in the overall number of teachers was accompanied with an ageing of the teaching force in upper secondary education (see Figure 2.16). This trend reflects the fact that some Brazilian professionals moved into teaching to overcome unemployment problems in their area and also suggests that the country failed to attract young teachers in large numbers, possibly as a result of insufficient incentives to enter the teaching occupation.

In 2003, upper secondary teachers in Chile and the Philippines were older than those in Argentina, Brazil, China, Indonesia, Jamaica, Malaysia and Paraguay.

The demography of teachers is important wherever education participation is expected to increase – either as a result of increasing enrolment rates or demographic pressure. If a large proportion of the teaching force is concentrated in the older age cohorts, countries have to develop effective means of replacing the retired teachers and attract new people to the teaching profession. The age structure of the teaching force also has important implications for education expenditure given that seniority in the teaching profession is often an important

Figure 2.16
Age distribution of teachers, 1995 and 2003
Distribution of teachers in public and private institutions by age group, level of education and year (%)

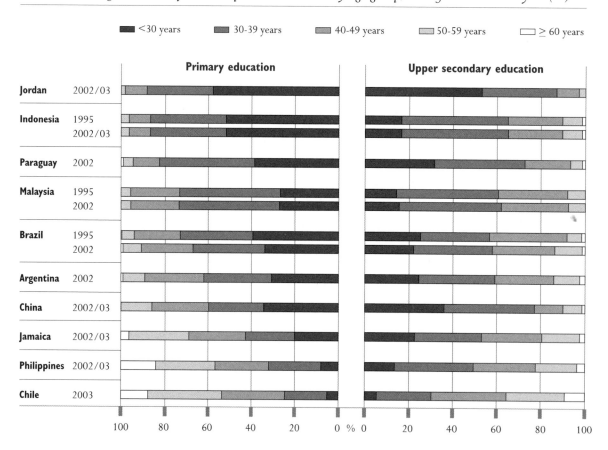

Countries are ranked in descending order of the 2003 percentage of primary teachers aged 39 and under.
Source: OECD/UNESCO WEI, Table 2.10 in Annex A4.

criterion in teacher salary scales. In this respect, the main challenge for WEI countries lies at the upper secondary and tertiary levels of education, where both demographic and participation pressures are still expected to grow in the coming years (see Chapter 1). In this respect, while more than one-half of upper secondary teachers in Argentina, Brazil, China, Indonesia, Jamaica, Malaysia and Paraguay were younger than 39 years of age, Chile and the Philippines had comparatively older teachers, with more than two-thirds of them aged 40 years and above in the case of Chile (see Figure 2.16).

The recruitment of new teachers in most WEI countries has permitted an upgrading of WEI teachers' qualifications in relative terms (see Box 2.2).

In most WEI countries, the recruitment of new teachers permitted an upgrading of their qualifications.

Box 2.2

Trends in WEI teachers' qualifications

All WEI countries have succeeded in increasing the amount of teachers with tertiary qualifications between 1995 and 2003.

In the Philippines, Tunisia and Uruguay, all teachers were in possession of tertiary qualifications in 1995 and this was still the case in 2003.

In Malaysia, the goal of universal tertiary qualifications for teachers was almost achieved over the period. All secondary and tertiary teachers held tertiary qualifications in 2003, while at the primary level this was the case for 99 per cent of teachers (compared with 92 per cent in 1995). Similarly, the percentage of teachers qualified at tertiary level was close to 100 per cent at all levels in Jordan, and close to 90 per cent in Jamaica for primary and secondary education.

Some WEI countries, however, still have some way to go before all teachers hold a tertiary qualification, particularly at the primary level. In 2003, less than one-half of primary teachers in Brazil, Egypt and Indonesia had tertiary-level educations. Despite this, significant improvements have been made since 1995, with the amount of tertiary-qualified teachers in primary education increasing by over one-third in Brazil, doubling in Egypt and tripling in Indonesia. In the case of Brazil, this improvement can be attributed to *Fundescola*, a fund for strengthening schools that was launched in 1999 with the goal of ensuring that by 2006 only university graduates or those with specific teacher training qualifications be eligible to teach. The problem of under-qualified teachers in Brazil is mainly region-specific and therefore the federal government is working with respective municipalities to train unqualified primary teachers by way of a two-year long-distance teacher training course (*Proformacao*).

At the secondary and tertiary levels of education, between 65 per cent (Argentina) and 100 per cent (Indonesia) of teachers held tertiary qualifications in 2003.

Improvement of teachers' working conditions in some WEI countries

The challenge of recruiting new teachers raises questions on the attractiveness of their working conditions.

The challenge of attracting large numbers of new teachers raises the question of the attractiveness of the teaching profession relative to other occupations in WEI countries. This can be apprehended through indicators of teachers' working conditions, as well as monetary incentives and career paths offered to them.

In assessing teachers' working conditions, the ratio of students to teaching staff and class size shall be considered together because there is a connection between them. The ratio of students to teaching staff is the number of students divided by the number of full-time equivalent teachers. It does not take into account instruction time received by students nor the length of a teacher's working day, so it can be interpreted as an indicator of the teaching resources available in a country on average. Overall, fewer students per teacher suggest that students have better access to teaching resources. By contrast, class sizes reflect the average size of groups in a class given student instruction time and teachers' teaching time.

In primary education, WEI student to teaching staff ratios are significantly higher than in OECD countries, except in Argentina, Malaysia, the Russian Federation and Thailand.

For student to teaching staff ratios, WEI countries were characterised by significantly higher ratios than on average in OECD countries. In primary and lower secondary education, the difference between WEI and OECD countries was about 8 to 10 students in 2003, while the ratios were more than twice the OECD average in Chile, India, the Philippines and Zimbabwe (at primary level). By contrast, Argentina, Malaysia, the Russian Federation and Thailand had student to teaching staff ratios fairly close to the OECD reference benchmark (see Annex A4, Table 2.8). At higher levels of education, the gap between WEI and OECD countries was less. The difference in student to teaching staff ratios was about six students in upper secondary education and less than four students in tertiary education (see Figure 2.17).

It is often the case that more teachers are supplied at the lower secondary level than at the primary level. The same phenomenon can occur between lower and upper secondary education. In WEI countries, this pattern was found in all countries except Argentina, the Philippines and Thailand.

The ratio of students to teaching staff is also an important indicator of policy priorities in different countries. Indeed, the supply and allocation of teachers is a policy matter that depends on how the ministries of education view the importance of different levels of education. In dealing with expanding participation in education, education authorities often have to weight smaller ratios of students to teaching staff against higher salaries for teachers, greater investment in teaching technology or more widespread use of assistant teachers and other paraprofessionals whose salaries are often considerably lower than

Figure 2.17
Ratio of students to teaching staff in educational institutions, 1995 and 2003
Ratio of students to teaching staff based on full-time equivalents, by level of education and year

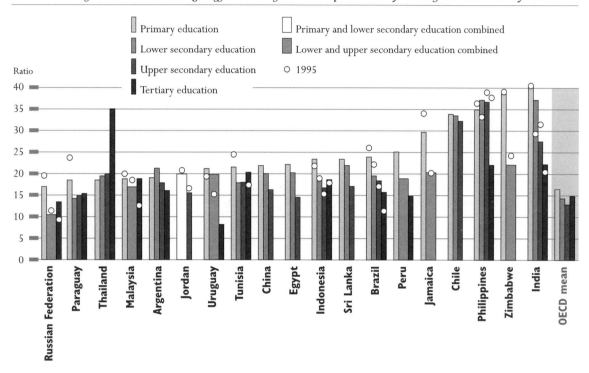

Countries are ranked in ascending order of the 2002 student to teaching staff ratio in primary education.
Source: OECD/UNESCO WEI, Table 2.8 in Annex A4.

those of qualified teachers. Moreover, as larger numbers of children with special educational needs are integrated into normal classes, more use of specialised personnel and support services may limit the resources available for reducing the ratio of students to teaching staff.

In many developing countries with the onset of 'Education for All' (EFA), the focus of 'better' education has been on primary education and efforts have been directed at improving the student to teaching staff ratios and class sizes. Between 1995 and 2003, there were significant drops in primary student to teaching staff ratios in Brazil, Jamaica, the Russian Federation (as a result of declining school-age population) and Tunisia, but increases in Indonesia and Uruguay over the period, and no significant improvements in India, the Philippines and Zimbabwe – the WEI countries displaying the highest ratios in 2003.

Between 1995 and 2003, primary student to teaching staff ratios dropped significantly in Brazil, Jamaica, the Russian Federation and Tunisia, but increased in Indonesia and Uruguay, and did not improve in India, the Philippines and Zimbabwe.

In Brazil, student to teaching staff ratios increased in upper secondary and tertiary education while policy emphasis focused on deploying more human resources in basic education and reducing primary and lower secondary student to teaching staff ratios. By contrast, the Indian education authorities put emphasis on reducing student to teaching staff ratios in upper secondary education while student to teaching staff ratios increased in lower secondary and tertiary education between 1995 and 2003, and did not decline in primary education despite high levels.

Policy choices regarding teacher supply have an impact on the working conditions of teachers since student to teaching staff ratios are an important component of class sizes.

The policy choices related to the supply of teachers have had an impact on the daily working conditions of teachers in WEI countries. Indeed, student to teaching staff ratios are an important component of class sizes. Class sizes are widely debated in many countries. Smaller classes are valued by parents because they are believed to allow students to receive more individual attention from their teachers and thus to lead to higher achievement. Teachers also prefer smaller classes because they are easier to teach and reduce the disadvantage of managing large numbers of students and their work. In this respect, class size is usually considered as an indicator that can be used to assess the quality of school systems, although it must also be recognised that there is a great deal of controversy about the importance of class size as a determinant of student achievement when compared with other factors (Finn and Voelkl, 1995 and Hanushek, 1998).

However, the predominance of staff costs in educational expenditure means that reducing class sizes leads to sharp increases in the costs of education unless this is done by increasing teaching time (see Figure 2.13). This is because the reduction of class sizes requires more teaching staff, more textbooks and often additional classrooms and capital investments in some schools. In assessing how WEI countries have responded to increased demand for education and managed to keep education expenditure within budgetary constraints, it is important to review trends in class sizes and in teaching time together (see Figure 2.18). In addition, from the perspective of the attractiveness of teaching, class sizes and teaching hours are two components of teachers' working conditions, and trade-offs between these two variables may well affect the attractiveness of teaching to potential candidates.

In 2003, primary class sizes were similar to those of OECD countries in Paraguay, the Russian Federation and Uruguay, while classes of 40 or more were common in China, Egypt, India, Jamaica and the Philippines.

In 2003, class sizes in public institutions were larger in WEI countries than in OECD countries on average, with the exceptions of Paraguay and Uruguay in primary education, and the Russian Federation in both primary and lower secondary education. At the other end of the spectrum, class sizes of more than 40 students were commonplace in China, Egypt, India, Jamaica and the Philippines at the primary level of education, and in China, Egypt, the Philippines and Thailand at the lower secondary level.

Not only did primary teachers have to deal with large class sizes in India, Jamaica and the Philippines, but they also taught comparatively long hours by WEI standards. Considering that total teacher time spent on school matters includes both teaching hours in school and also the preparation of lessons and the marking of homework and assignments, the combination of large classes and long teaching hours imply an even heavier workload and burden for teachers in these countries. By contrast, primary teachers in Paraguay, the Russian Federation, Thailand and Uruguay taught small class sizes and comparatively few hours and, therefore, enjoyed more attractive working conditions compared with their Indian, Filipino and Jamaican colleagues. But, in the case of Paraguay and Uruguay, the smaller class sizes and fewer working hours were offset by the fact that several teachers taught more than one shift per day. Other WEI countries had different trade-offs. In Egypt, primary teachers taught large class sizes but worked comparatively few hours by WEI standards (see Figure 2.18).

In India, Jamaica and the Philippines, long teaching hours added to large classes in primary education, while in Paraguay, the Russian Federation, Thailand and Uruguay, primary teachers enjoyed smaller classes and short teaching hours.

As was the case for working conditions, class sizes in primary education were reduced in all countries for which data were available, except in Brazil and the Philippines where class sizes increased, and India, Jordan and Thailand where they did not significantly change. In the Russian Federation and Uruguay both class sizes and teaching time decreased between 1995 and 2003, suggesting an improvement in teachers' working conditions. In the Philippines, by contrast, the increase in primary class size was counterbalanced by a reduction in teaching hours. Overall, however, teaching hours remained fairly stable over the period, probably due to the stability of educational curricula over time, as well as to the resistance of teachers' unions against increasing teaching time. Yet official teaching time can be an important cost factor and maintaining low official teaching hours can be more expensive than increasing the salaries of existing teachers in exchange for additional hours. In this respect, WEI countries varied widely in the teaching load that was required from their teachers. In 2003, annual hours of instruction ranged from 656 in the Russian Federation to 1 260 in Indonesia, compared with an average of 795 hours in OECD countries (see Annex A4, Table 2.11).

In the Russian Federation and Uruguay, primary teachers' working conditions improved between 1995 and 2003, with a decrease in class sizes and teaching time. In the Philippines, larger class sizes were offset by reduced teaching hours.

At the lower secondary level of education, class sizes only increased in the Philippines and Thailand, again with a decrease in teaching time in the Philippines. Lower secondary teachers' working conditions improved in Paraguay and Uruguay due to smaller classes and lower teaching time, and as a result of significantly smaller classes in the case of Brazil and Tunisia. In Peru and the Russian Federation, however, teaching hours increased significantly between 1995 and 2003.

Lower secondary teachers' working conditions improved in Brazil, Paraguay, Tunisia and Uruguay.

Trends in teachers' compensation

Class sizes and teaching time are only part of the attractiveness of teaching to both newcomers and current teachers. Monetary incentives, in the form of salaries and additional bonuses, are also an important determinant of the teacher supply. Indeed, education systems employ a large number of professionals in an increasingly competitive market, and ensuring that there are a sufficient number of skilled teachers is a key concern in all countries, OECD and WEI alike. Starting

Teachers' compensation is a critical aspect of teaching attractiveness and teacher supply, but also the largest single cost in providing education.

Figure 2.18
Class size and teaching time, 1995 and 2003
Average class size and teaching time (hours) in public institutions, by level of education and year

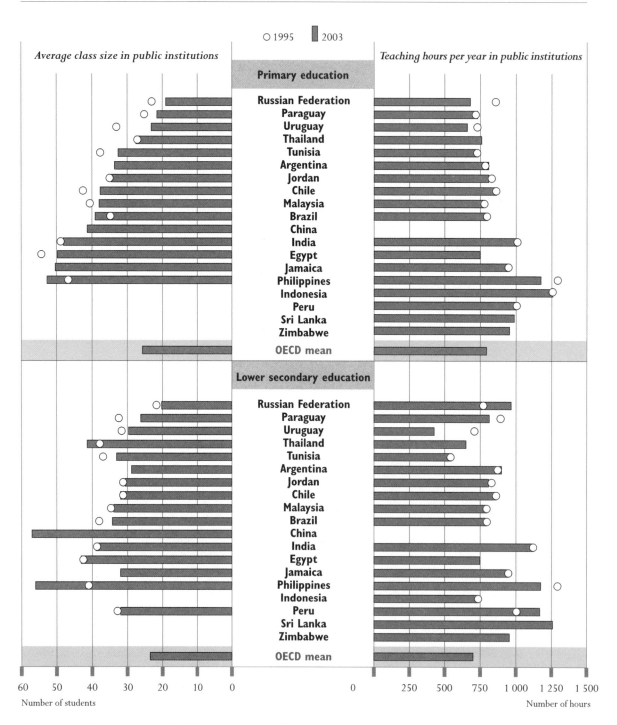

Countries are ranked in ascending order of class size at primary education.

Source: OECD/UNESCO WEI, Tables 2.9 and 2.11 in Annex A4.

salaries, pay scales and the costs incurred by individuals in becoming teachers, compared to salaries and costs in other high-skill occupations are key factors in determining the supply of qualified teachers. Both affect the career decisions of potential teachers and the types of people who are attracted to the teaching profession. But teachers' salaries are also the largest single cost in providing education, making teacher compensation a critical consideration for policy-makers seeking to maintain the quality of teaching and a balanced education budget. Although the size of education budgets reflects trade-offs among many interrelated factors, including teachers' salaries, the ratio of students to teaching staff, the instruction time planned for students and the designated number of teaching hours, salaries are a critical variable in this equation.

A first indication of the attractiveness of teaching as a profession at different levels of education can be obtained by comparing the statutory salaries of teachers holding the minimum level of qualifications required for certification in public primary and secondary education, according to official pay scales. These are gross salaries (total sum of money paid by the employer) less the employer's contribution to social security and pension. These statutory salaries must be distinguished from teachers' average salaries, which are also influenced by the age structure of the teaching force, the prevalence of part-time work, and the prevalence of bonuses in different countries (see Box 2.3). To permit international comparisons, these salaries have been expressed in USD converted using Purchasing Power Parities (PPPs) to account for differences in the cost of living across countries.

There were wide differences among WEI countries in the levels of compensation offered to teachers. Considering mid-career salaries as a proxy for average levels of compensation in 2003, primary teachers' gross salaries ranged from about PPP$ 1 600 in Indonesia to more than PPP$ 16 000 in Jamaica, a more than ten-fold increase (see Annex A4, Table 2.12a). On average, WEI primary teachers earned PPP$ 8 600 annually, nearly four times less than in OECD countries in PPP terms. Among them, primary teachers in Chile, Jamaica, Malaysia, Thailand and Tunisia enjoyed comparatively high salaries, while the levels of teacher compensation appeared to be fairly low for teachers in Egypt, Indonesia, Peru, Sri Lanka and Uruguay (see Figure 2.19).

Primary teachers' salaries are comparatively large in Chile, Jamaica, Malaysia, Thailand and Tunisia, and low in Egypt, Indonesia, Peru, Sri Lanka and Uruguay.

Caution should be exercised when comparing salaries, despite the conversion into purchasing power parities. Indeed, there are hidden factors that are unknown. For example, teaching time and teachers' workload vary considerably among countries (see Figure 2.18). There are also large differences between the taxation schemes and social charges prevailing in different countries. Many teachers also supplement their incomes by teaching several shifts in another school or by providing extra tuition, while income from these secondary sources was excluded from the data. Lastly, many countries provide bonuses and entitlements in addition to the gross salary, such as regional allowances for teaching in remote

Figure 2.19
Teachers' salaries, 2003
Annual statutory gross salaries of teachers with minimum level of training
at starting salary, after 15 years of experience and at the top of the salary scale,
in US\$ PPP converted, by level of education

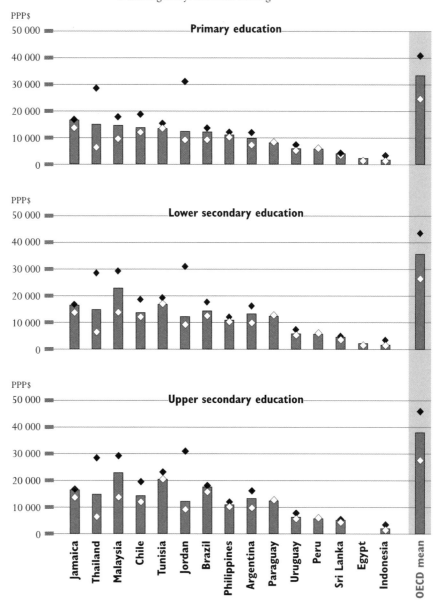

Countries are ranked in descending order of the salary of primary teachers with minimum level of training after 15 years of experience.

Source: OECD/UNESCO WEI, Table 2.12a in Annex A4.

regions, family allowances, reduced rates on public transportation, tax allowances on purchasing cultural goods, free or heavily subsidised teacher housing, etc. (see Box 2.3). These bonuses and entitlements contribute to a teacher's basic income and are not accounted for in the comparisons of basic salaries. All of these factors need to be taken into account when interpreting teachers' salaries in terms of monetary incentives. For instance, among WEI countries with the lowest salaries in primary education, Egypt and Indonesia resort extensively to extra bonuses, while bonuses are also used to top up gross salaries in Argentina, Paraguay, Peru, the Philippines and Uruguay. In addition, the levels of salaries reported for Paraguay and Uruguay were for a teaching load of 20 hours per week, while in practice most teachers work two shifts and thereby double their real income.

Box 2.3
The role of bonuses in WEI teachers' compensation schemes

In 2003, several WEI countries from various continents used bonuses to reward teachers. Teachers could obtain these salary increments in addition to the gross salary for working in educational priority areas, participating in school improvement projects or special activities, displaying excellent performance, etc.

In four WEI countries, teachers could earn significantly more than their gross salary with the application of the bonus system. In Chile, Egypt and Uruguay the maximum bonus available for starting primary teachers with minimum training represented between 63 and 95 per cent of the gross salary, thereby allowing those eligible for the maximum bonus to almost double their income. Bonuses were available throughout teachers' careers but their importance relative to the gross salary tended to decrease as teachers moved up the salary scale. Indonesia also awarded significant bonuses to teachers, allowing teachers to increase their gross salary by 40 to 60 per cent. However in contrast to Chile, Egypt and Uruguay, the maximum possible bonus was higher for teachers at the top of the pay scale. Bonuses in Indonesia were also partly dependant upon family status: extra money was allocated for those having a dependant partner and/or children, as is common in other civil service positions in Indonesia.

Other South American countries (Argentina, Paraguay and Peru) also used a bonus system to reward their teachers, although the size of bonuses was less significant than in Chile and Uruguay. In Peru, teachers could earn up to 15 per cent more at all levels of education. This was also the case in Paraguay, but the bonus only applied to teachers with at least 15 years of experience. In Argentina, bonuses representing 4 to 11 per cent of the gross salary were awarded at the discretion of the local authorities. They were higher at the bottom of the salary scale. Finally, a bonus system also existed in Brazil, but the magnitude of bonuses was unknown given variations across states.

In Asia, bonuses could contribute up to approximately 30 per cent of the gross salary in the Philippines. India and Malaysia also had a bonus system in addition to the statutory salary, however it represented between only 1 and 4 per cent of the gross salary.

Salaries are the same at all levels of education in Jamaica, Jordan, Peru, the Philippines and Thailand, but increase at each level taught in Argentina, Brazil, Sri Lanka and Tunisia.

Different patterns of salary incentives at different levels of education could be observed among WEI countries. In Jamaica, Jordan, Peru, the Philippines and Thailand, teachers' salaries were the same at all levels of education. Likewise, Chile, Egypt, Indonesia and Uruguay offered similar salaries to their primary and lower secondary teachers, while this was the case for all secondary teachers in Malaysia and Paraguay. Argentina, Brazil, Sri Lanka and Tunisia were the only countries where salaries increased at each level of education taught (see Annex A4, Table 2.12a).

Upper secondary salaries were highest in Brazil, Malaysia and Tunisia where teachers' numbers increased most between 1995 and 2003.

Since most WEI countries faced stronger growth in enrolments at the upper secondary and tertiary levels of education and therefore had to recruit large numbers of new teachers at these levels, it is interesting to see how upper secondary salaries compared in different countries in relation to the recruitment pressure they faced between 1995 and 2003. Interestingly upper secondary salaries were highest in Brazil, Malaysia and Tunisia. These countries also had the largest increases in teachers' numbers between 1995 and 2003, suggesting that high levels of upper secondary salaries may have helped attract large numbers of newcomers to the teaching profession (see Figure 2.15). By contrast, the number of upper secondary teachers decreased in Tunisia despite comparatively high salaries at this level by WEI standards.

A comparison of starting, mid-career and maximum statutory salaries of teachers also provides information on the influence of teaching experience on salary scales, as well as an indication of the career prospects offered to new teachers entering the profession. In Argentina, Brazil, Egypt, Jamaica, Paraguay, Peru, the Philippines, Sri Lanka, Tunisia and Uruguay, teachers' salaries were fairly stable throughout their careers and did not increase dramatically with experience. In Jordan and Thailand, however, salaries increased a great deal with experience and salaries at the top of the scale were more than double the amount that teachers received at mid-point in their careers. A similar pattern of salary increases with experience was found – although to a lesser extent – in Chile (mainly at the end of teachers' careers) and in Malaysia. These patterns in salaries at different points in a teacher's career can be related to the demographic characteristics of WEI teaching forces (see Figure 2.16). Interestingly, Chile rewarded experience in monetary terms and had the highest proportion of teachers in the older age groups of all WEI countries. Jordan and Malaysia had comparatively young teaching forces.

WEI teachers saw their real salaries improve between 1995 and 2003 in Brazil, Chile, Jamaica and the Philippines, while they worsened in Argentina, Indonesia and Paraguay.

Another way of looking at the attractiveness of teaching in relation to growth in enrolments and the need to recruit large numbers of new teachers is to examine trends in teachers' salaries between 1995 and 2003 at different levels of education and for different categories of teachers. To permit comparisons over time, changes in salaries have been adjusted by the GDP deflator to control for changes in price levels and inflation between the two dates and obtain changes in real incomes of teachers. Overall, WEI teachers in Brazil,

Figure 2.20
Change in teachers' salaries, 2003
Index change in statutory gross salaries of teachers with minimum level of training
at starting salary, after 15 years of experience and at the top of the salary scale
adjusted for inflation, by level of education (1995 = 100)

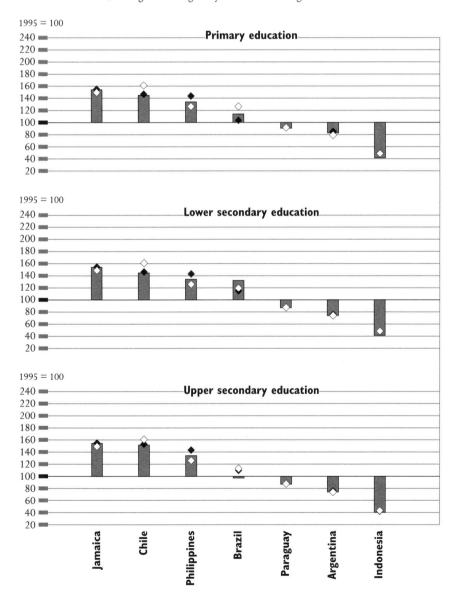

Countries are ranked in descending order of the index change in salary of primary teachers with
minimum level of training after 15 years of experience.
Source: OECD/UNESCO WEI, Table 2.12b in Annex A4.

Chile, Jamaica and the Philippines saw their real salaries improve – sometimes drastically – over the period, while in Argentina, Indonesia and Paraguay, their purchasing power actually worsened, quite dramatically so in the case of Indonesia (see Figure 2.20).

In Chile, Jamaica and the Philippines, a salary revalorisation of 30 to 50 per cent took place between 1995 and 2003 in primary and secondary education. Increases in teachers' salaries were more modest in Brazil and focused mainly on primary and lower secondary education, reflecting the strong emphasis of Brazil on improving its basic education.

Starting salaries increased faster than those of older teachers in Brazil and Chile, suggesting specific incentives to attract newcomers.

Another interesting pattern was that starting salaries increased faster than salaries of other categories of teachers in Brazil at primary and upper secondary education levels and in Chile at all levels. These peculiar trends may reflect a desire to attract younger individuals into the profession in Chile where the teaching force is ageing, as well as strong incentives to attract large numbers of new individuals to the profession in the case of Brazil – where large recruitment took place over the period (see Figure 2.15).

Trends in expenditure per student as an overall summary of policy trade-offs

The trade-offs and policy choices made by WEI education authorities that have been discussed above are reflected in levels and trends in expenditure per student. Indeed, expenditure per student can be seen as a summary outcome of these policy priorities and trade-offs between the level of teacher supply and the resulting students to teaching staff ratios and class sizes, the designated number of teaching hours, and the levels and trends in teachers' compensation.

Levels of expenditure per student vary by a factor of 20 among WEI countries.

Given the wide variation observed in levels of teacher compensation between WEI countries (see Figure 2.19) and the fact that teachers' salaries were the largest single cost in providing education (see Figure 2.13), levels of expenditure per student were expectedly very different across WEI countries (see Figure 2.21). In primary education, expenditure per student ranged from a mere PPP$ 110 in Indonesia to more than PPP$ 2 000 in Chile and Tunisia in 2002, *i.e.* more than 20 times more. India, Indonesia, Peru and the Philippines spent least per primary student – with less than PPP$ 500. Argentina, Chile, Malaysia, the Russian Federation and Tunisia spent more than PPP$ 1 000 on average and OECD countries, PPP$ 5 300 on average. This grouping of countries by level of expenditure per student mirrors their grouping according to levels of GDP per capita (see Figure 1.8), thereby underling the specific constraints of providing universal primary education for countries at lower stages of economic development.

Figure 2.21
Annual expenditure per student, 2002
Annual expenditure on educational institutions per student, in US$ PPP converted,
by level of education

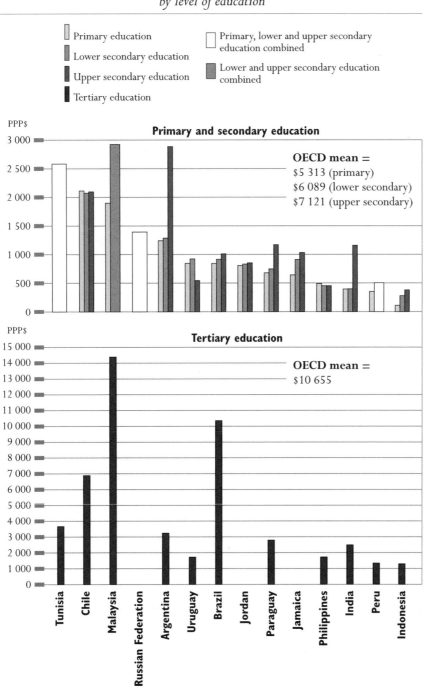

□ Primary education

□ Lower secondary education

■ Upper secondary education

■ Tertiary education

□ Primary, lower and upper secondary education combined

■ Lower and upper secondary education combined

Primary and secondary education

OECD mean =
$5 313 (primary)
$6 089 (lower secondary)
$7 121 (upper secondary)

Tertiary education

OECD mean =
$10 655

Countries are ranked in descending order of annual expenditure per student at the primary level of education.

Source: OECD/UNESCO WEI, Table 2.13 in Annex A4.

High levels of spending in Chile, Malaysia, the Russian Federation and Tunisia can be explained by low student to teaching staff ratios and teaching hours and comparatively high levels of salaries.

Levels of economic development and national wealth are not the only determinants of expenditure per student, however. The comparatively high levels of spending by Chile, Malaysia, the Russian Federation and Tunisia on primary education in 2002 can also be explained by the low primary student to teaching staff ratios and low teaching hours of Malaysia, the Russian Federation and Tunisia (see Figures 2.17 and 2.18), the comparatively high levels of teachers' salaries in Chile, Malaysia and Tunisia (see Figure 2.19), and the practice of supplementing salaries with generous bonuses in Chile (see Box 2.3). At the other end of the spectrum, low levels of expenditure per primary student in India, Indonesia, Peru and the Philippines derive from high student to teaching staff ratios in India and the Philippines, teaching hours above 1,000 hours annually in all four countries, and comparatively low salaries in Indonesia and Peru despite the practice of supplementing the low salaries with bonuses in Peru.

Expenditure per student did not differ drastically from primary to upper secondary education in Brazil, Chile, Jordan and the Philippines, whereas it was significantly higher for upper secondary students in Argentina, India, Malaysia and Paraguay.

Levels of expenditure per student increased at higher levels of education, which is not surprising given the stronger specialisation of teaching staff in secondary and tertiary education and the lower student to teaching staff ratios that it incurred. Besides lower student to teaching staff ratios (see Annex A4, Table 2.8), teachers tended to receive higher salaries at higher levels of education. These higher salaries resulted from either progressive salary scales (see Annex A4, Table 2.12a), higher qualifications (see Box 2.2) or demographic structures skewed towards older, more experienced teachers in Indonesia, Malaysia and Paraguay (see Annex A4, Table 2.10). Yet, this general pattern translated differently across WEI countries. In Brazil, Chile, Jordan and the Philippines, levels of expenditure per student did not differ drastically from primary to upper secondary education, whereas Argentina, India, Malaysia and Paraguay spent significantly more per upper secondary student than at lower levels of education.

At the tertiary level of education, Argentina, Brazil, Chile, Malaysia and Tunisia were the highest spenders per student. By contrast, Uruguay spent less than one-fifth of what Brazil devoted to each tertiary student, despite having a similar level of GDP per capita.

Lastly, changes in expenditure per student can help assess the impact that the growth in education participation that most WEI countries faced between 1995 and 2003 had on these countries' levels of education expenditure per student (see Figure 2.22).

Overall, expenditure per student in primary and secondary education increased in all countries, reflecting structural changes in the composition of enrolments.

Overall, expenditure per student in primary, secondary and post-secondary non-tertiary education increased in all countries for which data were available. This increase partly reflects structural changes in the composition of enrolments, with a relative increase in the proportion of students enrolled in secondary – especially upper secondary – education where levels of expenditure per student tend to be higher than in primary education (see Figure 2.21). The situations of Chile,

Figure 2.22
Change in expenditure per student and underlying factors, 2002
*Index change in expenditure per student, expenditure on educational institutions
and enrolment aligned to finance data, by level of education (1995 = 100)*

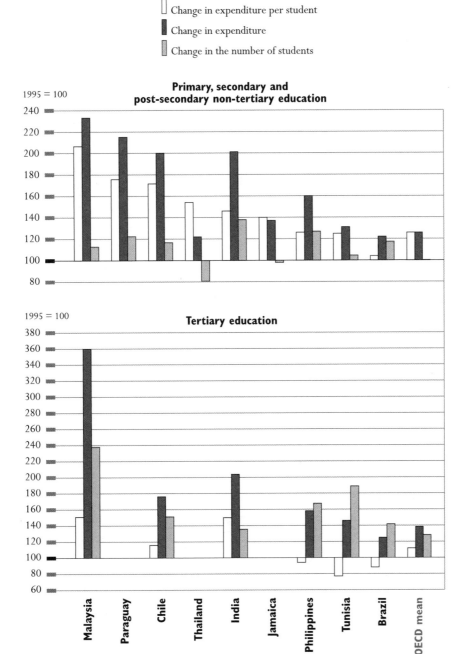

Countries are ranked in descending order of the index change in expenditure per student in primary
education

Source: OECD/UNESCO WEI, Table 2.14 in Annex A4.

Malaysia and Paraguay illustrate this mechanism. Indeed, these countries faced some of the largest increases in enrolments at the lower secondary (Paraguay) and upper secondary (Malaysia, Paraguay, Chile to a lesser extent) levels of education between 1995 and 2003. Enrolments in secondary education increased more than in primary (see Figures 1.12 and 1.16). Meanwhile, Malaysia and Paraguay also had significantly higher expenditure per student in secondary (Malaysia) and upper secondary (Paraguay) education. Thus, changes in the composition of the student body that were skewed towards upper secondary education automatically increased overall expenditure per student for primary, secondary and post-secondary non-tertiary education. In Brazil, however, a similar structural change in the composition of enrolments resulted in a very moderate increase in expenditure per student, highlighting the many other determinants of expenditure per student, *i.e.* trends in student to teaching staff ratios and class sizes, teachers' salaries and teaching hours, and levels of investment in education infrastructures and capital.

In tertiary education, expenditure per student increased only in Chile, India and Malaysia, while in other countries it could not keep pace with the growth in enrolments.

For tertiary education the picture was different. While expenditure per student increased by about 50 per cent in India and Malaysia, and to a lesser extent in Chile, other countries were not able to increase expenditure on tertiary education to keep pace with enrolment. As a result, expenditure per tertiary student decreased in Brazil, the Philippines and Tunisia over the period (see Figure 2.22). Meanwhile, student to teaching staff ratios in tertiary education increased in Brazil and Tunisia, highlighting one way by which these countries managed to reduce unit costs in tertiary education and to respond to increased demand for education under strict budgetary constraints (see Annex A4, Table 2.8).

The above discussion underlines the strong constraints borne by emerging countries in responding to increases in education demand. At a time when the importance of education for economic growth is widely recognised, as are the high returns that education yields for individuals, the demand for education is deemed to increase in response to individual strategies of human capital investment in addition to public growth-driven incentives. But in the case of emerging countries, this increase in education demand as a result of growing participation rates is combined with an increase in education demand resulting from demographic dynamics. These two factors combined result in a massive expansion of education systems – in particular at the upper secondary and tertiary levels of education – which places a strong burden on public education budgets. Indeed, public authorities need to take fiscal and budgetary constraints into account when responding to increased demand for education. Difficult trade-offs have to be made in allocating limited financial and human resources to different levels and sectors of education. The above discussion has illustrated how WEI countries have solved this equation during the 1995 to 2002 period, quite successfully overall given the difficult macroeconomic circumstances experienced by some countries.

REFERENCES

Falch, T. (2004), *Main driving forces of education expenditures*, presentation for The Ageing Working Group attached to the Economic Policy Committee of the European Union, Brussels, 17 June 2004.

Finn, J. and **K. Voelkl** (1995), "Class Size", *International Encyclopaedia of Teaching and Teacher Education*, 2nd edition, Pergamon Press, Oxford.

IMF (1998), *World Economic Outlook*, May 1998, International Monetary Fund, Washington, DC.

Hanushek, E. (1998), "The Evidence on Class Size", Occasional Paper Number 98-1, University of Rochester, Rochester, NY.

OECD/UNESCO Institute for Statistics (2003), *Financing Education – Investments and Returns*, OECD, Paris.

OECD (2005a), "Fifteen years of economic reform in Russia: what has been achieved? What remains to be done?", OECD Economics Department Working Paper No. 430, OECD, Paris.

OECD (2005b), "Education attainment in Brazil: the experience of FUNDEF", OECD Economics Department Working Paper No. 424, OECD, Paris.

Snyder, J. and **I. Yackovlev** (2000), *Political and economic determinants of government spending on social protection programs*, MIT Department of Political Science and Economics occasional paper, Cambridge, MA.

Verbina, I. and **A. Chowdhury** (2004), "What determines public education expenditure in a transition economy?", *Economics of Transition* 12 (3), pp. 489-508.

Chapter 3

COUNTRY PROFILES

Prepared by the UNESCO Institute for Statistics

About the profiles

The profile for each WEI country is comprised of a statistical chart and a one-page analytical text. Together they provide a snapshot of the current education system and changes since the mid-1990s.

Each chart has two parts:
- key indicators on the current situation with comparisons to other WEI countries, and the WEI and OECD means;
- key indicators that track changes since the mid-1990s, where data are available, along with comparisons to other WEI countries.

The indicators focus primarily on upper secondary education and education finance. The text, prepared with the collaboration of UNESCO and country representatives, provides contextual information and interprets the data.

Each indicator on the current situation has four components:
- The vertical axis represents the average for WEI countries;
- The horizontal axis shows:
  - the value for the profiled country;
  - the minimum and maximum values among WEI countries;
  - the relative position of other WEI countries, according to level of GDP per capita, represented by black triangles (higher GDP per capita than the profiled country) and white triangles (lower GDP per capita than the profiled country).

- The blue bar reflects the difference between the value of the profiled country and the WEI average.
- The black dot with a vertical line represents the OECD average.

Each indicator related to change over time has three components:
- The vertical axis represents "no change" in 2002 compared to the mid-1990s mark;
- The horizontal axis shows:
  - the value for the profiled country, and
  - the relative positions of other WEI countries, according to GDP per capita, again represented by black triangles (higher) and white triangles (lower);
- The blue bar reflects the amount of change in the profiled country since the mid-1990s.

Cross-references between indicators in the country profile charts and data tables in Annex A4

Indicators on the current situation

GDP per capita	Table 2.1
Expenditure per student in secondary education	Table 2.13
Expenditure per student in upper secondary education	Table 2.13
Percentage of students in private institutions in upper secondary education	Table 1.13
Population aged 5-14 as a percentage of total population	Table 1.3
Population aged 15-19 as a percentage of total population	Table 1.3
Population that has attained at least upper secondary education	Table 1.2
Ratio of students to teaching staff in upper secondary education	Table 2.8
School life expectancy	Table 1.4
Total public expenditure on education as a percentage of GDP	Table 2.2
Upper secondary graduation rate	Table 1.16

Indicators on change

Change in school life expectancy	Table 1.4
Change in population aged 5-14	Table 1.6
Change in population aged 15-19	Table 1.6
Change in primary enrolment	Table 1.9
Change in upper secondary enrolment	Table 1.9
Change in tertiary enrolment	Table 1.9
Change in total public expenditure on education (constant 1995 prices, local currency)	Table 2.3
Change in total public expenditure on education, ISCED 1-4 (constant 1995 prices, local currency)	Table 2.3
Change in upper secondary graduation rate	Table 1.16
Change in number of upper secondary teachers	Table 2.8
Change in expenditure per student, ISCED 1-4	Table 2.14

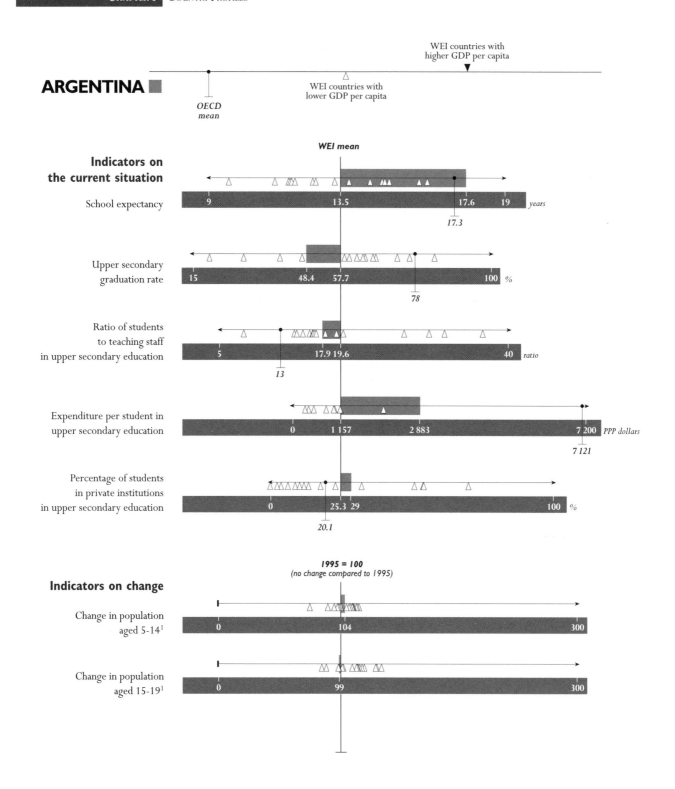

ARGENTINA

WEI countries with
higher GDP per capita

WEI countries with
lower GDP per capita

*OECD
mean*

WEI mean

**Indicators on
the current situation**

School expectancy
9   13.5   17.6   19   *years*
17.3

Upper secondary
graduation rate
15   48.4   57.7   100   *%*
78

Ratio of students
to teaching staff
in upper secondary education
5   17.9 19.6   40   *ratio*
13

Expenditure per student in
upper secondary education
0   1 157   2 883   7 200   *PPP dollars*
7 121

Percentage of students
in private institutions
in upper secondary education
0   25.3 29   100   *%*
20.1

Indicators on change

1995 = 100
(no change compared to 1995)

Change in population
aged 5-14[1]
0   104   300

Change in population
aged 15-19[1]
0   99   300

1. For 1995, United Nations Population Division (UNPD) population estimates were used given that national
population figures were not available.

ARGENTINA

The impact of recent economic and social problems is still evident in Argentina. GDP per capita decreased, in real terms, by more than 10 per cent between 1995 and 2002. Some 46 per cent of the population fall under the national poverty line, a sharp contrast to conditions in 1992-1995 when 22 per cent of the population was poor. And, yet, Argentina still has the highest GDP per capita (PPP$ 11 240) among WEI countries.

School life expectancy is longer in Argentina than in any other WEI country and many OECD countries. Children can expect to be in school for 17.6 years, more than 1.5 years longer than in other WEI countries in Latin America. Virtually all children go to school for at least 10 years, longer than in any other WEI country. Participation in education is universal at both primary and lower secondary levels. Among these students, 6 per cent repeat a grade, slightly more than the WEI average but much lower than in other WEI countries in the region.

Participation in secondary and tertiary education is also high. On average, young persons participate 2.4 years in upper secondary and 3.5 years in tertiary education, the fifth-longest and longest duration, respectively, in WEI countries. Yet, efficiency at these higher levels is a concern: upper secondary graduation rates are below the WEI average and substantially lower than in WEI neighbours, such as in Brazil, Chile and Peru. Entry rates to tertiary education are very high and at least every second young person starts tertiary education. Yet, dropout levels are also high – the graduation rate from type A programmes is 8 per cent, the second-lowest among reporting WEI countries.

Argentina has the highest annual expenditure per upper secondary student (PPP$ 2 883) among WEI countries. Expenditure at the pre-primary, primary and lower secondary levels is also high. By comparison expenditure per tertiary student is modest at PPP$ 3 235. Nonetheless, given the level of national wealth, education expenditure is moderate. Public and private expenditure account for 4.7 per cent of GDP, about one percentage point below the WEI and OECD averages. School staff salaries account for almost 90 per cent of education spending while capital expenditure is negligible – just 0.9 per cent compared to 8.7 per cent, on average, in WEI countries.

Teaching conditions in Argentina are slightly better than in most WEI countries. Student-teacher ratios are close to the WEI average at all levels while class sizes are below average. However, teacher salaries fell by 20 per cent, in real terms, over 1995.

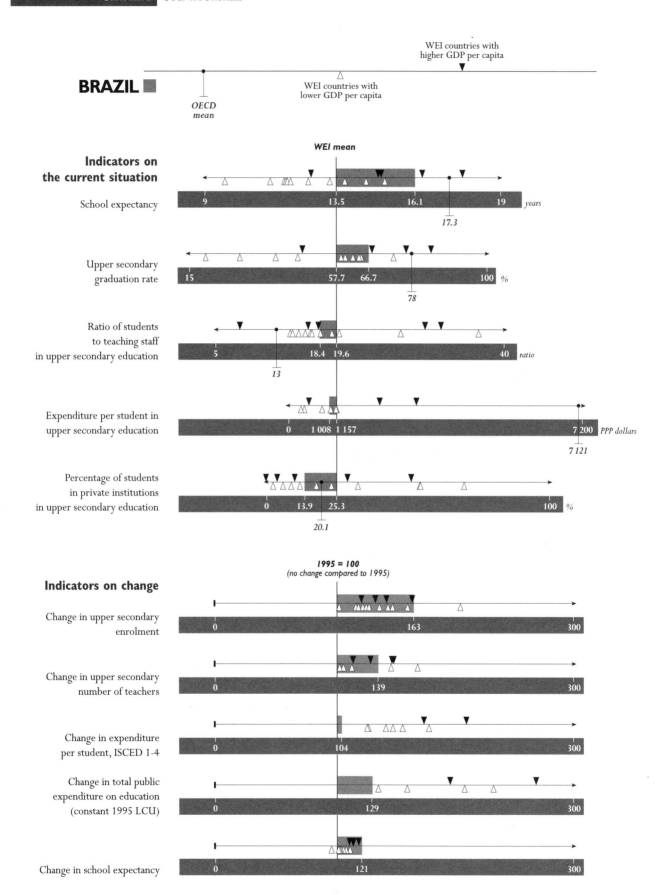

BRAZIL ▨

OECD
mean

WEI countries with
lower GDP per capita

WEI countries with
higher GDP per capita

WEI mean

**Indicators on
the current situation**

School expectancy
9   13.5   16.1   19   years
17.3

Upper secondary
graduation rate
15   57.7   66.7   100   %
78

Ratio of students
to teaching staff
in upper secondary education
5   18.4   19.6   40   ratio
13

Expenditure per student in
upper secondary education
0   1 008   1 157   7 200   PPP dollars
7 121

Percentage of students
in private institutions
in upper secondary education
0   13.9   25.3   100   %
20.1

Indicators on change

1995 = 100
(no change compared to 1995)

Change in upper secondary
enrolment
0   163   300

Change in upper secondary
number of teachers
0   139   300

Change in expenditure
per student, ISCED 1-4
0   104   300

Change in total public
expenditure on education
(constant 1995 LCU)
0   129   300

Change in school expectancy
0   121   300

BRAZIL

This country has the leading economy and the largest population in South America. GDP per capita is in the top third of WEI countries, but income distribution is highly unequal. The poorest 20 per cent of the population accounts for only 2.2 per cent of national income. Education indicators also present an uneven picture – with signs of significant progress tempered by significant challenges remaining.

The share of youths who have not completed primary education is one of the highest among WEI countries, about 10 per cent of 15 to19-year-olds. Nonetheless, this represents a reduction by one-half of the share in 1995. At the same time, the share of young persons completing upper secondary grew from just 23 per cent in 1995 to 41 per cent in 2003.

Since 1995, school life expectancy grew more in Brazil than in any other WEI country – by 2.7 years to 16.1 years, the third-highest span in the WEI group. At the same time, education is virtually universal to the end of compulsory schooling and the reduction of late entries has extended the span of universal education by one year. However, the age range in which all children are in school is two to three years shorter than in neighbouring WEI countries. Also, one in five students in primary school repeats grades and, overall, students repeat two years over the span of primary and secondary school. Recent PISA results show that one-half of 15-year-olds lack basic knowledge and skills in math literacy.

Education expanded rapidly at the upper secondary and tertiary levels between 1995 and 2003. On average, young people stay in upper secondary education a full year more than in 1995, and half a year longer in tertiary education. In absolute terms, student numbers grew by more than 50 per cent at the upper secondary level and doubled at the tertiary level.

The number of secondary teachers also increased rapidly, by 40 and 50 per cent at the lower and upper secondary levels, respectively. Student-teacher ratios improved at primary and lower secondary levels and remained relatively stable at the upper secondary level.

Unlike all other reporting WEI countries, financial resources in Brazil barely kept pace with the expanding participation from pre-primary to secondary levels. Spending per tertiary student is more than 10 times expenditure per primary or secondary student.

CHILE

WEI countries with higher GDP per capita

WEI countries with lower GDP per capita

OECD mean

Indicators on the current situation

WEI mean

School expectancy

9   13.5   15   19   *years*

17.3

Upper secondary graduation rate

15   57.7   67.4   100   %

78

Ratio of students to teaching staff in upper secondary education

5   19.6   32.3   40   *ratio*

13

Expenditure per student in upper secondary education

0   1 157   2 094   7 200   *PPP dollars*

7 121

Percentage of students in private institutions in upper secondary education

0   25.3   51.2   100   %

20.1

Indicators on change

1995 = 100
(no change compared to 1995)

Change in upper secondary enrolment

0   141   300

Change in expenditure per student, ISCED 1-4

0   171   300

Change in total public expenditure on education (constant 1995 LCU)

0   193   300

Change in school expectancy

0   110   300

CHILE

Chile has been among the best economic performers in the WEI group of countries. GDP expanded by more than 30 per cent from 1995 to 2002, giving Chile the second-highest GDP per capita in the group. Meanwhile, efforts to expand education have been facilitated by the fact that population growth has slowed almost to a halt.

High levels of education among the adult population continued to expand. In 1995 more than two-thirds of adults had attained at least lower secondary education and 41 per cent had attained upper secondary education. Since 1995, the share of 20 to 24-year-olds who completed upper secondary school increased from 59 to 71 per cent.

Access to education is relatively high. On average, children can expect to be in school for 15 years, 1.4 years longer than in 1995. Nearly every child is enrolled for at least nine years, indicating that universal participation in compulsory education is a reality. At the upper secondary level, entry rates are greater than 90 per cent and graduation rates are among the highest of WEI countries. However, the pattern is different for pre-primary education. Enrolment rates at this level are lower than in other WEI countries with high access to education, primarily because enrolment remained unchanged since 1995.

Access to tertiary education is also high and has grown since 1995. More than one-half of the youth population enters tertiary type A education and graduation rates for type A programmes doubled since 1995.

The education system relies heavily on private provision and funding of education. Around one-half of the students in primary and secondary education are enrolled in private institutions. More than 25 and 80 per cent of funds at the primary to upper secondary and tertiary levels, respectively, come from private sources. The latter is the highest share among both WEI and OECD countries.

Also among both WEI and OECD countries, Chile spends the second-highest share of GDP on education, after Jamaica. With public expenditure somewhat below the OECD average, the high overall spending is mainly due to the high share of private funding for education.

Expenditure on educational institutions has increased significantly at the primary, secondary and post-secondary non-tertiary levels, from 3.1 per cent in 1995 to 4.8 per cent of GDP in 2002. Notably, the share of public expenditure that goes to education increased from 14.5 per cent to 18.7 per cent over the same period.

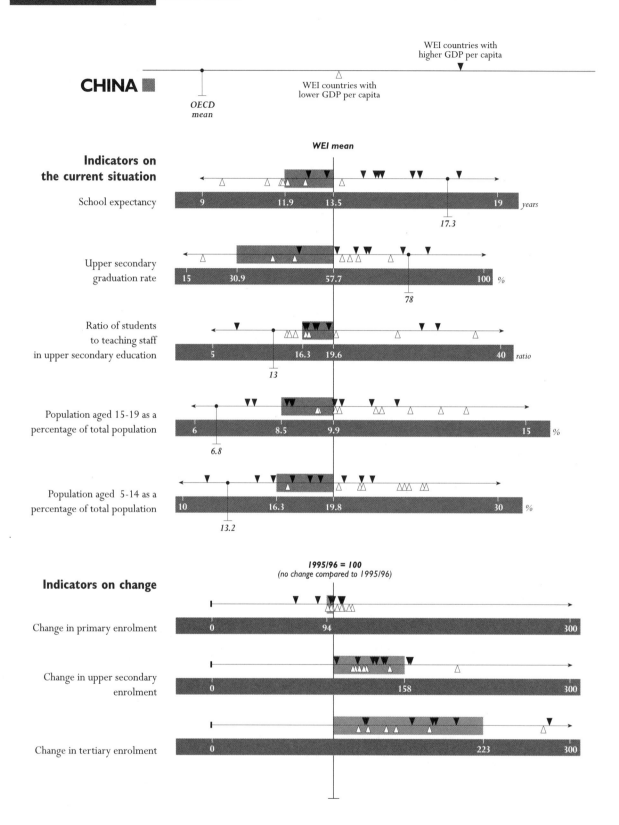

CHINA

Enrolment in education in China has expanded by 25 per cent since 1995, the third-strongest growth rate among WEI countries since the mid-1990s. With the exception of primary education, enrolment grew at every level of education. At the tertiary level, the number of students more than doubled. The number of primary school pupils declined as did the population of primary school age.

In the mid-1990s, China extended compulsory schooling to nine years. The reported increase in lower secondary enrolment reflects this extension: the number of students grew by 42 per cent over 1995. However, the goal of universal compulsory education is not yet met – more than 10 per cent of children covered by the last three years of compulsory education are, in fact, out of school.

Teaching resources have not expanded as rapidly as enrolment, resulting in big class sizes getting even bigger – a condition that can significantly impact the quality of education. Average class size grew from 52 pupils in 1995 to 57 in 2002, the highest WEI ratio at the lower secondary level.

School life expectancy is almost 12 years which is 1.5 years less than the WEI average. With its fast-growing economy and favourable demographic conditions, China has a ready opportunity to close this gap. For example, China and Paraguay have similar levels of per capita income but the average participation in education in China is two years less than in Paraguay.

China has the lowest tertiary graduation rate in the WEI group but, given the large increase in entry and participation rates, this will likely grow in the near future.

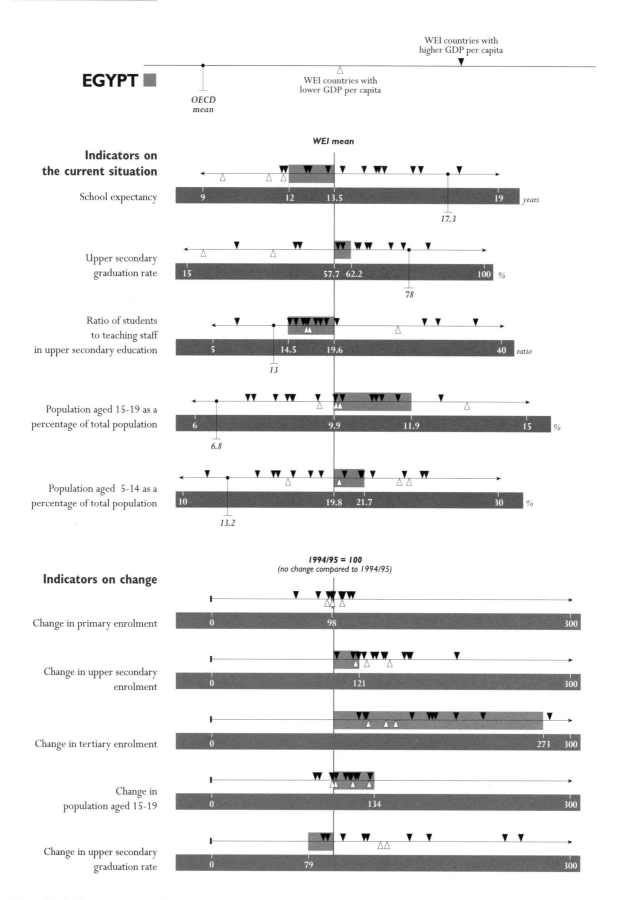

WEI countries with
higher GDP per capita

EGYPT

WEI countries with
lower GDP per capita

*OECD
mean*

WEI mean

**Indicators on
the current situation**

School expectancy

9   12   13.5   19   *years*

17.3

Upper secondary
graduation rate

15   57.7 62.2   100 *%*

78

Ratio of students
to teaching staff
in upper secondary education

5   14.5   19.6   40 *ratio*

13

Population aged 15-19 as a
percentage of total population

6   9.9   11.9   15 *%*

6.8

Population aged 5-14 as a
percentage of total population

10   19.8 21.7   30 *%*

13.2

Indicators on change

1994/95 = 100
(no change compared to 1994/95)

Change in primary enrolment

0   98   300

Change in upper secondary
enrolment

0   121   300

Change in tertiary enrolment

0   273   300

Change in
population aged 15-19

0   134   300

Change in upper secondary
graduation rate

0   79   300

EGYPT

The education system in Egypt operates within the contexts of limited national resources and growing demographic pressures. The GDP per capita of PPP$ 3 669 is 33 per cent lower than the WEI average while the youth population keeps growing. Yet, compared to other WEI countries, Egypt enjoyed substantial economic growth during the period 1995 to 2001. Growth slowed after 2001, but GDP still grew by 3 per cent in 2002.

A 5-year-old in Egypt can expect to receive 12 years of schooling, 1.5 years less than the WEI average. Participation in primary education is virtually universal, but universal participation in compulsory education, up to age 13, has not been reached. More than 10 per cent of children aged 11 to 13 are out of school. Yet, the upper secondary graduation rate is relatively high at 62 per cent. Secondary education is characterised by a concentration on vocational programmes, which represent almost 64 per cent of total enrolment and graduates in upper secondary education.

According to international assessments, average school performance is comparable to other WEI countries. Egypt participated in TIMSS 2003 and the mathematics achievement for Grade 8 was lower than the average of OECD countries but higher than scores in WEI countries with a higher GDP per capita, including Chile.

Overall, enrolment grew substantially from 1995 to 2003. At the pre-primary and tertiary levels, it grew faster than the relevant age groups in the population. However, at the upper secondary level, enrolment and graduation rates decreased: an increase of 20 per cent in student numbers at the lower and upper secondary levels was outpaced by an increase of 34 per cent in the corresponding age group and upper secondary graduation rates fell by 20 percentage points. Meanwhile, participation rates in tertiary education nearly tripled, a sign of growing inequity. Population projections indicate that the growth of the upper secondary population will slow by 2006, thereby reducing demand.

Working conditions for teachers are characterised by a combination of low salaries (by international standards) and a low number of teaching hours. Teacher salaries at primary and lower secondary levels – both at entry into the profession and after 15 years of experience – are among the lowest in the WEI countries. The workload for primary school teachers is 748 hours per year, the fourth-lowest amount in the WEI countries. Despite a low pupil-teacher ratio, the average class size in Egypt, both in primary and lower secondary, is almost 42 students – one of the highest ratios among WEI countries. This is because the low pupil-teacher ratios are more than offset by the low numbers of hours that teachers teach.

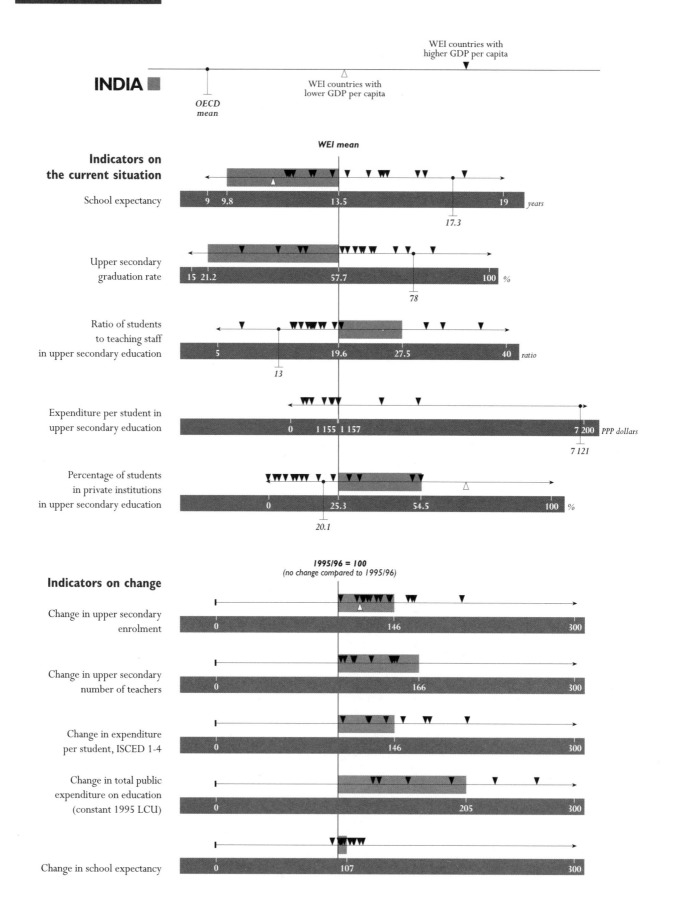

INDIA

WEI countries with
higher GDP per capita

WEI countries with
lower GDP per capita

OECD
mean

WEI mean

Indicators on
the current situation

School expectancy

9   9.8   13.5   19   *years*

17.3

Upper secondary
graduation rate

15   21.2   57.7   100   %

78

Ratio of students
to teaching staff
in upper secondary education

5   19.6   27.5   40   *ratio*

13

Expenditure per student in
upper secondary education

0   1 155   1 157   7 200   *PPP dollars*

7 121

Percentage of students
in private institutions
in upper secondary education

0   25.3   54.5   100   %

20.1

1995/96 = 100
(no change compared to 1995/96)

Indicators on change

Change in upper secondary
enrolment

0   146   300

Change in upper secondary
number of teachers

0   166   300

Change in expenditure
per student, ISCED 1-4

0   146   300

Change in total public
expenditure on education
(constant 1995 LCU)

0   205   300

Change in school expectancy

0   107   300

INDIA

The Indian economy grew rapidly during the 1990s, averaging 6 per cent a year. Progress in many social indicators was also registered, *e.g.* the poverty rate was significantly reduced and the literacy rate rose[1]. However, more than one in four Indians still live in poverty, and there are significant social disparities.

School life expectancy was only 9.8 years in 2002, almost 4 years below the WEI average. Education is compulsory for children aged 6-14 years, but the enrolment rate for 5 to14-year-olds is only 66 per cent – the lowest rate among WEI countries. Almost half of primary pupils drop out of school[2]. In 2001, India launched a national initiative called Sarva Shiksha Abhiyan (SSA) intended to universalise primary education across the country. A 2002 amendment to the Constitution made free and compulsory basic education a fundamental right for all children aged 6-14.

The number of enrolments has increased significantly at all education levels. Upper secondary and tertiary levels registered increases of 46 per cent and 51 per cent, respectively. Teacher numbers at the upper secondary level increased by 66 per cent. Female participation in education, however, did not increase significantly and a substantial gender gap still exists at all levels of education.

Despite a growing economy, India has the second-lowest GDP per capita among WEI countries at PPP$ 2 572 in 2002. Total expenditure on education represents 4.8 per cent of GDP, almost one percentage point below the WEI average. This translates into an expenditure of PPP$ 712 per secondary student, almost 42 per cent less than the WEI average. Nonetheless, between 1995 and 2002, expenditure per student at primary, secondary and tertiary levels increased considerably and total public expenditure on education more than doubled.

Relative to other WEI countries, secondary education in India is provided in large measure by private institutions. Upper secondary private institutions provide 55 per cent of education at this level, but two-thirds of the schools depend on government funding. Still, private expenditures account for almost 30 per cent of total expenditure on all levels of education.

India has the highest student-teacher ratios of all WEI countries at the primary and lower secondary levels, 40.2 and 37.2 students per teacher respectively. Teachers at these levels also have one of the highest annual workloads among WEI countries.

---

1. World Bank (2004). Poverty in India

2. Government of India (2004). Education for All, India Marches Ahead.

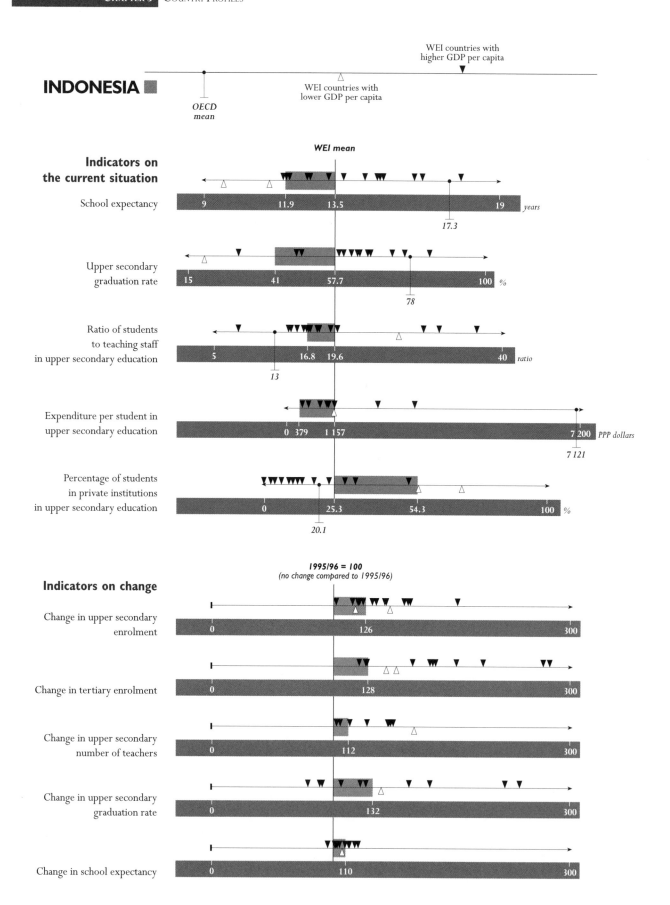

INDONESIA

WEI countries with higher GDP per capita

WEI countries with lower GDP per capita

OECD mean

Indicators on the current situation

WEI mean

School expectancy

9   11.9   13.5   19   *years*

17.3

Upper secondary graduation rate

15   41   57.7   100   %

78

Ratio of students to teaching staff in upper secondary education

5   16.8   19.6   40   *ratio*

13

Expenditure per student in upper secondary education

0 379 1 157   7 200   *PPP dollars*

7 121

Percentage of students in private institutions in upper secondary education

0   25.3   54.3   100   %

20.1

Indicators on change

1995/96 = 100
(no change compared to 1995/96)

Change in upper secondary enrolment

0   126   300

Change in tertiary enrolment

0   128   300

Change in upper secondary number of teachers

0   112   300

Change in upper secondary graduation rate

0   132   300

Change in school expectancy

0   110   300

INDONESIA

Between 1995 and 2002, development in Indonesia was dominated by the Asian economic crisis of 1997 and an ensuing national political crisis. However, growth in real GDP per capita was substantial before the crisis and income per capita rebounded by 2000 and began increasing again. Still, Indonesia has the second-lowest income per person among WEI countries at less than one-half of the group average. Despite the crises, poverty reduction has been considerable with extreme poverty falling from 21.0 to 6.7 per cent between 1990 and 2000. These data imply that the UN Millennium Development Goal target for halving extreme poverty has been achieved.[1]

School life expectancy grew slowly to 12 years, among the lowest in WEI countries. Still, participation in education is almost universal at the primary and lower secondary levels. It is, however, low at upper secondary and tertiary levels compared to other WEI countries. This fact is reflected in a relatively low graduation rate of 41 per cent from upper secondary school.

Due to the economic situation, financial resources have been tight for all sectors. Still, only a relatively small share of these limited resources is devoted to education – just 1.2 per cent of GDP or 5.9 per cent of government expenditures are spent on education, the lowest shares by far among both WEI and OECD countries. This translates into very low expenditure per student, PPP$ 379 or one-third of the WEI average at the upper secondary level. Such low expenditures also reflect very low teacher salaries. Student-teacher ratios are relatively favourable.

Private institutions that are independent of government funding play an important role in the provision of education. The share of pupils in such institutions jumps significantly by level of education, from 16 per cent at the primary level to 36 per cent at the upper secondary and to more than 50 per cent at the tertiary level. However, this situation is not a new trend.

The 1995-2002 period saw important, but mixed, trends. Little or no improvements are observed in enrolment and graduation rates, compared to dramatic growth in other WEI countries. Participation at primary and lower secondary levels failed to meet the goals set with the extension of compulsory education from six to nine years. And, despite growth of 28 per cent in upper secondary graduation, Indonesia did not keep pace with growth in other WEI countries.

Student-teacher ratios increased but given the relatively good ratio in the first place the small increase does not appear to be worrying. Of greater concern is the dramatic fall in teacher salaries which in 2003, adjusted for inflation, were one-half of what they were in 1995. This decrease in base salaries has, however, been partially offset by additional bonuses.

At the same time, there has been substantial investment in in-service teacher training, increasing the educational attainment of teachers. Minimum training requirements for new teachers were also improved. Primary teachers now need a tertiary degree to enter the teaching profession.

---

1. World Bank (2003), "Supporting Sound Policies With Adequate And Appropriate Financing", DC2003-0016.

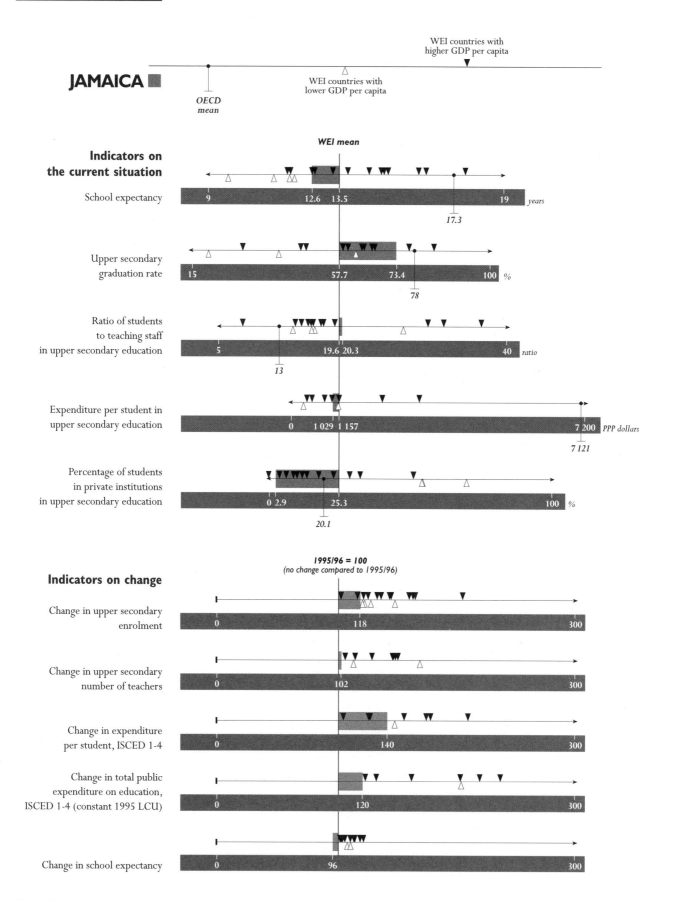

JAMAICA

WEI countries with higher GDP per capita

WEI countries with lower GDP per capita

OECD mean

WEI mean

Indicators on the current situation

School expectancy — 9 · 12.6 · 13.5 · 19 · years · 17.3

Upper secondary graduation rate — 15 · 57.7 · 73.4 · 100 · % · 78

Ratio of students to teaching staff in upper secondary education — 5 · 19.6 20.3 · 40 · ratio · 13

Expenditure per student in upper secondary education — 0 · 1 029 1 157 · 7 200 · PPP dollars · 7 121

Percentage of students in private institutions in upper secondary education — 0 2.9 · 25.3 · 100 · % · 20.1

Indicators on change

1995/96 = 100
(no change compared to 1995/96)

Change in upper secondary enrolment — 0 · 118 · 300

Change in upper secondary number of teachers — 0 · 102 · 300

Change in expenditure per student, ISCED 1-4 — 0 · 140 · 300

Change in total public expenditure on education, ISCED 1-4 (constant 1995 LCU) — 0 · 120 · 300

Change in school expectancy — 0 · 96 · 300

JAMAICA

Jamaica's education system operates in the context of difficult economic conditions. Inflation and unemployment rates are high and the economy, which is heavily dependent on the service sector, especially tourism, declined sharply after the 2001 downturn in global trade and tourism. Economic growth between 1995 and 2003 was negligible and income per capita decreased slightly. Today, Jamaica stands at the lower end of WEI countries with a GDP per capita of PPP$ 3 800.

The number of years a child can expect to spend in school is 12.6 years, less than the WEI average but relatively high given Jamaica's per capita income. However, the fact that school life expectancy in Jamaica has declined by half a year compared to 1995 is cause for concern. Enrolment numbers at the lower secondary level dropped while the relevant age group in the population continued to grow. The share of 5 to14-year-olds who are in school dropped by 5 percentage points and is among the lowest in WEI countries. This indicates that an increasing share of children is out of school. Meanwhile, the upper secondary graduation rate of 73 per cent is the third-highest in the WEI countries; however, most graduate with an ordinary level (O-level) which does not qualify students directly for tertiary education. In the near future, demographic pressures will be light due to slow population growth.

Jamaica shows – by far – the highest investment in education relative to national wealth among both WEI and OECD countries. Education expenditure accounted for 12.1 per cent of GDP in 2002, the highest share among WEI countries. The share of private funding for education has also increased, accounting for almost one-half of the expenditure at primary and secondary levels in 2002.

In public primary schools, there are 42 students on average per classroom, the second-highest ratio among WEI countries. However, due to the growth in the number of teachers, the student-teacher ratio at the primary level improved from 34:1 in 1995 to 30:1 in 2003.

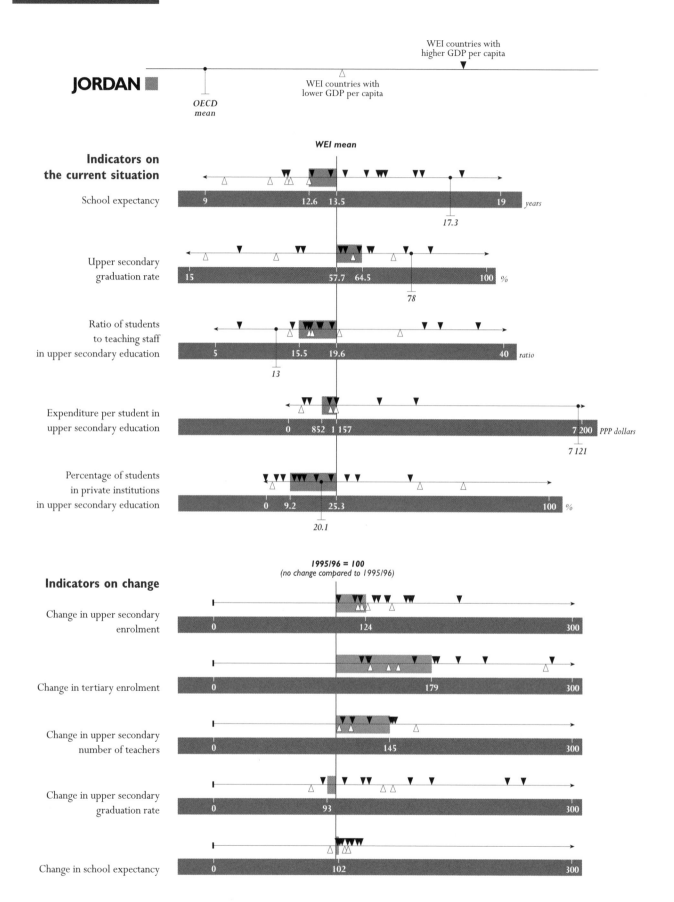

JORDAN

The education system in Jordan faces considerable demographic pressures. Almost 6 in 10 persons are 5 to 29-year-olds, the second-highest share in WEI countries. Over the next decade, the 5 to 19-year-old age group is projected to grow faster than any other WEI country, creating additional demand for education providers.

The country suffered economically during the Gulf wars of the 1980s and early 1990s. The poverty rate rose sharply from 3 per cent at the end of the 1980s to about 14 per cent in 1992[1]. Since 2000, Jordan has undertaken economic reforms, but regional instability has created economic uncertainty in the region. Given this context, Jordan has experienced relatively robust economic growth. Still, the GDP per capita of PPP$ 4 063 is almost one-third lower than the WEI average.

Compared to 1995, school life expectancy increased slightly to 12.6 years – one year less than the WEI average but better than two other WEI countries with higher GDP per capita. This increase is almost entirely due to growth in tertiary-level enrolment. Jordan has very low rates of grade repetition, at both primary and secondary levels, compared to other WEI countries. Moreover, mathematics and science achievement, as measured by TIMSS 2003, was higher than other WEI countries with higher GDP per capita that participated in the study.

The level of public expenditure on primary and secondary education is, relatively speaking, one of the highest among WEI countries. Public expenditure on these levels of education equals 4.4 per cent of GDP. However, in terms of expenditure per student in secondary education, the country spends only PPP$ 837 – 32 per cent below the WEI average.

In public primary and secondary institutions, staff compensation accounts for 95 per cent of current expenditure, one of the highest shares among WEI countries. The high proportion reflects in part favourable student-teacher ratios at primary and secondary levels as well as teaching workloads, which are among the lightest in WEI countries.

---

1. World Bank (2004). *Jordan: An evaluation of World Bank Assistance for Poverty Reduction, Health and Education.*

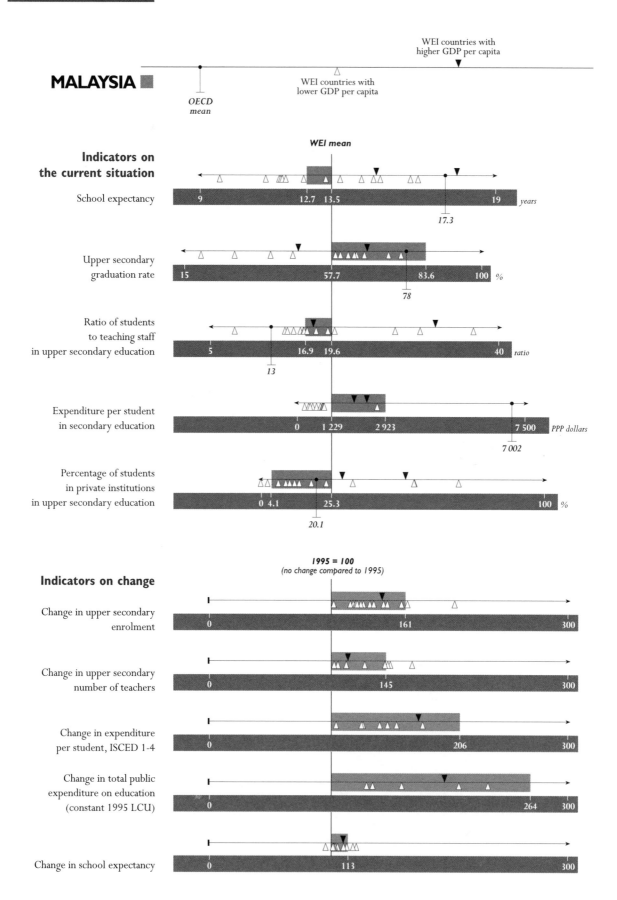

MALAYSIA ▪

WEI countries with
higher GDP per capita

WEI countries with
lower GDP per capita

*OECD
mean*

WEI mean

Indicators on
the current situation

School expectancy

9 12.7 13.5 19 *years*
17.3

Upper secondary
graduation rate

15 57.7 83.6 100 *%*
78

Ratio of students
to teaching staff
in upper secondary education

5 16.9 19.6 40 *ratio*
13

Expenditure per student
in secondary education

0 1 229 2 923 7 500 *PPP dollars*
7 002

Percentage of students
in private institutions
in upper secondary education

0 4.1 25.3 100 *%*
20.1

1995 = 100
(no change compared to 1995)

Indicators on change

Change in upper secondary
enrolment

0 161 300

Change in upper secondary
number of teachers

0 145 300

Change in expenditure
per student, ISCED 1-4

0 206 300

Change in total public
expenditure on education
(constant 1995 LCU)

0 264 300

Change in school expectancy

0 113 300

MALAYSIA

Malaysia has returned to robust economic growth after the 1997 Asian financial crisis. It enjoys some of the most favourable economic conditions in the WEI: GDP per capita (PPP$ 8 811) is third-highest in the group.

Malaysia has virtually achieved universal completion rates at primary and lower secondary levels of education – 99 and 93 per cent respectively. Efforts to expand participation have now shifted to upper secondary and tertiary education. In the period 1995-2003, the share of the 20 to 24-year-olds who completed upper secondary education increased from 60 to 71 per cent. The share of 25 to 34-year-olds who attained tertiary education almost doubled, surpassing the WEI average.

School life expectancy is 12.7 years, below the WEI average and five years short of the OECD average. However, Malaysia is catching up: school expectancy increased by 1.5 years over 1995. Growth in upper secondary enrolment was third-highest among WEI countries. Still, most of these students attain ordinary-level qualifications (O-level) which means that they do not qualify for direct entry into tertiary type A programmes. As a result, Malaysia has the second-lowest graduation rate (15.5 per cent) in the WEI countries from programmes (A-level) that qualify for type A tertiary studies.

The growth of tertiary education in Malaysia since the mid-1990s has been the fastest of both WEI and OECD countries. It must be noted, however, that the expansion started from very low levels of participation and completion. Tertiary enrolment has doubled, type A enrolment has tripled, and tertiary graduation rates have grown fourfold – pulling Malaysia from the last rank among reporting WEI countries in 1995 to almost reaching the WEI average for tertiary graduation.

The relative growth in public expenditure on education was higher in Maylasia than in any other WEI or OECD country. In 2002, Malaysia's public expenditure on education, at 8.1 per cent of GDP, was the highest among all WEI and OECD countries. This represents an impressive increase of 3.6 percentage points. For all levels of education, Malaysia now has higher per-student expenditures than any other WEI country. Expenditure per tertiary student even exceeded the OECD average, despite a doubling of student numbers.

High expenditure can partially be explained by heavy investments in education infrastructure. Almost 40 per cent of expenditure from primary to upper secondary levels is classified as capital; 47 per cent at the tertiary level.

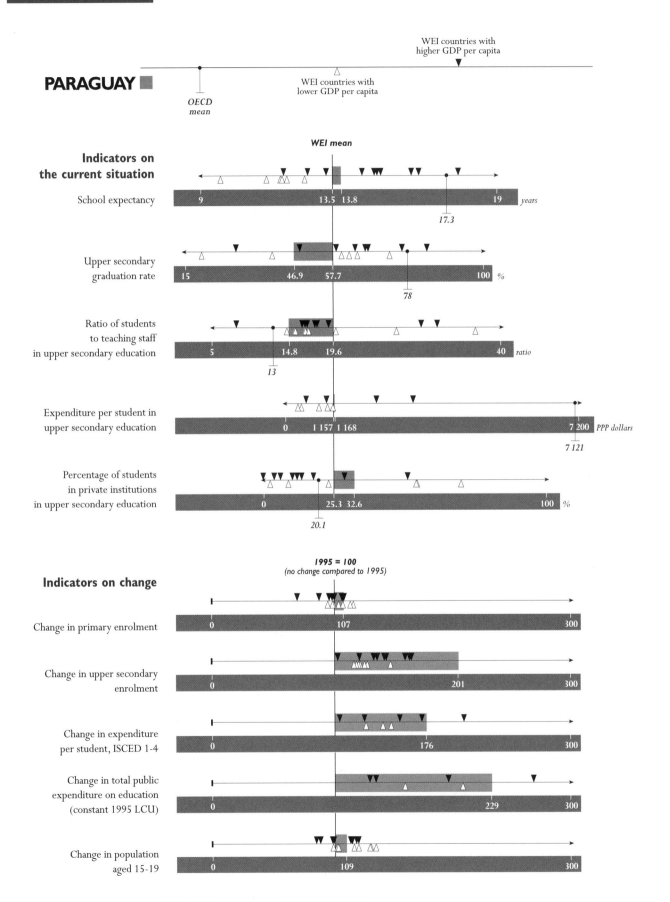

PARAGUAY

WEI countries with
higher GDP per capita

WEI countries with
lower GDP per capita

OECD
mean

WEI mean

Indicators on the current situation

School expectancy

| 9 | 13.5 13.8 | 19 | years |

17.3

Upper secondary
graduation rate

| 15 | 46.9 57.7 | 100 | % |

78

Ratio of students
to teaching staff
in upper secondary education

| 5 | 14.8 19.6 | 40 | ratio |

13

Expenditure per student in
upper secondary education

| 0 | 1 157 1 168 | 7 200 | PPP dollars |

7 121

Percentage of students
in private institutions
in upper secondary education

| 0 | 25.3 32.6 | 100 | % |

20.1

Indicators on change

1995 = 100
(no change compared to 1995)

Change in primary enrolment

| 0 | 107 | 300 |

Change in upper secondary
enrolment

| 0 | 201 | 300 |

Change in expenditure
per student, ISCED 1-4

| 0 | 176 | 300 |

Change in total public
expenditure on education
(constant 1995 LCU)

| 0 | 229 | 300 |

Change in population
aged 15-19

| 0 | 109 | 300 |

PARAGUAY

Paraguay's economy has stagnated, with GDP per capita averaging negative growth of -1.2 per cent per year for the decade 1993-2003. Poverty and income inequality are exceptionally high in Paraguay compared to other WEI countries. According to 2001 data, nearly one-third of the population – 2 million people – live in poverty.

The level of educational attainment among the adult population is one of the lowest in the WEI group of countries. More than a one-third of the working-age population fail to complete primary education and less than one in ten persons complete tertiary education. Low levels of education are widespread among the young – almost 20 per cent of the 15 to 19-year-olds do not complete primary education. Although progress has been made since 1995, other WEI countries with low levels of attainment have demonstrated stronger growth.

Expanding participation in education in Paraguay has been challenged by continuing population growth – and the school-age population is projected to grow until 2015 and even beyond. Still, Paraguay has expanded participation in school since 1995: student numbers at pre-primary, lower and upper secondary levels have doubled. Children can expect to receive 13.8 years of schooling, slightly more than the WEI average. Participation is almost universal for children aged 5-14 years, but continues to be low at upper secondary and tertiary levels compared to other WEI countries. The upper secondary graduation rate also improved substantially, rising from 19.4 per cent in 1995 to 46.9 per cent in 2002.

Expansion of enrolment has been paralleled by increases in education expenditure: in real terms, expenditure more than doubled over 1995, the second-biggest increase among reporting WEI countries. Growth in public expenditure on education was substantially faster than expenditure growth in other public sectors. The share of government expenditure spent on education increased from 7.6 per cent in 1995 to 11.4 per cent in 2002. As a percentage of GDP, expenditure grew substantially, from 3.2 per cent to 4.5 per cent, reaching the WEI average. Funding actually grew faster than enrolment: annual expenditure per student was PPP$ 676 at the primary level and PPP$ 919 at the secondary level, just below the WEI average.

The improvements in expenditure translate into improvements in teaching conditions. The student-teacher ratio in primary school is 17.3 pupils per teacher, one of the lowest among WEI countries, decreasing from 24.2 in 1995. The student-teacher ratio in secondary school is the second-lowest among WEI countries. Class sizes are also relatively small – second-smallest among WEI countries at primary (18.1 students per class) and lower secondary (25.5 students per class) levels.

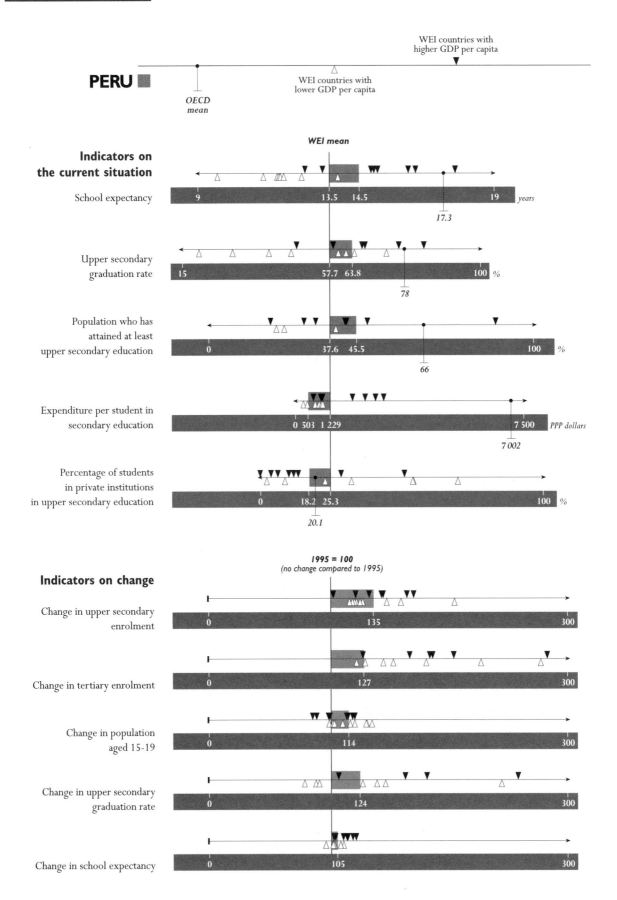

PERU

WEI countries with higher GDP per capita

WEI countries with lower GDP per capita

OECD mean

WEI mean

Indicators on the current situation

School expectancy — 9 | 13.5 | 14.5 | 19 years — 17.3

Upper secondary graduation rate — 15 | 57.7 | 63.8 | 100 % — 78

Population who has attained at least upper secondary education — 0 | 37.6 | 45.5 | 100 % — 66

Expenditure per student in secondary education — 0 503 | 1 229 | 7 500 PPP dollars — 7 002

Percentage of students in private institutions in upper secondary education — 0 | 18.2 | 25.3 | 100 % — 20.1

Indicators on change

1995 = 100
(no change compared to 1995)

Change in upper secondary enrolment — 0 | 135 | 300

Change in tertiary enrolment — 0 | 127 | 300

Change in population aged 15-19 — 0 | 114 | 300

Change in upper secondary graduation rate — 0 | 124 | 300

Change in school expectancy — 0 | 105 | 300

PERU

Peru enjoyed positive economic development for most of the 1990s, but experienced a slowdown after 1998. Political crisis followed in 2000-2001, resulting in new elections and a new government. The economy has since responded positively to government fiscal policy and social programmes have targeted the poor. Annual growth in real GDP per capita was substantial, rising from 3.4 per cent in 1993 to 4.9 per cent in 2002.

The share of 15 to 19-year-olds who had not completed primary education is 10 per cent. Still, this represents substantial progress since 1995 when the share was twice as high. The percentage of the population that have attained at least upper secondary education is 42 per cent, third-highest among WEI countries. However, this is roughly the same level as 1993, so Peru's standing relative to other WEI countries is actually declining.

School life expectancy is 14.5 years, one year more than the WEI average. Participation in education is almost universal at the primary and lower secondary levels. Yet, expansion was slower than in other WEI countries, especially at the upper secondary and tertiary levels of education.

Due to Peru's economic situation, public financial resources for education are limited. Although 16 per cent of the total public budget is spent on education, this represents a relatively small share of GDP, 2.7 per cent. As a consequence, the education burden on households is high. Private expenditure on education accounts for a further 1.9 per cent of GDP – or 40 per cent of total spending at primary and secondary levels and almost two-thirds at the tertiary level.

Despite relatively low expenditure per student – PPP$ 503 in secondary education – Peru reports a relatively good student-teacher ratio with 18.9 pupils per teacher, well below the WEI average. The situation of low expenditure per student and improved student-teacher ratios can be explained by very low teacher salaries and a low share of the education budget allocated to teaching materials or capital expenditure.

Grade repetition remains high in Peru. Students can expect to spend one full year repeating grades in primary and secondary school.

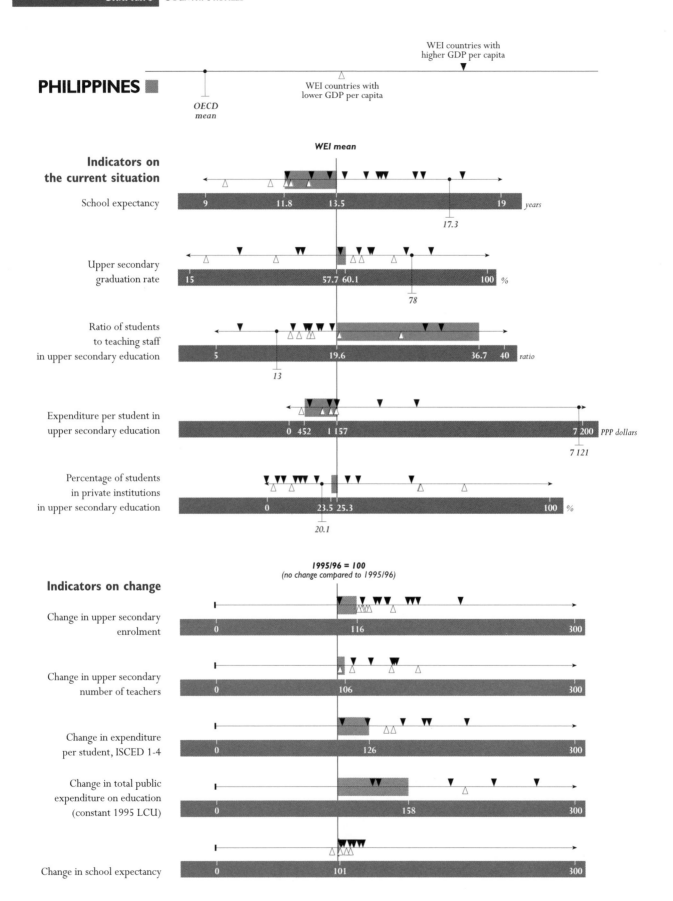

PHILIPPINES

WEI countries with
higher GDP per capita

WEI countries with
lower GDP per capita

OECD
mean

WEI mean

**Indicators on
the current situation**

School expectancy

| 9 | 11.8 | 13.5 | 19 | *years* |

17.3

Upper secondary
graduation rate

| 15 | 57.7 | 60.1 | 100 | % |

78

Ratio of students
to teaching staff
in upper secondary education

| 5 | 19.6 | 36.7 | 40 | *ratio* |

13

Expenditure per student in
upper secondary education

| 0 | 452 | 1 157 | 7 200 | *PPP dollars* |

7 121

Percentage of students
in private institutions
in upper secondary education

| 0 | 23.5 | 25.3 | 100 | % |

20.1

Indicators on change

1995/96 = 100
(no change compared to 1995/96)

Change in upper secondary
enrolment

| 0 | 116 | 300 |

Change in upper secondary
number of teachers

| 0 | 106 | 300 |

Change in expenditure
per student, ISCED 1-4

| 0 | 126 | 300 |

Change in total public
expenditure on education
(constant 1995 LCU)

| 0 | 158 | 300 |

Change in school expectancy

| 0 | 101 | 300 |

PHILIPPINES

The Philippines was immediately affected by the financial crisis in Asia in 1997, but to a less severe degree than other parts of the region – economic growth returned by 1999. Overall, the Philippines experienced robust growth in GDP (30 per cent) over the period 1995-2002. However, the country has also had strong population growth: the population aged 5-14 years grew by 15 per cent, the greatest increase in WEI countries. This puts pressure on the education system to increase student numbers at all levels.

Overall enrolment has grown by 20 per cent, but this has been barely enough – from primary to tertiary levels – to maintain the status quo. In 2003, school life expectancy was roughly 12 years, the third-lowest result among WEI countries and almost unchanged from 1995.

An exception to this pattern is the change at the pre-primary level. Student numbers grew by more than 50 per cent and enrolment rates doubled. The pattern is mixed for basic education. Enrolment in primary education grew less than the relevant population, but lower secondary education expanded. Overall, the changes resulted in a decrease of net enrolment rates for 5 to 14-year-olds.

Access to upper secondary education, rapidly growing in most WEI countries, was stagnant in the Philippines and the graduation rate declined. Growth of tertiary education was also slowest in the Philippines. However, since access to tertiary education was already widespread in 1995, tertiary graduation rates are still among the highest in the WEI group.

With low public expenditure on education as a percentage of GDP (3.1 per cent) and low growth in tertiary education, it is not surprising that public expenditure on tertiary education as a percentage of GDP (0.4 per cent) is third-lowest among WEI countries and half of the WEI mean – a situation that has been virtually unchanged since 1995. Low capital expenditure in primary and secondary education as well as tertiary education is also not surprising given the low level of public spending and above-average starting salaries for teachers.

To ensure the quality of teachers, a tertiary degree is designated as the minimum teacher qualification. However, this selectivity also makes it more difficult to alleviate the shortage of teachers. Class sizes of more than 40 students are common in primary and lower secondary education.

Teachers in the Philippines also work comparatively long hours by WEI standards. The annual teaching load has decreased since 1995 due to a shortening of the school year, but class sizes grew over the same period. The student-teacher ratio at secondary education is the highest of all WEI countries, at 37 students per teacher.

In recent years, the private sector has shrunk at all levels, but it still plays a significant role compared to other countries. For instance, 23.5 per cent of upper secondary students are enrolled in independent private institutions compared to the WEI mean of 13.3 per cent. It represents a drop of almost 12 percentage points since 1995.

The shrinking of the private sector has somewhat influenced expenditure per student which has increased by 26 per cent in primary and secondary education between 1995 and 2002 but has not increased as much as most other WEI countries during the same period.

RUSSIAN FEDERATION

WEI countries with higher GDP per capita

WEI countries with lower GDP per capita

OECD mean

WEI mean

Indicators on the current situation

School expectancy
9 13.5 14.9 19 *years*
17.3

Upper secondary graduation rate
15 57.7 87.3 100 %
78

Ratio of students to teaching staff in upper secondary education
5 10.8 19.6 40 *ratio*
13

Expenditure per student in secondary education
0 1 229 1 327 7 500 *PPP dollars*
7 002

Percentage of students in private institutions in upper secondary education
0 0.3 25.3 100 %
20.1

Indicators on change

1995/96 = 100
(no change compared to 1995/96)

Change in upper secondary enrolment
0 120 300

Change in tertiary enrolment
0 181 300

Change in upper secondary number of teachers
0 103 300

Change in upper secondary graduation rate
0 104 300

Change in school expectancy
0 118 300

RUSSIAN FEDERATION

The Russian economy has made an impressive recovery since its 1998 crisis. Between 1998 and 2005, GDP expanded by an estimated 48 per cent, while real incomes grew by 46 per cent. Poverty rates were cut in half and regional disparities declined somewhat. While living standards have begun to get better, improving education and health has been more difficult, and significant social risks remain for some segments of society.

The Russian education system also has to respond to huge changes in its demographic context. Population projections suggest that by 2015 the number of children aged 5-14 years will be half of the level of 1995. Such a rapid decrease will require big adjustments in the education system, as well as other sectors of society; it also provides an opportunity to improve the quality of educational provision.

The educational attainment of the adult population and the current output of education in Russian have been very high historically and remain so. Educational attainment exceeds the OECD average for all levels of education. Of the adult population, 96 per cent has completed lower secondary education and most also have an upper secondary education. Furthermore, more than one-half of all adults have attained type A or type B tertiary education. Graduation rates are at or above OECD standards – 87, 29 and 33 per cent for upper secondary, tertiary type B and tertiary type A, respectively.

International student achievement tests, namely PISA and TIMSS, also show high results for Russian children in Grades 4 and 8 and at age 15. However, TIMSS results indicate that mathematics and science achievement of Grade 8 students decreased compared to 1995.

The relatively good performance of Russia in education is achieved at a limited cost relative to GDP. With public expenditure on education amounting to 3.7 per cent of GDP, the Russian Federation stands slightly below the WEI average (4.3 per cent) and well below the OECD average (5.4 per cent). The main factors behind the low expenditure are the relatively small school-age population and, given national income levels, relatively low teacher salaries.

Teaching conditions in terms of class size and student-teacher ratios are well above WEI and OECD averages. With 16 students per class, primary school classes are the second-smallest among both WEI and OECD countries. At the primary level, the decrease in the number of teachers was proportionately less than the decrease in student numbers – resulting in a further drop in the already low pupil-teacher ratio. This illustrates the difficulties in meeting new demographic realities.

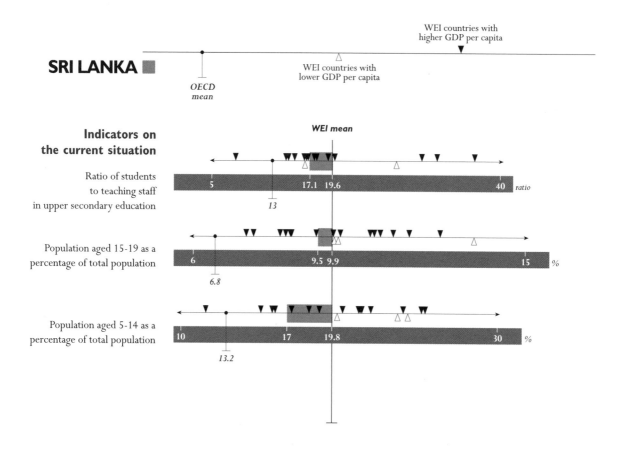

SRI LANKA ▪

WEI countries with higher GDP per capita ▼

WEI countries with lower GDP per capita △

OECD mean

Indicators on the current situation

WEI mean

Ratio of students to teaching staff in upper secondary education

5   17.1 19.6   40   ratio

13

Population aged 15-19 as a percentage of total population

6   9.5 9.9   15   %

6.8

Population aged 5-14 as a percentage of total population

10   17   19.8   30   %

13.2

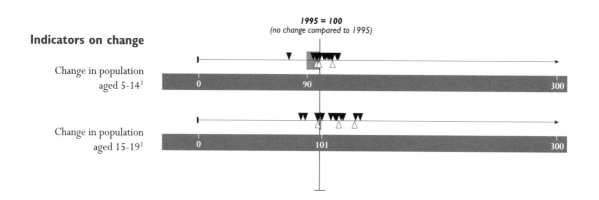

Indicators on change

1995 = 100
(no change compared to 1995)

Change in population aged 5-14[1]

0   90   300

Change in population aged 15-19[1]

0   101   300

1. For 1995, United Nations Population Division (UNPD) population estimates were used given that national population figures were not available.

SRI LANKA

Economically, Sri Lanka is growing but remains in the bottom quarter of WEI countries in terms of GDP per capita – PPP\$ 3 426 in 2002. Between 1996 and 2002, per capita income grew by 2.5 per cent. However, during the same period, poverty reduction was modest, with the share of the population living in poverty falling from 28.8 to 22.7 per cent.[1]

Universal participation in education among 5 to 14-year-olds has largely been achieved due to the introduction in 1998 of compulsory education for this age group. Another contributing factor was the decrease in the size of this age group since 1996, reducing demographic demand on the education system at the primary and lower secondary levels. However, enrolment rates for 15 to 19-year-olds remain relatively low compared to other WEI countries. This indicates the need for both greater access to and expansion of upper secondary education. The government has also emphasised the provision of equitable opportunities for participation in education.

Primary and lower secondary schools are characterised by lower-than-average class sizes and higher-than-average instruction time. Rates of repetition are very low, only 0.9 per cent of pupils repeat their current grade.

Teachers salaries are low both at entry level and after 15 years of experience, third-lowest in the WEI group for both primary and lower secondary education.

---

1. World Bank, "Sri Lanka Development Forum 2005: The Economy, the Tsunami and Poverty Reduction".

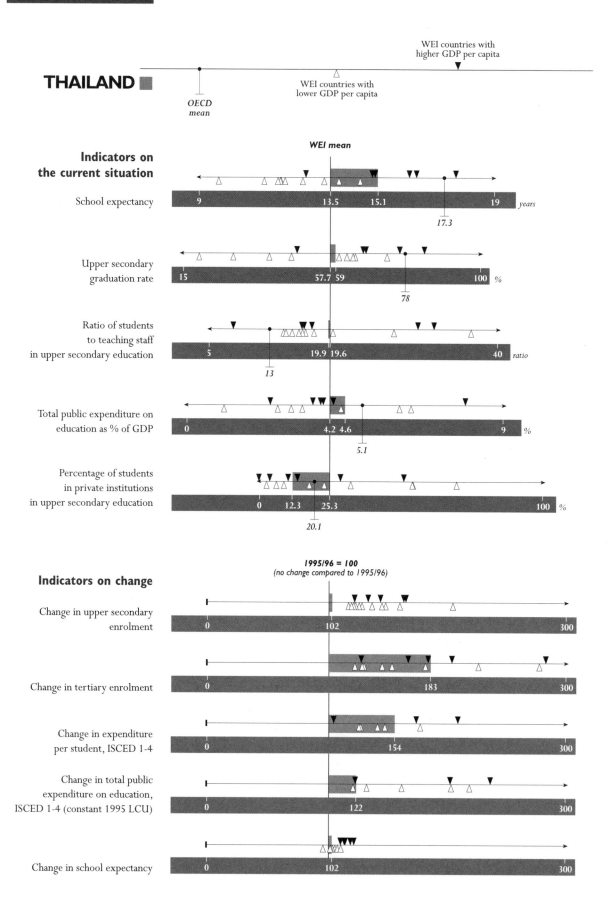

THAILAND

WEI countries with higher GDP per capita

WEI countries with lower GDP per capita

OECD mean

Indicators on the current situation

WEI mean

School expectancy

| 9 | 13.5 | 15.1 | 19 | years |

17.3

Upper secondary graduation rate

| 15 | 57.7 59 | 100 | % |

78

Ratio of students to teaching staff in upper secondary education

| 5 | 19.9 19.6 | 40 | ratio |

13

Total public expenditure on education as % of GDP

| 0 | 4.2 4.6 | 9 | % |

5.1

Percentage of students in private institutions in upper secondary education

| 0 | 12.3 | 25.3 | 100 | % |

20.1

Indicators on change

1995/96 = 100
(no change compared to 1995/96)

Change in upper secondary enrolment

| 0 | 102 | 300 |

Change in tertiary enrolment

| 0 | 183 | 300 |

Change in expenditure per student, ISCED 1-4

| 0 | 154 | 300 |

Change in total public expenditure on education, ISCED 1-4 (constant 1995 LCU)

| 0 | 122 | 300 |

Change in school expectancy

| 0 | 102 | 300 |

THAILAND

The 1997 Asian financial crisis had severe consequences in Thailand where the currency lost half of its value. Although the economy rebounded with GDP growth of 6.9 per cent in 2003, the SARS crisis contributed to continuing uncertainty. However, with GDP per capita of PPP$ 6 740, Thailand is one of the wealthiest WEI countries.

In the last decade, Thailand has also experienced a tremendous increase in human capital. The share of 25 to 34-year-olds who have completed primary education grew from 54 per cent in 1995 to 91 per cent in 2003. At the same time, completion of primary education was virtually universal among 15 to 19-year-olds. The share of youths who have attained upper secondary education doubled in just eight years.

Thailand has aimed to provide all citizens with at least 12 years of basic education and has extended the duration of compulsory education from six to nine years. Unfortunately, as the Asian economic crisis occurred just when educational reforms were being implemented, many projects were delayed or halted. Efforts to increase access to education are helped by the fact that Thailand has a relatively small school-age population.

With respect to access to education, reforms have largely been successful. Almost all children aged 5-14 years are enrolled in school. School life expectancy has increased since 1995 to 15.1 years, fourth-highest among WEI countries. Participation rates and consequently graduation rates in upper and post-secondary education have also increased.

TUNISIA

WEI countries with
higher GDP per capita

WEI countries with
lower GDP per capita

OECD
mean

**Indicators on
the current situation**

WEI mean

School expectancy

| 9 | 13.4 13.5 | 19 | *years* |

17.3

Total public expenditure
on education as % of GDP

| 0 | 4.2 | 6.4 | 9 | *%* |

5.1

Ratio of students
to teaching staff
in upper secondary education

| 5 | 18 19.6 | 40 | *ratio* |

13

Expenditure per student
in secondary education

| 0 | 1 229 | 2 583 | 7 500 | *PPP dollars* |

7 002

Percentage of students
in private institutions
in upper secondary education

| 0 | 7 | 25.3 | 100 | *%* |

20.1

Indicators on change

1995/96 = 100
(no change compared to 1995/96)

Change in upper secondary
enrolment

| 0 | 142 | 300 |

Change in total public
expenditure, ISCED 1-4
(constant 1995 LCU)

| 0 | 131 | 300 |

Change in expenditure
per student, ISCED 1-4

| 0 | 125 | 300 |

Change in total public
expenditure on education
(constant 1995 LCU)

| 0 | 134 | 300 |

Change in school expectancy

| 0 | 103 | 300 |

TUNISIA

Between 1961 and 2002, the Tunisian economy grew annually by 5 per cent while per capita income tripled by 2001. During this period, literacy levels and educational attainments increased significantly, especially among women[1]. The country has reduced the overall incidence of poverty from 16 per cent in 1990 to 10 per cent in 2000, which reflects progress towards the achievement of the MDG target of halving poverty by 2015.

In 2002, a 5-year-old in Tunisia can expect to receive 13.4 years of schooling, almost exactly the average for WEI countries. This result is partly due to the long duration of compulsory education from age 6 to 16 years. However, school expectancy includes a full year of schooling that is attributed to repetition. At the primary and secondary levels, Tunisia has the third- and second-highest repetition rates respectively among WEI countries.

The mathematics achievement of 8th graders in Tunisia, as measured by the TIMSS 2003, is close to the average among the participating WEI countries, but better than some countries with higher GDP per capita. PISA 2003, which tested 15-year-olds, shows that the between-school difference in mathematics performance is lower than the OECD average. However, there seems to be a significant gender difference in favor of boys in terms of Grade 8 mathematics achievement.

Public expenditure on education, for all levels combined, represents 6.4 per cent of GDP, which exceeds both the WEI and OECD averages. The high level of spending translates into relatively high expenditure per student. At the primary and secondary levels expenditure per student (PPP$ 2 583) is well above the WEI average. The high level of spending has not changed compared to other WEI countries, which made gains since 1995.

Teacher salaries in Tunisia are high relative to both national GDP per capita and the WEI average. The starting salary for primary teachers with minimum training was PPP$ 13 120 in 2003, second-highest among WEI countries. High salaries are partly explained by the high levels of teacher qualifications and training: all primary and secondary teachers have tertiary qualifications. Teachers also have a relatively light workload. Primary and secondary teachers have an annual teaching load of 735 and 548 hours respectively, third- and second-lowest among WEI countries.

---

1. *Tunisia's Path to Development* : 1961-2001. Shanghai Poverty Conference, Shanghai 25-27 May 2004, World Bank.

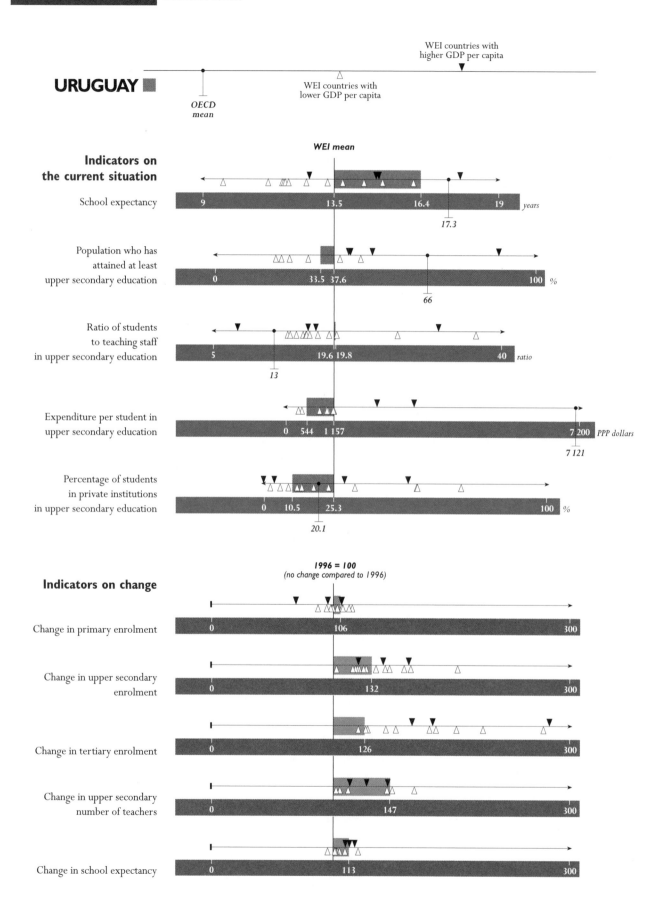

URUGUAY

WEI countries with
higher GDP per capita ▼

WEI countries with
lower GDP per capita △

*OECD
mean*

WEI mean

Indicators on
the current situation

School expectancy
9   13.5   16.4   19   *years*
17.3

Population who has
attained at least
upper secondary education
0   33.5 37.6   100   *%*
66

Ratio of students
to teaching staff
in upper secondary education
5   19.6 19.8   40   *ratio*
13

Expenditure per student in
upper secondary education
0   544 1 157   7 200   *PPP dollars*
7 121

Percentage of students
in private institutions
in upper secondary education
0   10.5   25.3   100   *%*
20.1

1996 = 100
(no change compared to 1996)

Indicators on change

Change in primary enrolment
0   106   300

Change in upper secondary
enrolment
0   132   300

Change in tertiary enrolment
0   126   300

Change in upper secondary
number of teachers
0   147   300

Change in school expectancy
0   113   300

URUGUAY

Uruguay still struggles to recover from economic recessions of 1999-2001 and the 2002 crisis which precipitated a drop in GDP per capita of 11 per cent. The recession left one-third of the population living below the poverty line. Yet, there have been substantial improvements in the economic situation since then. And, demographic demands are relatively light – 5 to 14-year-olds represent only 16 per cent of the total population, third-lowest in the WEI, and 15 to 19-year-olds represent 8 per cent, second-lowest in the WEI group.

The rate of school participation in Uruguay is the second-highest among WEI countries. School life expectancy, at 16.4 years, is almost two years more than in 1996 and almost three years more than the WEI average and longer than in some OECD countries. Participation in primary and lower secondary education is almost universal with 99 per cent of children aged 5-14 years enrolled in school.

Grade repetition, however, remains a problem: on average, children repeat one full year. Completion of primary school is high; however, attainment decreased slightly among 15 to 19-year-olds, from 99 per cent in 1996 to 96 per cent in 2003. The share of youths who have attained lower or upper secondary education is below the WEI average. Similarly, the graduation rate for tertiary type A programmes was around 9 per cent, more than 5 percentage points below the WEI average.

In terms of Uruguay's national income, only 2.8 per cent of GDP is invested in education, half of the WEI and OECD averages. Different from most other Latin American countries, education is largely publicly funded: only 3 per cent of expenditure on tertiary education and 8 per cent of expenditure on primary/secondary institutions is private. The low level of investment is also reflected in the annual expenditure per student, which is very low given Uruguay's level of national income. Expenditure per secondary student (PPP$ 732) is less than one-third of the average in WEI countries with comparable GDP, such as Chile, Malaysia or Tunisia.

The education system in Uruguay is distinguished by its combination of low education expenditure and short instruction time. In essence, education expenditures can be kept low because the volume of services provided is very small. Instruction time at both primary and secondary levels is the shortest among all WEI countries. With teaching time continuing to decrease between 1995 and 2003, secondary students ended up spending little more than one-half of the hours in school per year than students in other WEI countries. Teachers have the shortest work hours in the WEI and, in turn, very low salaries.

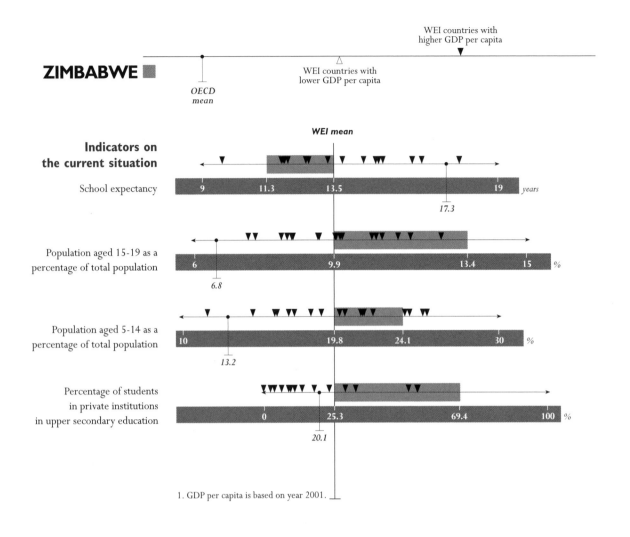

ZIMBABWE

WEI countries with
higher GDP per capita

WEI countries with
lower GDP per capita

OECD
mean

WEI mean

**Indicators on
the current situation**

School expectancy

9   11.3   13.5   19   *years*

17.3

Population aged 15-19 as a
percentage of total population

6   9.9   13.4   15   *%*

6.8

Population aged 5-14 as a
percentage of total population

10   19.8   24.1   30   *%*

13.2

Percentage of students
in private institutions
in upper secondary education

0   25.3   69.4   100   *%*

20.1

1. GDP per capita is based on year 2001.

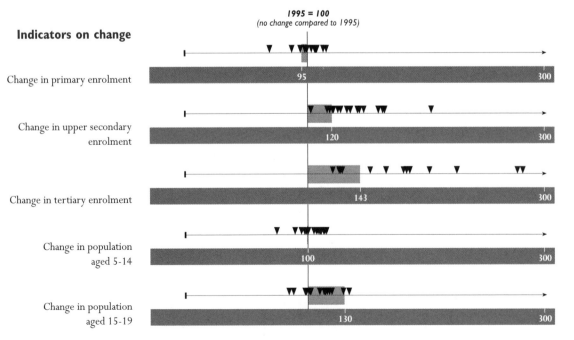

1995 = 100
(no change compared to 1995)

Indicators on change

Change in primary enrolment

95   300

Change in upper secondary
enrolment

120   300

Change in tertiary enrolment

143   300

Change in population
aged 5-14

100   300

Change in population
aged 15-19

130   300

ZIMBABWE

Since the late 1990s, Zimbabwe has been struggling with a wide range of economic and social problems, including soaring inflation and an HIV/AIDS pandemic. The education system faces high demand due to a large school-age population. More than one-third of the population is between the ages of 5 and 19 years. However, due primarily to the impact of HIV/AIDS, the population of 5 to 14-year-olds has not grown since 1995.

Participation in education in Zimbabwe is low compared to other WEI countries. In 2003, school life expectancy was 11.3 years, more than two years less than the WEI average. In the primary school-age range (7-13 years), more than 90 per cent of the relevant population is enrolled in school. Officially, compulsory education includes lower secondary education, but many children do not participate at this level. Entry rates to lower secondary education are 62 per cent and only 6 per cent to upper secondary school, the lowest rate – by far – in WEI countries. Despite an increase of 20 per cent in upper secondary enrolment numbers since 1995, enrolment rates remained the same because of a commensurate increase in the population of eligible age.

Participation in tertiary education is almost negligible in Zimbabwe. The entry rate to type A programmes is just 2 per cent, by far the lowest rate among WEI countries. Relative to other WEI countries, tertiary student numbers have grown only slightly since 1995.

Zimbabwe is one of the few WEI countries with substantially lower participation of females in education. On average, girls can expect to receive 1.2 years less schooling than boys. Disparities are stronger at higher levels of education: two out of three tertiary type A students are male. Yet, compared to 1995 the share of female students has increased.

ANNEXES

These annexes provide the data used in this publication as well as important information on the definitions and methods underlying these data. The full documentation of national data sources and calculation methods is published in the OECD 2005 edition of *Education at a Glance* and on the OECD web site:

www.oecd.org/edu/eag2005

Five annexes are presented:

- **Annex A1** provides general notes pertaining to the coverage of the data, the reference periods and the main sources for the data.
- **Annex A2** provides definitions and technical notes that are important for the understanding of the indicators presented in this publication (the notes are organised alphabetically).
- **Annex A3** provides a cross-reference between data tables and technical notes.
- **Annex A4** provides the full set of data tables used in this publication.
- **Annex A5** documents the classification of the 19 WEI countries' educational programmes according to the 1997 International Standard Classification of Education (ISCED97).

Further resources

The full documentation of national data sources and calculation methods is published in the OECD 2005 edition of *Education at a Glance* and on the OECD web site: *www.oecd.org/edu/eag2005*. It provides a rich source of information on the methods employed for the calculation of indicators, the interpretation of indicators in the respective national contexts and the data sources involved. It also provides further indicators for OECD countries.

Any post-production changes to this publication are listed at: *www.uis.unesco.org/wei2005*.

The full set of questionnaires used to gather the education data for this publication and data complementing the presented tables, such as data by gender or additional age groups, are available at *www.uis.unesco.org/wei2005*.

ANNEX A1 – GENERAL NOTES

Coverage

Although a shortage of data still limits the scope of some indicators in many WEI countries, the coverage extends, in principle, to the entire national education system regardless of the ownership or sponsorship of the institutions concerned and regardless of education delivery mechanisms.

With one exception described below, all types of students and all age groups are meant to be included: children (including those classified as exceptional), adults, nationals, foreigners, as well as students in open distance learning, special education programmes or educational programmes organised by ministries other than the Ministry of Education provided that the main aim of the programme is the educational development of the individual. Vocational and technical training in the workplace, with the exception of combined school- and work-based programmes that are explicitly deemed to be parts of the education system, are not included in the basic education expenditure and enrolment data.

Educational activities classified as "adult" or "non-regular" are covered, provided that the activities involve studies or have subject-matter content similar to "regular" education studies or that the underlying programmes lead to potential qualifications similar to corresponding regular educational programmes. Courses for adults that are primarily for general interest, personal enrichment, leisure or recreation are excluded.

Reference periods

Unless specified otherwise in the indicator table notes, the reference year for the financial data is the calendar year 2002 and the school year which has the greatest overlap with the year 1995 for both WEI and OECD countries. The reference year for all data on entry, enrolment, completion and education personnel is the school year ending in 2003 and again the school year which has the greatest overlap with the year 1995. As a convention, those years were referred to as 2003 and 1995 in the text and table headings. Note that this convention is different from other publications by the UNESCO Institute for Statistics. For WEI countries the exact school year is provided in most tables, *i.e.* start and end of the year. For OECD countries this information is available from Table X1.2a in the OECD 2005 edition of *Education at a Glance*. Where the financial data year does not coincide with this target reference period, GDP and total public expenditure data have been adjusted accordingly.

Data on national expenditure in this publication have been converted using World Bank *World Development Indicators* purchasing power parities (PPPs).

Sources

Most numerical data used in this report are based on the annual WEI/UOE data collection. Government officials in OECD and WEI countries provide these data annually to the OECD and the UNESCO Institute for Statistics in detailed and highly structured electronic questionnaires. These questionnaires consist of several electronic workbooks organised by topic - demographic background, education finance, enrolments, entrants, graduates, curriculum and personnel.

Sources used by government officials to complete the electronic questionnaires consist most often of labour force surveys, population censuses, or, in the case of demographic background and educational attainment data, population projections based on censuses. In most cases, education system records, such as school censuses, provide the data on enrolments, entrants, graduates, curriculum and personnel. Education finance data often come from sources outside education ministries such as government ministries that specialise in finance.

Additional financial and economic background data used in this report come from World Bank databases, some of which are published in its *World Development Indicators* publication. Specific indicators borrowed from World Bank databases include purchasing power parity indices and gross domestic product (GDP) per capita.

National data sources are:

Argentina

Ministry of Education, 2002 school census and programme on improvement of university information systems.

Brazil

Ministry of Education *(MEC),* National Institute for Educational Studies and Research *(INEP),* 2002 school census, 2002 higher education census*,* 2002 Data Collection on Advanced Studies. Brazilian Institute for Geography and Statistics *(IBGE),* 2002 National Household Survey *(PNAD)* and National Treasure Secretariat.

Chile

Ministry of Education: enrolment, graduates, achievement, education personnel and finance (ISCED 0-6); Central Bank - National Accounts (ISCED 0-6), National Council on Science and Technology – CONICYT (ISCED 5-6), Ministry of Internal Affairs (ISCED 0-6), and JUNJI and INTEGRA (ISCED 0).

Institute of National Statistics, INE: demographic information.

China

Ministry of Education, Department of Development and Planning, *Education Statistics Yearbook of China*, 2002

Egypt

Ministry of Education.

Ministry of Higher Education.

India

Ministry of Human Resource Development. Selected Educational Statistics 2002-03.

National Institute of Educational Planning and Administration.

Department of Education, Planning and Monitoring Unit.

Indonesia

Ministry of Education, school statistics and census.

Jamaica

Ministry of Education, Youth and Culture.

Jordan

Ministry of Education, Statistical Yearbook 2002/2003, Department of Statistics, Directorate of Planning, Division of Planning, Division of Salaries, MOE/Budget Division.

Malaysia

Ministry of Education, Education Planning and Resources Division (*ERPD*), Teacher Education Department (*TED*), Polytechnic Management Division, Community College, National Institute of Educational Management and Leadership (*IAB*), Matriculation Department, Higher Education Department (*HED*), Ministry of Rural Development (*KEMAS*), National Unity Department, Ministry of Youth and Sports, Agriculture Department, Council of Trust of the Indigenous People (*MARA*), Ministry of Human Resource, Rescue and Fire Academy, JAKIM, KUSZA, Ministry of Health, Private Education Department (*PED*).

JPN, JPS, KOMMUNITI, JTM, KBS, PERTANIAN, JPT, BPG, POLITEKNIK

Paraguay

Ministry of Education and Culture, Education Statistics Yearbook 2002, Department of Educational and Cultural Planning.

National General Budget of Expenditures.

Peru

Ministry of Education: Basic Statistics 2002 – School census 2002.

National Institute for Statistics *(INEI), Compendium 2003*.

Ministry of Economy and Finance: Integrated System of Financial Management, 2002.

Philippines

Department of Education, Basic Education Information System, school year 2002/2003.

Technical Education and Skills Development Authority (TESDA) Statistical Bulletins.

Commission of Higher Education (CHED) Statistical Bulletins.

Russian Federation

Ministry of Education, Centre for Monitoring and Statistics of Education.

National Statistics Agency.

Sri Lanka

Ministry of Education.

School Census 2002.

Thailand

Ministry of Education.

Office of the National Education Commission (ONEC).

Tunisia

Ministry of Education.

Ministry of Economic Development.

National Institute of Statistics.

Uruguay

Ministry of Education and Culture, Education Division, Statistics Department.

National Institute for Statistics *(INE)*.

Zimbabwe

Ministry of Education, Sport and Culture.

For a full documentation of national data sources and calculation methods for the OECD countries, refer to the OECD 2005 edition of *Education at a Glance* or the OECD web site: *www.oecd.org/edu/eag2005*.

■ ANNEX A2 – DEFINITIONS, METHODS AND TECHNICAL NOTES

Annual growth rate (Table 1.10)

Annual growth rates allow better comparison of change over time between countries where the change refers to periods of different duration. Annual growth rates are calculated as geometric growth rates. They express the ► *index of change* as an average annual change. Index of change can be converted to annual growth rates as $r = \exp((\ln(i/100)/n)-1$, where r is the annual growth rate, i is the index of change and n is the duration of the reference period in years.

Attainment

► *Educational attainment.*

Class size (Table 2.9)

Class sizes have been calculated by dividing the number of students enrolled by the number of classes for the whole country. In order to ensure comparability among countries, special needs programmes have been excluded. Data include only regular programmes at primary and lower secondary levels of education and exclude teaching in sub-groups outside the regular classroom setting.

The class size indicator in the report is different from previous WEI reports, where the class size presented was a theoretical constructed figure.

Compulsory education (Table 1.7)

Number of years or the age-span during which children and young people are legally obliged to attend school.

Current and capital expenditure (Table 2.7)

The distinction between current and capital expenditure is the standard one used in national accounting.

Current expenditure is expenditure on educational institutions' goods and services consumed within the current year, that needs to be made recurrently to sustain the production of educational services. Minor expenditure on items of equipment, below a certain cost threshold, is also reported as current spending.

Capital expenditure represents the portion of ► *expenditure on educational institutions'* capital assets acquired or created during the year in question – *i.e.*, the amount of capital formation, regardless of whether the capital outlay was financed from current revenue or by borrowing. Capital expenditure includes outlays on construction, renovation, and major repair of buildings and expenditure for new or replacement equipment. Although capital investment requires a large initial expenditure, the plant and facilities have a lifetime that extends over many years. Capital expenditure does not include debt servicing.

Educational attainment (Tables 1.1-1.2)

The levels of educational attainment present the highest ► *level of education*, defined according to ► *ISCED97* (see Annex A5), completed by people in different sub-groups of the total population (*e.g.* age-groups, labour force, unemployed). Note that many educational programmes cannot be easily classified and the contents of a specific ISCED level may differ between countries, and even within countries over time and between age groups.

Educational institution (Tables 2.2-2.8, 2.13-2.14)

Educational institutions are defined as entities that provide instructional services to individuals or education-related services to individuals and other educational institutions. Whether or not an entity qualifies as an educational institution is not contingent upon which public authority (if any) has responsibility for it.

Educational institutions are subdivided into ► *public and private educational institutions.*

Educational institutions comprise instructional educational institutions and non-instructional educational institutions, the latter being of special importance for comparable coverage of the data on educational finance. The term "instructional" is used simply to imply the direct provision of teaching and learning.

Instructional educational institutions are those that provide individuals with educational programmes that fall within the scope of the WEI/UOE data collection. In this report, the generic term "school" is often used to refer to instructional institutions at the primary, secondary, and post-secondary non-tertiary levels, and "university" to those at the tertiary level.

Non-instructional educational institutions are educational institutions that provide administrative, advisory or professional services, frequently for other educational institutions. Non-instructional educational institutions include the following:

- Entities administering educational institutions, including institutions such as national, state and provincial ministries or departments of education; other bodies that administer education at various levels of government and analogous bodies in the private sector (*e.g.* diocesan offices that administer Catholic schools and agencies administering admissions to universities).

- Entities providing support services to other educational institutions, including institutions that provide educational support and materials as well as operation and maintenance services for buildings. These are commonly part of the general purpose units of public authorities.

- Entities providing ancillary services, covering separate organisations that provide such education-related services as vocational and psychological counselling, placement, transportation of students, and student meals and housing. In some countries, housing and dining facilities for tertiary students are operated by private organisations, usually non-profit, that may be subsidised out of public funds.

- Institutions administering student-loan or scholarship programmes.

- Entities performing curriculum development, testing, educational research and educational policy analysis.

Educational personnel (staff) (Tables 2.7-2.8)

Educational personnel includes staff employed in both public and private schools and other educational institutions. Educational personnel is subdivided into ► *teacher* and other personnel categories. The latter comprises teachers' aides, teaching/research assistants and non-instructional personnel.

Teachers' aides and teaching/research assistants include non-professional personnel or students who support teachers in providing instruction to students.

Non-instructional personnel comprises four categories:

• *Professional support* for students includes professional staff who provide services to students that support their learning. This category also includes all personnel employed in education systems who provide health and social support services to students, such as guidance counsellors, librarians, doctors, dentists, nurses, psychiatrists and psychologists and other staff with similar responsibilities

• *School and higher level management* include professional personnel who are responsible for school management and administration and personnel whose primary responsibility is the quality control and management of higher levels of the education system.

• *School and higher level administrative personnel* include all personnel who support the administration and management of schools and of higher levels of the education system.

• *Maintenance and operations personnel* include personnel who support the maintenance and operation of schools, the transportation of students to and from school, school security and catering.

► *Student-teacher ratios* do account for only teachers and therefore underestimate the human resources involved in education.

Enrolment (Tables 1.6, 1.9-1.12, 2.8)

Number of pupils or students officially enrolled in a given ► *level of education*. Typically, these data are collected at the beginning of the school year.

Enrolment rate (net) (Tables 1.6, 1.8)

Net enrolment rates (also referred to as enrolment rates) are calculated by dividing the number of students of a particular age group enrolled in all ► *levels of education* by the number of persons in the population in that age-group (multiplied by 100). Figures are based on ► *headcounts*, *i.e.* they do not distinguish between full-time and part-time students.

Net enrolment rates for primary and secondary education are calculated for different age groups for different countries, dependent on the ► *typical ages* of participants at the corresponding level. This can influence the results, *e.g.* in countries with longer programme duration, the typical age for upper secondary education may include ages 17 and 18, while in other countries only age 16 is included. As a result, countries with longer duration may show lower rates due to the drop out of the 17 and 18-year-olds, although they have higher enrolment rates at all ages.

Entry rate (Table 1.15)

Gross entry rates are the ratio of all ► *new entrants*, regardless of age, to the size of the population at the ► *typical age* of entry (multiplied by 100). Gross entry rates are more easily influenced by differences in the size of population by single year of age, however, data requirements for the calculation of gross rates are lower and, therefore, more countries can provide the necessary data. Since entry to lower and upper secondary school takes place within a narrower age band than entry to tertiary education, demographic changes are less important at those levels.

Net entry rate of a specific age, used for tertiary education, is obtained by dividing the number of new entrants to the university level of that given age by the total population in the corresponding age group (multiplied by 100). The sum of net entry rates is calculated by adding the net entry rates for each single year of age. The result represents the proportion of persons of a synthetic age cohort who enter the tertiary level of education, irrespective of changes in the population sizes and differences between countries in the typical entry age. The sums of net entry rates are more robust against demographic factors, such as changes in the cohort sizes of the ages of entrants. Since entry to tertiary education takes place within a wider age band these rates are a more preferable measure than gross rates.

Expected years of repeating an educational level (Table 1.18)

The percentage of ► *repeaters* can be translated into the expected number of years repeating a grade, which is related to the ► *school life expectancy* indicator. Even low levels of grade repetition can cumulate to a substantial number of years over the course of both primary and secondary cycles. To calculate the indicator school life expectancy for each ► *level of education* separately, we multiplied it by the rate of repeaters for that level. Summing up the result for primary, lower secondary and upper secondary provides the number of years children spend on average repeating grades in primary and secondary education combined.

Expenditure, educational

Ideally, expenditure would cover both direct private costs (such as tuition and other education related fees and the costs of textbooks, uniforms and transport) as well as indirect private costs (lost output when employees participate in on-the-job training). But many of these private costs are difficult to measure and to compare internationally. The main focus of most indicators is therefore on public and private ► *expenditure on educational institutions*. Exceptions are indicators on ► *public expenditure* which include transfers to households for living costs (► *public subsidies*). Data on private payments other than to ► *educational institutions*, including direct purchases of personal items used in education or subsidised expenditure on student living expenses, are too scarce to be considered here.

- *Expenditure on educational institutions* (Tables 2.2-2.6)

  Expenditure on educational institutions covers expenditure on ► *public and private educational institutions*. It covers expenditure by institutions from all sources, public, private and international. However, educational institutions are, in many countries, embedded in wider institutional arrangements (*e.g.* general purpose units of local governments, institutions that provide both education-related services as well as child-care services). Expenditure on educational institutions is thus defined by the functions of specific expenditure.

  Included in expenditure on educational institutions are: expenditure on instruction and provision of educational goods by institutions (books, materials); training of apprentices and other participants in mixed school and work-based educational programmes at the workplace; administration; ► *capital expenditure* and rent; provision of ancillary services (student transportation, school meals, student housing, boarding); provision of guidance, student health services and special educational needs; provision of services for the general public provided by educational institutions; educational research and curriculum development; and ► *research and development activities* performed at higher education institutions.

Conversely, this category excludes expenditure on: child care or day care provided by schools and other instructional institutions; educational activities outside the scope of the WEI/UOE data collection; teaching hospitals; and debt servicing.

Direct public expenditure on educational institutions may take one of two forms: purchases by the government agency itself of educational resources to be used by educational institutions (*e.g.* direct payment of ► *teachers' salaries* by a central or regional education ministry); or payments by the government agency to educational institutions that have responsibility for purchasing educational resources themselves (*e.g.* a government appropriation or block grant to a university which the university then uses to compensate staff and buy other resources).

Direct private expenditure on educational institutions includes tuition payments received from students (or their families) enrolled in public schools under that agency's jurisdiction, even if the tuition payments flow, in the first instance, to the government agency rather than to the institution in question. It also includes payments by other private entities to educational institutions, either as support for educational institutions or paid as rent for the use of resources by educational institutions. Direct private expenditure on educational institutions is net of subsidies received from ► *public sources*. Such subsidies are accounted as indirect public expenditure and included in public expenditure.

Indirect public expenditure on educational institutions includes ► *public subsidies* to students, families or other private entities that are used by the recipients for payments to educational institutions.

• **Expenditure on educational institutions as a percentage of GDP (Table 2.2)**

In Table 2.2, expenditure on educational institutions is expressed as a percentage of ► *GDP* and is presented by source of funds and by ► *level of education*. The distinction by source of funds is based on the initial source of funds and does not reflect subsequent public-to-private or private-to-public transfers. (► *Public subsidies*).

• **Expenditure on personnel compensation (Table 2.7)**

Current expenditure on compensation of personnel includes gross salaries (net of employee contributions for pensions, social security and other purposes) plus expenditure on non-salary compensation (benefits such as health care, health insurance, disability insurance, unemployment compensation, maternity and childcare benefits, free or subsidised housing) and retirement. Expenditure on retirement is estimated on the basis of expenditure for the retirement of current employees rather than current retirees.

Teaching staff includes only personnel directly involved in the instruction of students. Under expenditure on compensation of teachers, countries report the full compensation of full-time teachers plus appropriate portions of the compensation of staff who teach part-time. Non teaching staff include head-teachers, school administrators, supervisors, counsellors, school psychologists, school health personnel, librarians, educational media specialists, curriculum developers, inspectors, educational administrators at the local, regional and national levels, clerical personnel, building operations and maintenance staff, security personnel, transportation workers, food service workers. The exact list of occupations included in this category varies from one country to another.

The proportions of ► *current expenditure* allocated to the compensation of teachers, compensation of other staff, total staff compensation and other (non-personnel) current outlays are calculated by expressing the respective amounts as percentages of total current expenditure.

• *Expenditure per student (Tables 2.13-2.14)*

The data used in calculating expenditure per student include only direct public and private expenditure on ▶ *educational institutions*. ▶ *Public subsidies* for students' living expenses have been excluded.

For some countries, expenditure data for students in private educational institutions were not available (indicated by notes in the tables). In some cases, where data collection still covers a very small number of independent private institutions, only expenditure on public and government-dependent private institutions (▶ *public and private educational institutions*) is taken into account.

Expenditure per student at a particular ▶ *level of education* is calculated by dividing the total expenditure at that level by the corresponding ▶ *full-time-equivalent* ▶ *enrolment*. Only those types of educational institutions and programmes for which both enrolment and expenditure data are available are taken into account. The result in national currency is then converted into equivalent PPP dollars by dividing the national currency figure by the ▶ *purchasing power parities (PPP)* index.

Full-time equivalents (Tables 2.8, 2.13)

• *Students*

The *full-time equivalent* (FTE) measure attempts to standardise a student's actual load against the normal load. For the reduction of ▶ *headcount* data to FTEs, where data and norms on individual participation are available, course load is measured as the product of the fraction of the normal course load for a full-time student and the fraction of the school/academic year. [FTE =(actual course load/normal course load)*(actual duration of study during reference period/normal duration of study during reference period)]. When actual course load information is not available, a full-time student is considered equal to one FTE.

• *Teachers*

Full-time equivalents are generally calculated in person years. The unit for the measurement of full-time equivalents is full-time employment, *i.e.* a full-time teacher equals one FTE. The full-time equivalence of part-time educational staff is then determined by calculating the ratio of hours worked over the statutory hours worked by a full-time employee during the school year.

Graduates (Tables 1.16-1.17)

Graduates are those who were enrolled in the final year of a ▶ *level of education* and completed it successfully during the reference year. However, there are exceptions (especially at the tertiary level of education) where graduation can also be recognised by the awarding of a certificate without the requirement that participants are enrolled.

Completion is defined by each country. In some countries, completion occurs as a result of passing an examination or a series of examinations. In other countries, completion occurs after a requisite number of course hours have been accumulated (although completion of some or all of the course hours may also involve examinations).

Success is also defined by each country. In some countries it is associated with the obtaining of a degree, certificate, or diploma after a final examination. In other countries, it is defined by the completion of programmes without a final examination.

Graduation rates (Tables 1.16-1.17)

Gross graduation rates are estimated by dividing the number of all ▶ *graduates* by the population at the ▶ *typical graduation age* (multiplied by 100). In many countries, defining a typical age of graduation is difficult because ages of graduates vary. In that case, the average cohort size for a wider age band is used as denominator.

Gross Domestic Product (GDP) (Tables 2.1-2.2, 2.5, 2.13)

Gross domestic product (GDP) refers to the total output of goods and services for final use occurring within the domestic territory of a given country, regardless of the allocation to domestic and foreign claims. Gross domestic product is the sum of gross value added by all resident producers in the economy plus any taxes and minus any subsidies not included in the value of the products. It is calculated without making deductions for depreciation of fabricated assets or for depletion and degradation of natural resources. The residency of an institution is determined on the basis of economic interest in the territory for more than a year.

GDP deflator (Tables 2.1, 2.3, 2.12, 2.14)

The GDP deflator (implicit price deflator for ▶ *GDP*) is a price index measuring changes in prices of all new, domestically produced, final goods and services in an economy. Using the GDP deflator expenditure that occurred in different years are expressed in constant prices before calculating the ▶ *index of change*. The GDP deflators have been taken from the World Bank.

GDP per capita (Table 2.1)

GDP per capita is the ▶ *gross domestic product* divided by mid-year population, expressed in ▶ *purchasing power parity* terms.

Headcounts (Table 2.10)

The total number of individuals, ▶ *teacher* or students irrespectively of their study- or work-mode. Headcounts do not distinguish between full-time and part-time study and therefore overestimate the volume of enrolment or human resources. For a number of indicators it is preferable to convert headcounts to ▶ *full-time equivalents.*

Index of change (Tables 1.4, 1.6, 1.9, 2.1, 2.3, 2.8, 2.12, 2.14)

The index of change measures changes in indicators or absolute numbers, such as enrolment numbers or expenditure. It expresses the measure for the current year as a percentage of the same measure for the base year. An index of 100 per cent indicates no change, an index greater than 100 per cent indicates results higher than in the base year, an index below 100 per cent indicates decreasing results.

Base year and current year used for the index of change are the first and last year of the reference period used for this report. The duration of the reference period is different for different countries. A strict comparison of change can be done using ▶ *annual growth rates*.

ISCED: International Standard Classification of Education

A classification system that provides a framework for the comprehensive statistical description of national educational systems and a methodology that translates national educational programmes into internationally comparable ► *levels of education*. The basic unit of classification in ISCED is the educational programme. ISCED also classifies programmes by field of study, ► *programme orientation* and ► *programme destination*. For details see Annex A5.

Level of education (Tables 1.1-1.2, 1.4, 1.8-1.11, 1.13, 1.18, 2.2-2.14)

Educational programmes are classified by level of education according to ► *ISCED*.

A "level" of education is broadly defined as the gradations of learning experiences and competencies built into the design of an educational programme. Broadly speaking, the level is related to the degree of complexity of the content of the programme. This does not, however, imply that levels of education constitute a ladder, where access of prospective participants to each level necessarily depends on the successful completion of the previous level, though such progression is more likely between the lower ISCED levels. It also does not preclude the possibility that some participants in educational programmes at a given level – most probably at post-compulsory level – may have previously successfully completed programmes at a higher level.

The notion of "levels" of education, therefore, is essentially a construct based on the assumption that educational programmes can be grouped, both nationally and cross-nationally, into an ordered series of categories broadly corresponding to the overall knowledge, skills and capabilities required of participants if they are to have a reasonable expectation of successfully completing the programmes in these categories. These categories represent broad steps of educational progression from very elementary to more complex experiences with the more complex the programme, the higher the level of education.

The only concept that can meaningfully underlie an international level taxonomy is the educational content of the educational activities involved.

Mode of study (Tables 1.4, 1.14)

A student's mode of study is part-time or full-time. The part-time/full-time classification is regarded as an attribute of student participation rather than as an attribute of the educational programmes or the provision of education in general. It is recognised however, that many countries still make the full-time/part-time distinction based on characteristics of the educational programmes and use corresponding conversion factors at the programme level to transform the measures into ► *full-time equivalents*.

Four elements are used to decide whether a student is enrolled full-time or part-time: the units of measurement for course load; a normal full-time course load, which is used as the criterion for establishing full-time participation; the student's actual course load; and the period of time over which the course loads are measured. In general, students enrolled in primary and secondary level educational programmes are considered to participate full-time if they attend school for at least 75 per cent of the school day or week (as locally defined) and would normally be expected to be in the programme for the entire academic year. Otherwise, they are considered part-time. When determining full-time/part-time status, the work-based component in combined school- and work-based programmes is included. At the tertiary level an individual is considered full-time if he or she is taking a course load or educational programme considered to require at least 75 per cent of a full-time commitment of time and resources. Additionally, it is expected that the student will remain in the programme for the entire year.

New entrants (Table 1.15)

New entrants to a ▶ *level of education* are students who are entering any programme leading to a recognised qualification at this level of education for the first time, irrespective of whether students enter the programme at the beginning or at an advanced stage of the programme. Individuals who are returning to study at a level following a period of absence from studying at that same level are not considered new entrants.

Private expenditure (private sources) (Tables 2.2-2.4, 2.7)

Private expenditure refers to expenditure funded by private sources, *e.g.* households and other private entities. *Household* means students and their families. *Other private entities* include private business firms and non-profit organisations, including religious organisations, charitable organisations, and business and labour associations.

Private expenditure comprises school fees as well as fees for materials such as textbooks and teaching equipment, transportation to school (if organised by the school), meals (if provided by the school) and boarding; and expenditure by employers on initial vocational education (expenditure by private companies on the work-based element of school- and work-based training of apprentices and students). Note that private ▶ *educational institutions* are considered service providers, not funding sources.

Programme destination (Tables 1.1, 1.9-1.12, 1.14-1.16)

▶ *ISCED* allows to sub-classify educational programmes according to the types of subsequent education for which completers are eligible: the destination for which the programmes have been theoretically designed to prepare students. For details see Annex A5.

Programme orientation (Tables 1.12, 1.16)

▶ *ISCED* uses three categories to classify the orientation of educational programmes:

General programmes refer to education which is not designed explicitly to prepare participants for a specific class of occupations or trades or for entry into further vocational/technical education programmes. Less than 25 per cent of the programme content is vocational or technical.

Pre-vocational programmes refer to education mainly designed as an introduction to the world of work and as preparation for further vocational or technical education. Does not lead to a labour-market relevant qualification. Content is at least 25 per cent vocational or technical.

Vocational programmes refer to education which prepares participants for direct entry, without further training, into specific occupations. Successful completion of such programmes leads to a labour-market relevant vocational qualification.

For details see Annex A5.

Public and private educational institutions (Tables 1.13-1.14, 2.6, 2.9)

Educational institutions are classified as either public or private according to whether a public agency or a private entity has the ultimate power to make decisions concerning the institution's affairs.

An institution is classified as *public* if it is: controlled and managed directly by a public education authority or agency; or controlled and managed either by a government agency directly or by a governing body (council, committee, etc.) most of whose members are either appointed by a public authority or elected by public franchise.

An institution is classified as *private* if it is: controlled and managed by a non-governmental organisation (*e.g.* a church, trade union or business enterprise), or if its governing board consists mostly of members not selected by a public agency.

In general, the question of who has the ultimate management control over an institution is decided with reference to the power to determine the general activity of the school and to appoint the officers managing the school. The extent to which an institution receives its funding from public or private sources does not determine the classification status of the institution.

A distinction is made between government-dependent and independent private institutions on the basis of the degree of a private institution's dependence on funding from government sources. A *government-dependent private institution* is one that receives more than 50 per cent of its core funding from government agencies. An *independent private institution* is one that receives less than 50 per cent of its core funding from government agencies. *Core funding* refers to the funds that support the basic educational services of the institution. It does not include funds provided specifically for research projects, payments for services purchased or contracted by private organisations, or fees and subsidies received for ancillary services such as lodging and meals. Additionally, institutions should be classified as government-dependent if their teaching staff are paid by a government agency, either directly or indirectly.

Public expenditure (public sources) (Tables 2.2-2.7)

Public expenditure includes expenditure by all public agencies at local, regional and central levels of government. No distinction is made between education authorities and other government agencies. Thus, central government expenditure includes not only the expenditure of the national education ministry, but also all expenditure on education by other central government ministries and authorities. Similarly, educational expenditure by regional and local governments includes not only the expenditure of the regional or local agencies with primary responsibility for operation of schools (*e.g.* provincial ministries of education; or local education authorities) but also the expenditure of other regional and local bodies that contribute to the financing of education.

Public expenditure used for the calculation of the education indicators, corresponds to the non-repayable current and capital expenditure.

Public subsidies (to households and other private entities) (Tables 2.4-2.6)

Public subsidies to households and other private entities consists of transfers to the private sector for ▶ *educational institutions* and transfers for student living costs and other education related costs that occur outside educational institutions.

Public subsidies to households and other private entities for educational institutions are composed of government transfers and certain other payments to students/households, insofar as these translate into payments to educational institutions for educational services (for example, fellowships, financial aid or student loans for tuition). They also include government transfers and some other payments (mainly subsidies) to other private entities, including, for example, subsidies to firms or labour organisations that operate apprenticeship programmes and interest subsidies to private financial institutions that provide student loans, etc.

Public subsidies to households that are not attributable to payments to educational institutions include subsidies for student living costs and the value of special subsidies provided to students, either in cash or in kind, such as free or reduced-price travel on public transport or family allowances that are contingent on student status.

Purchasing Power Parity (PPP) (Tables 2.1, 2.12-2.13)

Purchasing power parities (PPPs) are the currency exchange rates that equalize the purchasing power of different currencies. This means that a given sum of money, when converted into US dollar at the PPP rates (PPP dollars), will buy the same basket of goods and services in all countries. In other words, PPPs are the rates of currency conversion which eliminate the differences in price levels among countries. Thus, when expenditure on ► *GDP* for different countries is converted into a common currency by means of PPPs, it is, in effect, expressed at the same set of international prices so that comparisons between countries reflect only differences in the volume of goods and services purchased.

Repeater (Table 1.18)

Students enrolling in the same grade or year of study a second or further time are classified as repeaters except if the new programme is classified as "higher" than the previous one. "Higher" is thereby operationalised by the individual countries. ► *Expected years of repeating an educational level.*

Research and Development (R&D) activities (Table 2.13)

Expenditure on R&D activities is in many countries embedded within general university budgets and can not be separated from education expenditure. In fact, in many countries there is consensus that R&D activities are fundamental for instruction at the tertiary level. This embedded expenditure includes, for example, spending on the compensation of teaching staff who work part of their time on R&D.

In order to ensure international comparability, data on education finance include all expenditure on research performed at universities and other institutions of tertiary education, regardless of whether the research is financed from general institutional funds, through separate grants, or from contracts from public or private sponsors. Yet, expenditure on independent, organisationally separate, government research institutions are excluded in cases where the connection between universities and research institutions is purely administrative.

School-age population (Table 1.3)

Population of the age group corresponding to a given ► *level of education.* For WEI indicators standard age groups for all countries are used.

School life expectancy (Tables 1.4-1.5)

School life expectancy measures the average duration of formal education that a 5-year-old child can expect to enrol in over his or her lifetime, assuming that the probability of being enrolled in school at any particular age is equal to the current enrolment rates for that age for all ► *ISCED* levels. It is calculated by adding the net enrolment rates for each single year of age from age five onwards, and dividing by 100. Should there be a tendency to lengthen (or shorten) studies during the ensuing years, the actual average duration of schooling for the cohort will be higher (or lower). School expectancy for pre-primary education alone considers children below the age of five.

Figures are based on ► *headcounts*, *i.e.* they do not distinguish between full-time and part-time study. Countries who report comparably high proportions of part-time enrolment have therefore an overall higher school expectancy level.

It must also be noted that the expected number of years does not necessarily coincide with the expected number of grades of education completed because of grade repetition. Caution is required when data on school expectancy are compared. Neither the length of the school year nor the quality of education is necessarily the same in each country. In addition, as this indicator does not directly take into account the effects of repetition, it is not strictly comparable between countries with automatic promotion practices and those that permit grade repetition. ► *Expected years of repeating an educational level*.

Student (Tables 1.6, 1.13, 1.14, 2.8)

A student is defined as any individual participating in educational services covered by the data collection. The number of students enrolled refers to the number of individuals (► *headcount*) who are enrolled within the reference period and not necessarily to the number of registrations. Each student enrolled is counted only once.

Students are classified by their pattern of attendance, *i.e.*, full-time or part-time.

Student-teacher ratio (Table 2.8)

The student-to-teaching staff ratio is obtained by dividing the number of ► *full-time-equivalent* students at a given ► *level of education* by the number of full-time-equivalent teachers at the same level and for the same type of institution.

The concept of a ratio of students to teaching staff is different than the concept of class size. Although one country may have a lower ratio of students to teaching staff than another, this does not necessarily mean that classes are smaller in the first country or that students in the first country receive more teaching. The relationship between the ratio of students to teaching staff and both average class size and hours of instruction per student is complicated by many factors, including differences between countries in the length of the school year, the number of hours for which a student attends class each day, the length of a teacher's working day, the number of classes or students for which a teacher is responsible, the division of the teacher's time between teaching and other duties, the grouping of students within classes, and the practice of team teaching.

Student-teacher ratios do account for only ► *teachers* and underestimate the human resources involved in education. ► *Educational personnel*.

Teachers (Tables 2.8, 2.10)

A teacher is defined as a person whose professional activity involves the transmission of knowledge, attitudes and skills that are stipulated in a formal curriculum to students enrolled in an educational programme. The teacher category includes only personnel who are directly involved in instructing students.

This definition does not depend on the qualification held by the teacher or on the delivery mechanism. It is based on three concepts: *activity*, thus excluding those without active teaching duties with the exception of teachers temporarily not at work (*e.g.* for reasons of illness or injury, maternity or parental leave, holiday or vacation); *profession*, thus excluding people who work occasionally or in a voluntary capacity in educational institutions or as teacher's aid (► *educational personnel*); and *educational programme*, thus excluding people who provide services other than formal instruction to students (*e.g.* supervisors, activity organisers, etc.), whether the programme is established at the national or school level.

Head teachers without teaching responsibilities are not defined as teachers, but classified separately. Head teachers who do have teaching responsibilities are defined as (part-time) teachers, even if they only teach for 10 per cent of their time. Former teachers, people who work occasionally or in a voluntary capacity in schools, people who provide services other than formal instruction, *e.g.* supervisors or activity organisers, are excluded.

Teachers' salaries, statutory (Table 2.12)

Teachers' salaries are expressed as statutory salaries, which are scheduled salaries according to official pay scales. They refer to the average scheduled gross salary per year for a full-time teacher with the minimum training necessary to be fully qualified at the beginning of his or her teaching career. Reported salaries are defined as the sum of wages (total sum of money paid by the employer for the labour supplied) minus the employer's contribution to social security and pension funding (according to existing salary scales). Bonuses that constitute a regular part of the salary (such as a 13th month, holidays or regional bonuses) are included in the figures.

Additional bonuses (for example, remuneration for teachers in remote areas, for participating in school improvement projects or special activities, or for exceptional performance) are excluded from the reported gross salaries. Salaries at 15 years' experience refer to the scheduled annual salary of a full-time classroom teacher with the minimum training necessary to be fully qualified and with 15 years' experience. The maximum salaries reported refer to the scheduled maximum annual salary (top of the salary scale) of a full-time classroom teacher with the minimum training to be fully qualified for his or her job. Salary data are reported in accordance with formal policies for public institutions.

Teaching time, statutory (Table 2.11)

Statutory teaching time (sometimes also referred to as instructional time) is defined as the total number of hours per year for which a full-time classroom teacher is responsible for teaching a group or class of students, according to the formal policy in the specific country. Periods of time formally allowed for breaks between lessons or groups of lessons are excluded.

Teaching hours per year are calculated on the basis of teaching hours per day multiplied by the number of teaching days per year, or on the basis of teaching hours per week multiplied by the number of weeks per year that the school is open for teaching. The number of hours per year that fall on days when the school is closed for festivities and celebrations are excluded. When no formal data were available, the number of teaching hours was estimated from survey data.

Total public expenditure (Tables 2.1 2.5)

Total public expenditure, as used for the calculation of the education indicators, corresponds to the non-repayable current and capital expenditure of all levels of government.

Current expenditure includes final consumption expenditure (*e.g.* compensation of employees, consumption of intermediate goods and services, fixed capital, and military expenditure), property income paid, subsidies, and other current transfers paid (*e.g.* social security, social assistance, pensions and other welfare benefits).

Capital expenditure is spending to acquire and/or improve fixed capital assets, land, intangible assets, government stocks and non-military non-financial assets, and spending to finance net capital transfers.

The data on total public expenditure for all purposes (the denominator in all percentage calculations) was provided by countries.

Typical ages (Tables 1.16-1.17)

Typical ages refer to the ages that normally correspond to the age at entry and end of a cycle of education. These ages relate to the theoretical duration of a cycle, assuming full-time attendance and no repetition of a year. The assumption is made that, at least in the ordinary education system, a student can proceed through the educational programme in a standard number of years, which is referred to as the theoretical duration of the programme. The *typical starting age* is the age at the *beginning* of the first school/academic year of the relevant level and programme. The *typical ending* age is the age at the beginning of the last school/academic year of the relevant level and programme. The *typical graduation age* is the age at the end of the last school/academic year of the relevant level and programme when the qualification is obtained.

Vocational and technical education (Tables 1.12, 1.16)

▶ *Programme orientation.*

ANNEX A3 – CROSS-REFERENCE BETWEEN DATA TABLES AND TECHNICAL NOTES

Table 1.1 Educational attainment; level of education; programme destination.

Table 1.2 Educational attainment; level of education.

Table 1.3 School-age population.

Table 1.4 Index of change; level of education; mode of study; school life expectancy.

Table 1.5 School life expectancy.

Table 1.6 Enrolment; enrolment rate (net); index of change; student.

Table 1.7 Compulsory education.

Table 1.8 Enrolment rate (net); level of education; programme destination.

Table 1.9 Enrolment; index of change; level of education; programme destination.

Table 1.10 Annual growth rate; enrolment; level of education; programme destination.

Table 1.11 Enrolment; level of education; programme destination.

Table 1.12 Enrolment; programme destination; programme orientation.

Table 1.13 Level of education; public and private educational institutions, students.

Table 1.14 Mode of study; public and private educational institutions, students; programme destination.

Table 1.15 Entry rate; new entrants; programme destination.

Table 1.16 Graduates; graduation rates; programme destination; programme orientation; typical ages.

Table 1.17 Graduates; graduation rates; typical ages.

Table 1.18 Expected years of repeating an educational level; level of education; repeater.

Table 2.1 Gross Domestic Product (GDP); GDP deflator; GDP per capita; index of change; Purchasing Power Parity (PPP); total public expenditure.

Table 2.2 Educational institution; expenditure on educational institutions; expenditure on educational institutions as a percentage of GDP; Gross Domestic Product (GDP); level of education; private expenditure (private sources); public expenditure (public sources).

Table 2.3 Educational institution; expenditure on educational institutions; GDP deflator; index of change; level of education; private expenditure (private sources); public expenditure (public sources).

Table 2.4 Educational institution; expenditure on educational institutions; level of education; private expenditure (private sources); public expenditure (public sources); public subsidies (transfer).

Table 2.5	Expenditure on educational institutions; educational institution; Gross Domestic Product (GDP); level of education; public expenditure (public sources); total public expenditure; public subsidies (transfer).
Table 2.6	Educational institution; expenditure on educational institutions; level of education; public and private educational institutions; public expenditure (public sources); public subsidies (transfer).
Table 2.7	Current and capital expenditure; educational institution; educational personnel (staff); expenditure on personnel compensation; level of education; private expenditure (private sources); public expenditure (public sources).
Table 2.8	Educational institution; educational personnel (staff); enrolment; full-time equivalents; index of change; level of education; student; student-teacher ratio; teacher.
Table 2.9	Class size; level of education; public and private educational institutions.
Table 2.10	Headcounts; level of education; teacher.
Table 2.11	Level of education; teaching time (statutory).
Table 2.12	GDP deflator; index of change; level of education; Purchasing Power Parity (PPP); teacher's salaries (statutory).
Table 2.13	Educational institution; expenditure per student; full-time equivalents; Gross Domestic Product (GDP); level of education; Purchasing Power Parity (PPP); R&D activities.
Table 2.14	Educational institution; expenditure per student; GDP deflator; index of change; level of education.

■ ANNEX A4 – DATA TABLES

Symbols for missing data

Five symbols are employed in the tables and graphs to denote missing data:

a	Data not applicable because the category does not apply.
n	Magnitude is either negligible or zero.
...	Data not available from countries.
—	Data not requested from countries.
x (y)	Data included in another category/column (y) of the table.

ANNEX A4

Table 1.1

Educational attainment of the adult population

Distribution of the population aged 25 to 64 years, by highest level of education attained

	Year	No schooling	Incompleted primary	Primary	Lower secondary	Upper secondary	Tertiary (type B) education	Tertiary (type A) and advanced research programmes	Unknown
		1	**2**	**3**	**4**	**5**	**6**	**7**	**8**
WEI participants									
Argentina	2002	1.1	9.0	33.7	14.1	28.2	4.6	9.1	0.2
Brazil	2002	7.4	18.3	30.2	14.1	21.3	x(7)	8.2	0.5
	1995	12.9	22.0	30.6	12.8	14.8	x(7)	6.9	n
Chile	2003	2.0	11.6	11.4	25.7	36.1	1.2	11.9	0.2
	1995	2.9	15.9	13.7	26.1	29.3	2.2	9.4	0.5
Indonesia	2002/03	7.2	12.1	38.9	18.3	19.3	1.9	2.3	a
	1995/96	13.3	25.4	34.8	10.1	13.3	1.7	1.5	a
Jordan	2002/03	11.6	6.5	16.1	26.4	15.1	11.9	12.4	n
Malaysia	2002	8.3	a	28.7	20.7	31.1	x(7)	11.1	a
	1995	14.1	x(1)	34.5	19.8	25.3	x(7)	6.2	a
Paraguay	2002	5.0	32.0	31.0	9.7	13.7	2.6	4.9	1.1
	1995	5.1	38.0	30.3	8.4	11.2	0.2	6.7	0.2
Peru	2002	8.3	20.5	15.2	13.8	24.5	8.7	8.9	a
	1993	1.8	38.1	6.7	8.2	27.5	6.1	11.8	...
Russian Federation	2002/03	0.2	0.3	2.5	7.9	33.9	33.4	20.5	1.2
	1995/96	x(3)	x(3)	6.3	16.4	32.1	26.1	17.7	1.3
Thailand	2003/04	4.2	43.1	21.0	10.5	8.8	3.0	9.1	0.3
	1995/96	5.5	63.0	11.1	6.9	5.8	1.8	5.8	n
Uruguay	2002	0.7	9.1	32.0	24.8	23.8	9.7	x(6)	n
	1996	1.4	x(1)	48.1	23.0	12.3	14.1	x(6)	1.1
WEI mean	**2003**	**4.5**	**13.7**	**24.8**	**17.7**	**24.1**	**8.4**	**9.6**	**0.3**
OECD countries									
Australia	2003	x(4)	x(4)	x(4)	38	31	11	20	a
Austria	2003	x(4)	x(4)	x(4)	21	64	7	7	a
Belgium	2003	x(3)	x(3)	17	21	33	16	13	a
Canada	2003	x(3)	x(3)	6	11	40	22	22	a
Czech Republic	2003	x(3)	x(3)	n	11	76	n	12	a
Denmark	2003	x(3)	x(3)	1	17	51	7	25	a
Finland	2003	x(3)	x(3)	14	10	42	17	17	a
France	2003	x(3)	x(3)	16	20	41	9	15	a
Germany	2003	x(3)	x(3)	3	14	59	10	14	a
Greece	2003	x(3)	x(3)	37	10	36	6	12	a
Hungary	2003	x(3)	x(3)	2	24	59	n	15	a
Iceland[1]	2003	x(3)	x(3)	2	32	40	6	20	a
Ireland	2003	x(3)	x(3)	19	19	36	10	16	a
Italy[1]	2003	x(3)	x(3)	20	33	36	x(8)	10	a
Japan	2003	x(4)	x(4)	x(4)	16	47	17	21	a
Korea	2003	x(3)	x(3)	14	13	44	8	22	a
Luxembourg	2003	x(3)	x(3)	20	10	56	9	6	a
Mexico	2003	x(3)	x(3)	53	25	6	2	14	a
Netherlands	2002	x(3)	x(3)	12	22	42	3	22	a
New Zealand	2003	x(4)	x(4)	x(4)	22	46	15	17	a
Norway	2003	x(3)	x(3)	n	12	56	2	29	a
Poland	2003	x(4)	x(4)	x(4)	17	68	x(8)	14	a
Portugal	2003	x(3)	x(3)	64	13	12	2	9	a
Slovak Republic	2003	x(3)	x(3)	1	13	75	n	11	a
Spain	2003	x(3)	x(3)	30	27	17	7	18	a
Sweden	2003	x(3)	x(3)	7	10	49	15	18	a
Switzerland	2003	x(3)	x(3)	3	10	60	9	17	a
Turkey	2003	x(3)	x(3)	64	10	17	x(8)	10	a
United Kingdom	2003	x(3)	x(3)	n	16	56	9	19	a
United States	2003	x(3)	x(3)	5	8	49	9	29	a
OECD mean	**2003**	**x(3)**	**x(3)**	**14**	**17**	**44**	**8**	**16**	**a**

Note: Post-secondary non-tertiary is included in upper secondary education.
Source: OECD/UNESCO WEI.
Please refer to the Reader's Guide for information concerning the symbols replacing missing data. Data by gender are available at *www.uis.unesco.org/wei2005*.

Table 1.2
Educational attainment of the adult population, by age group
Percentage of the population that has attained a specific level of education

	Current year	Base year	2003							1995	
			1	**2**	**3**	**4**	**5**	**6**	**7**	**8**	**9**
			\<td colspan align>			Age group					
At least completed primary education			25-64	15-19	20-24	25-34	35-44	45-54	55-64	25-64	15-19
Argentina	2002		90	97	98	95	91	88	80	…	…
Brazil	2002	1995	74	89	87	81	79	70	51	65	77
Chile	2003	1995	86	97	96	94	90	84	70	81	94
Indonesia	2002/03	1995/96	81	97	93	93	84	73	48	61	89
Jordan	2002/03	1995/96	82	97	96	…	…	…	…	…	…
Malaysia	2002	1995	92	99	98	97	94	89	75	86	99
Paraguay	2002	1995	62	81	80	73	64	53	41	57	74
Peru	2002	1993	71	90	87	83	75	65	47	60	83
Russian Federation	2002/03	1995/96	98	98	98	98	98	98	98	99	100
Thailand	2003/04	1995/96	52	98	96	91	47	23	15	31	96
Uruguay	2002	1996	90	96	97	96	94	89	80	98	99
WEI mean			*81*	*95*	*94*	*91*	*83*	*74*	*62*	…	…
At least completed lower secondary education										25-64	20-24
Argentina	2002		56	67	74	68	58	51	38	…	…
Brazil	2002	1995	44	53	62	52	48	38	23	34	45
Chile	2003	1995	75	92	93	88	81	71	48	67	87
Indonesia	2002/03	1995/96	42	60	63	55	42	31	17	27	52
Jordan	2002/03	1995/96	66	87	87	…	…	…	…	…	…
Malaysia	2002	1995	63	93	88	82	68	46	25	51	85
Paraguay	2002	1995	31	38	49	39	32	24	18	26	37
Peru	2002	1993	56	81	77	70	59	47	29	54	68
Russian Federation	2002/03	1995/96	96	93	97	97	98	97	88	92	99
Thailand	2003/04	1995/96	31	74	70	46	32	19	12	20	36
Uruguay	2002	1996	58	65	72	70	63	55	42	49	70
WEI mean			*57*	*71*	*75*	*67*	*58*	*49*	*35*	…	…
At least completed upper secondary education			25-64	15-19	20-24	25-34	35-44	45-54	55-64	25-64	25-34
Argentina	2002		42	–	58	52	43	38	28	…	…
Brazil	2002	1995	30	–	41	35	32	27	16	22	26
Chile	2003	1995	49	–	71	63	51	44	30	41	52
Indonesia	2002/03	1995/96	24	–	36	32	24	17	8	16	24
Jordan	2002/03	1995/96	39	–	49	…	…	…	…	…	…
Malaysia	2002	1995	42	–	71	58	45	27	15	32	47
Paraguay	2002	1995	21	–	35	27	22	16	12	18	23
Peru	2002	1993	42	–	55	53	44	36	21	45	57
Russian Federation	2002/03	1995/96	88	–	88	91	94	89	71	76	93
Thailand	2003/04	1995/96	21	–	47	30	22	13	7	13	20
Uruguay	2002	1996	33	–	34	38	37	33	24	26	36
WEI mean			*38*	*–*	*53*	*44*	*40*	*33*	*23*	…	…
OECD mean			*66*	*–*	*–*	*75*	*70*	*62*	*51*	*–*	*–*
Completed tertiary education										25-64	25-34
Argentina	2002		14	–	–	15	15	14	9	…	…
Brazil	2002	1995	8	–	–	7	9	10	7	7	6
Chile	2003	1995	13	–	–	17	12	12	8	12	14
Indonesia	2002/03	1995/96	4	–	–	5	5	4	2	3	4
Jordan	2002/03	1995/96	24	–	–	…	…	…	…	…	…
Malaysia	2002	1995	11	–	–	16	11	7	5	6	8
Paraguay	2002	1995	7	–	–	9	8	6	5	7	8
Peru	2002	1993	18	–	–	22	19	15	8	18	21
Russian Federation	2002/03	1995/96	54	–	–	55	58	54	44	44	49
Thailand	2003/04	1995/96	12	–	–	16	13	9	5	8	10
Uruguay	2002	1996	10	–	–	9	11	11	8	14	17
WEI mean			*15*	*–*	*–*	*15*	*16*	*14*	*10*	…	…
OECD mean			*24*	*–*	*–*	*29*	*26*	*22*	*17*	*–*	*–*

Note: Data for OECD countries are available at *www.oecd.org/edu/eag2005*, Tables A1.2 and A1.3.
Source: OECD/UNESCO WEI.
Please refer to the Reader's Guide for information concerning the symbols replacing missing data. Data by gender are available at *www.uis.unesco.org/wei2005*.

Table 1.3
Relative size of school-age populations

Population at different age groups as a percentage of total population and as a percentage of the population aged 20 years and older

			Ratio of school-age population to total population (%)						Ratio of school-age population to working-age population (including 65 years and older)		
			5 to 14-year-olds		15 to 19-year-olds		20 to 29-year-olds		5-14	15-19	20-29
	Current year	Base year	2003	1995	2003	1995	2003	1995	2003		
			1	2	3	4	5	6	7	8	9
WEI participants											
Argentina	2002		19	...	9	...	16	...	30	14	26
Brazil	2002	1995	21	23	11	14	18	17	34	18	29
Chile	2003	1995	18	19	9	9	15	17	29	14	24
China	2002/03	1995/96	16	...	9	...	16	...	24	12	23
Egypt	2002/03	1994/95	22	25	12	10	19	17	39	21	34
India	2002/03	1995/96	25	25	10	10	17	17	44	18	30
Indonesia	2002/03	1995/96	20	22	10	11	19	18	33	17	31
Jamaica	2002/03	1995/96	21	21	9	10	16	19	36	16	27
Jordan	2002/03	1995/96	...	31	...	14	...	24	...	...	...
Malaysia	2002	1995	22	23	10	10	17	18	38	18	30
Paraguay	2002	1995	25	25	11	11	16	16	49	22	31
Peru	2002	1993	22	25	10	11	18	18	40	18	32
Philippines	2002/03	1995/96	24	25	11	11	20	17	46	21	...
Sri Lanka	2002		17	...	10	...	17	...	26	14	26
Russian Federation	2002/03	1995/96	12	16	9	7	15	13	16	12	20
Thailand	2003/04	1995/96	15	17	7	10	17	20	22	11	25
Tunisia	2002/03	1995/96	17	38	12	17	20	28	27	18	31
Uruguay	2002	1996	16	17	8	8	16	15	24	11	23
Zimbabwe	2003	1995	24	28	13	12	20	18	51	28	43
WEI mean	*2003*	*1995*	*20*	*23*	*10*	*11*	*17*	*18*	*34*	*17*	*29*
OECD countries											
Austria	2003	1995	12	12	6	6	12	16	15	8	16
Belgium	2003	1995	12	12	6	6	13	14	15	8	16
Czech Republic	2003	1995	11	...	7	...	16	...	14	8	21
Denmark	2003	1995	13	11	5	6	13	15	17	7	16
Finland	2003	1995	12	13	6	6	12	13	16	8	16
Greece	2003	1995	10	12	6	7	15	15	13	8	19
Hungary	2003	1995	11	12	6	8	16	14	15	8	20
Iceland	2003	1995	16	...	7	...	15	...	22	10	21
Ireland	2003	1995	14	17	8	9	16	15	19	11	23
Italy	2003	1995	10	10	5	6	13	16	12	6	16
Luxembourg	2003	1995	13	...	6	...	13	...	17	7	17
Mexico	2003	1995	22	24	10	11	19	19	38	18	32
Netherlands	2003	1995	12	12	6	6	12	16	16	8	16
New Zealand	2003	1995	15	15	7	7	13	16	22	10	19
Norway	2003	1995	14	12	6	6	13	15	18	8	17
Poland	2003	1995	13	17	8	8	16	14	18	11	22
Portugal	2003	1995	11	12	6	8	15	16	13	8	20
Slovakia	2003	1995	13	...	8	...	17	...	18	11	23
Sweden	2003	1995	14	...	8	...	16	...	19	11	23
Switzerland	2003	1995	12	...	6	...	12	...	15	7	16
Turkey	2003	1995	19	22	9	11	19	18	31	15	31
United Kingdom	2003	1995	13	13	6	6	12	15	17	8	17
United States	2003	1995	14	...	7	...	14	...	20	10	19
OECD mean			*13*	*14*	*7*	*7*	*14*	*15*	*18*	*9*	*20*

Source: OECD/UNESCO WEI.
Please refer to the Reader's Guide for information concerning the symbols replacing missing data.

Table 1.4

Education expectancy

Expected years of education under current conditions (excluding education for children under the age of five)

	Year	Full-time and part-time							Full-time	Part-time	Index of change in education expectancy for all levels of education (1995 = 100)
		All levels of education			Primary and lower secondary education	Upper secondary education	Post-secondary non-tertiary education	Tertiary education	All levels of education		
		M + F	Males	Females	M + F				M + F		M + F
		1	**2**	**3**	**4**	**5**	**6**	**7**	**8**	**9**	**10**
WEI participants											
Argentina	2002	17.6	16.9	18.4	10.7	2.4	a	3.5	15.1	2.6	...
Brazil	2002	16.1	15.8	16.4	10.8	2.8	a	1.2	16.1	n	121
	1995	13.4	12.6	13.8	9.7	1.7	n	0.7	–	–	–
Chile	2003	15.0	15.2	14.8	8.3	3.8	a	2.0	15.0	n	110
	1995	13.6	13.7	13.5	8.2	3.1	n	1.4	–	–	–
China	2002/03	11.9	...	...	9.0	1.4	...	0.7	...	...	...
Egypt	2002/03	12.0	10.8	10.4	8.1	2.2	0.1	1.5	...	...	...
India	2002/03	9.8	10.2	9.3	6.9	1.6	n	0.5	...	...	107
	1995/96	9.1	10.0	8.2	7.4	1.3	n	0.5	–	–	–
Indonesia	2002/03	11.9	12.0	11.7	9.2	1.4	a	0.8	11.9	n	110
	1995/96	10.8	11.1	10.4	9.5	1.0	n	0.6	–	–	–
Jamaica[1]	2002/03	12.6	12.6	12.5	8.4	1.6	0.1	...	12.6	...	96
	1995/96	13.2	13.1	13.2	9.0	1.4	0.1	...	–	–	–
Jordan	2002/03	12.6	12.3	13.0	9.4	1.4	a	1.5	12.6	n	102
	1995/96	12.3	12.2	12.4	9.6	1.4	n	1.1	–	–	–
Malaysia	2002	12.7	12.3	13.2	8.3	1.9	0.4	1.4	12.6	0.1	113
	1995	11.2	10.9	11.5	8.3	1.4	0.2	0.6	–	–	–
Paraguay	2002	13.8	13.7	13.9	9.9	1.8	...	1.2	12.8	n	...
	1995	...	...	...	9.1	0.8	n	–	–	–	–
Peru	2002	14.5	14.5	14.5	10.1	1.6	...	...	...	...	105
	1993	13.8	13.8	13.8	9.9	1.3	n	0.6	–	–	–
Philippines	2002/03	11.8	11.5	12.3	9.3	0.6	0.2	1.4	11.3	...	101
	1995/96	11.6	11.5	11.8	9.3	0.7	n	1.4	–	–	–
Russian Federation	2002/03	14.9	14.6	15.7	8.1	1.7	0.1	3.3	12.1	2.8	118
	1995/96	12.7	14.3	14.4	8.7	1.7	0.1	2.2	–	–	–
Thailand	2003/04	15.1	14.9	15.3	9.3	2.2	...	2.1	13.0	2.8	102
	1995/96	14.8	14.8	14.7	9.8	1.8	n	1.1	–	–	–
Tunisia	2002/03	13.4	13.1	13.6	9.5	2.5	n	1.2	13.4	n	103
	1995/96	12.9	...	...	10.4	2.0	n	0.6	–	–	–
Uruguay	2002	16.4	15.5	17.3	10.1	2.9	0.1	1.9	16.4	n	113
	1996	14.5	13.7	15.3	9.6	2.2	n	1.7	–	–	–
Zimbabwe	2002	11.3	11.9	10.7	8.8	1.1	...	0.2	12.3	0.1	...
	1995	...	...	...	...	...	...	...	...	...	...
WEI mean	**2003**	**13.5**	**13.4**	**13.7**	**9.1**	**1.9**	**...**	**1.6**	**13.4**	**...**	**108**
	1995	**12.6**	**12.7**	**12.6**	**9.1**	**1.5**	**...**	**1.0**	**–**	**–**	**–**
OECD countries											
Australia	2003	21.1	20.8	21.4	11.7	4.6	0.6	3.6	14.8	6.3	110
Austria	2003	16.1	16.0	16.2	8.1	3.9	0.6	2.2	15.9	0.2	103
Belgium	2003	19.7	19.1	20.2	9.4	5.9	0.4	2.9	16.4	3.3	110
Czech Republic	2003	16.6	16.5	16.8	9.0	3.7	0.5	1.9	16.3	0.3	117
Denmark	2003	18.3	17.6	18.9	9.7	3.7	n	2.9	17.2	1.0	108
Finland	2003	19.7	19.0	20.4	9.0	4.6	0.2	4.4	17.8	1.9	114
France	2003	16.8	16.5	17.0	9.5	3.3	n	2.7	16.8	n	101
Germany	2003	17.2	17.3	17.1	10.2	3.0	0.5	2.2	17.1	0.1	105
Greece	2003	16.5	16.2	16.8	8.9	2.9	0.2	3.6	16.3	0.1	118
Hungary	2003	17.2	16.8	17.6	8.1	4.0	0.6	2.7	15.3	1.9	120
Iceland	2003	19.2	18.2	20.2	9.9	5.1	0.1	3.1	16.9	2.4	115
Ireland	2003	16.7	16.1	17.4	10.8	2.3	0.8	2.8	15.7	1.0	109
Italy	2003	16.8	16.4	17.1	8.3	4.7	0.1	2.7	16.7	0.1	...
Japan	2003	...	...	...	9.1	3.0	...	...	...	...	...
Korea	2003	16.4	17.3	15.5	8.9	2.9	a	4.2	16.4	n	115
Luxembourg	2003	14.8	14.7	14.9	9.1	3.5	0.2	0.6	14.6	0.2	...
Mexico	2003	13.2	13.0	13.4	9.7	1.5	a	1.1	13.2	n	110
Netherlands	2003	17.3	17.4	17.2	10.5	3.2	n	2.6	16.7	0.6	...
New Zealand	2003	18.6	17.5	19.5	10.2	4.1	0.7	3.5	15.5	3.0	...
Norway*	2003	18.2	16.6	18.1	9.9	3.8	0.1	3.5	16.8	1.4	104
Poland	2003	17.2	16.7	17.7	9.0	3.3	0.3	3.2	14.4	2.8	119
Portugal	2003	16.9	16.5	17.3	10.4	2.9	a	2.6	16.2	0.7	103
Slovak Republic	2003	15.3	15.1	15.4	8.9	3.3	0.1	1.8	14.6	0.7	...
Spain	2003	17.0	16.6	17.4	10.8	2.2	a	3.0	16.4	0.6	100
Sweden	2003	20.1	18.7	21.6	9.8	4.8	0.1	3.7	16.9	3.3	146
Switzerland	2003	16.7	17.0	16.4	9.6	3.2	0.3	2.0	16.1	0.5	...
Turkey	2003	12.0	12.8	10.8	7.7	2.6	a	1.5	12.0	n	127
United Kingdom	2003	20.4	19.0	21.7	9.1	8.4	x(5)	2.9	14.9	5.5	119
United States	2003	16.8	16.3	17.4	9.2	2.7	0.1	4.1	14.9	2.0	...
OECD mean	**2003**	**17.3**	**16.9**	**17.6**	**9.5**	**3.7**	**0.2**	**2.8**	**15.8**	**1.5**	**113**

1. The total excludes tertiary education. Jamaica hosts the University of the West Indies, which serves students from the whole region.
* See Annex 3 of *Education at a Glance*, 2005, for notes (*www.oecd.org/edu/eag2005*).
Source: OECD/UNESCO WEI.
Please refer to the Reader's Guide for information concerning the symbols replacing missing data. More data by gender are available at *www.uis.unesco.org/wei2005*.

Table 1.5
Pre-primary education expectancy
Expected years of pre-primary education under current conditions
(including education for children under the age of five, full-time and part-time education)

	Current year	Base year	2003			1995		
			M + F	Males	Females	M + F	Males	Females
			1	2	3	4	5	6
WEI participants								
Argentina	2002		1.8	1.8	1.8	...	...	...
Brazil	2002	1995	1.7	1.7	1.7	1.8	1.5	1.5
Chile	2003	1995	1.4	1.4	1.3	1.3	1.3	1.3
China	2002/03	1995/96	1.1	...	...	...	...	...
Egypt	2002/03	1994/95	0.3	0.3	0.3	0.2	...	...
India	2002/03	1995/96	1.0	...	...	0.5	0.5	0.5
Indonesia	2002/03	1995/96	0.4	0.4	0.5	0.4	0.4	0.4
Jamaica	2002/03	1995/96	2.5	2.5	2.5	2.6	...	...
Jordan	2002/03	1995/96	0.7	0.7	0.6	0.5	...	...
Malaysia	2002	1995	1.0	1.0	1.1	0.9	0.9	0.9
Paraguay	2002	1995	1.0	1.0	1.0	0.6	0.6	0.6
Peru	2002	1993	1.7	1.7	1.7	1.5	1.5	1.5
Philippines	2002/03	1995/96	0.4	...	...	0.2	0.2	0.2
Russian Federation	2002/03	1995/96	2.9	...	...	3.2	...	...
Thailand	2003/04	1995/96	2.6	2.6	2.5	2.6	2.6	2.6
Uruguay	2002	1996	1.9	1.9	1.9	1.4	1.4	1.4
Zimbabwe	2003	1995	1.3	...	...	...	...	...

Source: OECD/UNESCO WEI.

Please refer to the Reader's Guide for information concerning the symbols replacing missing data.

Table 1.6

Changes in enrolment rates of different age groups and underlying factors

Enrolment rates by age group; enrolment, population and enrolment rates for current year expressed as a percentage of the respective value in the base year, by age
(full-time and part-time students in public and private institutions)

	Current year	Base year	5 to 14-year-olds					15 to 19-year-olds					20 to 29-year-olds				
			Enrolment as a percentage of the population of 5 to 14-year-olds		Index change in enrolment rate	Index change in enrolment	Index change in population	Enrolment as a percentage of the population of 15 to 19-year-olds		Index change in enrolment rate	Index change in enrolment	Index change in population	Enrolment as a percentage of the population of 20 to 29-year-olds		Index change in enrolment rate	Index change in enrolment	Index change in population
			2003	1995	(1995=100)	(1995=100)	(1995=100)	2003	1995	(1995=100)	(1995=100)	(1995=100)	2003	1995	(1995=100)	(1995=100)	(1995=100)
			1	2	3	4	5	6	7	8	9	10	11	12	13	14	15
WEI participants																	
Argentina	2002		104	...	...	...	...	71	...	...	...	...	28	...	...	...	...
Brazil	2002	1995	92	89	103	103	100	74	48	153	135	88	22	15	143	171	119
Chile	2003	1995	91	88	103	110	107	70	61	114	129	113	3	3	106	104	98
China	2002/03	1995/96	89	...	...	112	...	13	...	...	119	...	...	...	...	...	...
Egypt	2002/03	1994/95	87	...	...	...	98	...	...	...	...	134	...	...	...	...	129
India	2002/03	1995/96	66	63	104	115	111	...	...	...	...	116	...	5	...	...	112
Indonesia	2002/03	1995/96	89	82	107	104	97	51	44	116	115	99	4	4	105	120	114
Jamaica	2002/03	1995/96	82	87	95	102	108	40	36	113	115	102	...	...	...	...	91
Jordan	2002/03	1995/96	...	89	...	116	...	...	67	...	...	...	...	1	...	...	...
Malaysia	2002	1995	90	91	99	110	110	56	37	149	178	119	8	3	284	319	112
Paraguay	2002	1995	95	...	...	...	110	55	...	...	...	109	7	...	...	...	109
Peru	2002	1993	98	93	106	116	110	56	53	104	119	114	10	9	105	130	123
Philippines	2002/03	1995/96	82	86	96	110	115	52	55	95	114	119	4	5	78	107	137
Sri Lanka	2002		102	...	...	...	...	43	...	...	...	...	...	...	...	...	...
Russian Federation	2002/03	1995/96	94	...	...	...	74	29	...	...	...	118	...	...	...	...	111
Thailand	2003/04	1995/96	97	97	100	98	97	60	...	...	...	84	14	...	...	...	94
Uruguay	2002	1996	99	97	102	107	105	72	55	130	127	98	23	17	134	153	114
Zimbabwe	2003	1995	82	...	...	...	100	30	...	...	...	130	...	...	...	...	135
WEI mean	*2003*	*1995*	*92*	*...*	*102*	*108*	*104*	*55*	*...*	*...*	*128*	*108*	*15*	*...*	*...*	*...*	*114*
OECD countries (countries with 1995 data only)																	
Austria	2003	1995	98	...	...	...	100	77	...	...	...	104	18	13	134	104	78
Belgium	2003	1995	100	99	101	103	102	94	93	100	99	99	29	24	121	109	90
Denmark	2003	1995	99	98	101	122	120	85	79	107	93	87	32	25	127	110	86
Finland	2003	1995	95	90	105	105	100	86	82	105	103	99	40	29	137	134	98
Greece	2003	1995	97	88	110	96	87	83	77	108	92	85	26	13	204	214	105
Hungary	2003	1995	100	100	101	91	91	83	64	130	98	75	22	10	215	238	110
Ireland	2003	1995	100	97	103	90	88	84	81	105	96	91	19	15	130	158	121
Mexico	2003	1995	97	94	103	108	104	44	36	123	129	105	10	8	116	129	111
Norway	2003	1995	98	97	101	115	114	85	83	103	103	100	29	26	109	94	87
Poland	2003	1995	94	89	106	82	77	88	78	113	115	101	29	16	180	212	118
Portugal	2003	1995	105	105	100	90	89	71	68	105	82	79	22	21	102	103	101
Turkey	2003	1995	82	71	116	116	101	35	30	117	114	97	6	7	88	107	122
United Kingdom	2003	1995	101	99	102	103	101	77	72	107	117	110	28	17	163	136	84
OECD mean (countries with 1995 data only)	*2003*	*1995*	*97*	*94*	*104*	*102*	*98*	*76*	*70*	*110*	*103*	*95*	*24*	*17*	*141*	*142*	*101*

Note: Data for more OECD countries are available at *www.oecd.org/edu/eag2005*, Table C1.2.
Source: OECD/UNESCO WEI.
Please refer to the Reader's Guide for information concerning the symbols replacing missing data. Data by gender are available at *www.uis.unesco.org/wei2005*.

Table 1.7

Age range of universal primary and secondary education

Number of age years and age range at which over 90 per cent are enrolled in primary and secondary education[1]

	Year	2003			1995	
		Ending age of compulsory education (in years)	Number of years at which over 90% of the population is enrolled	Age range at which over 90% of the population is enrolled (in years)	Number of years at which over 90% of the population is enrolled	Age range at which over 90% of the population is enrolled (in years)
		1	**2**	**3**	**4**	**5**
WEI participants						
Argentina	2002	14	10	6-15	...	...
Brazil	2002	14	7	8-14	6	9-14
Chile	2003	13	9	7-15	9	7-15
China	2002/03	14	5	7-11	...	...
Egypt	2002/03	13	5	6-10	...	...
India	2002/03	14	2	6-16	...	...
Indonesia	2002/03	15	6	7-13	6	7-13
Jamaica	2002/03	11	7	7-13	8	7-14
Jordan	2002/03	15	...	...	8	6-13
Malaysia[2]	2002	12	7	6-12	7	6-12
Paraguay	2002	14	6	7-12	6	7-12
Peru	2002	16	9	6-14	8	6-13
Philippines	2002/03	12	7	7-13	6	8-13
Russian Federation	2002/03	15	8	7-14	...	...
Thailand	2003/04	14	6	7-13	6	7-13
Uruguay	2002	15	9	7-15	7	7-13
Zimbabwe	2003	12	7	7-13	...	...

1. Data are not comparable with Indicator C1.2 in *Education at a Glance*, 2005. Here pre-primary is excluded.
2. Compulsory schooling until 12 years of age was introduced in the school year 2003.
Source: OECD/UNESCO WEI.
Please refer to the Reader's Guide for information concerning the symbols replacing missing data.

Table 1.8

Transition characteristics at ages 15, 16, 17, 18, 19 and 20

Net enrolment rates by level of education in public and private institutions (based on headcounts)

	Year	Age 15	Age 16			Age 17			Age 18			Age 19			Age 20		
		Secondary education	Secondary education	Post-secondary non-tertiary education	Tertiary education	Secondary education	Post-secondary non-tertiary education	Tertiary education	Secondary education	Post-secondary non-tertiary education	Tertiary education	Secondary education	Post-secondary non-tertiary education	Tertiary education	Secondary education	Post-secondary non-tertiary education	Tertiary education
		1	2	3	4	5	6	7	8	9	10	11	12	13	14	15	16
WEI participants																	
Argentina	2002	87	82	a	n	72	a	3	34	a	20	18	a	28	9	a	31
Brazil	2002	78	73	a	n	70	a	1	59	a	5	41	a	8	27	a	10
	1995	48	44	a	n	37	a	n	32	a	3	36	a	6	23	a	5
Chile	2003	96	89	a	n	83	a	n	57	a	...	19	a	...	7	a	...
	1995	91	82	a	n	70	a	n	41	a	...	15	a	...	8	a	...
China	2002/03	46	9	n	n	2	...	...	n	...	...	...	...	...	...	...	...
Egypt	2002/03	75	61	...	...	35	...	...	n	...	...	n	...	...	n	...	...
Indonesia	2002/03	55	53	a	n	55	a	n	33	a	22	11	a	27	3	a	25
	1995/96	53	39	a	n	43	a	n	29	a	17	13	a	22	5	a	20
Jamaica	2002/03	78	67	3	...	34	5	...	8	2	...	1	1	...	n	n	...
	1995/96	76	56	2	...	28	3	...	8	2	...	2	n	...	n	n	...
Jordan	2002/03	...	...	a		...	a		...	a		...	a		n	a	...
	1995/96	82	73	a	n	57	a	n	18	a	35	5	a	65	n	a	...
Malaysia	2002	81	78	n	n	17	13	8	12	13	25	1	7	20	n	1	17
	1995	63	54	n	n	11	6	3	11	6	14	1	4	12	n	n	8
Paraguay[1]	2002	67	62	n	n	56	n	n	47	...	1	17	...	3	9	...	5
	1995	44	35	...	...	29	...	...	16	...	...	7	...	...	...	...	...
Peru	2002	79	67	...	1	40	...	4	22	...	8	13	...	10	7	...	11
	1993	69	63	...	1	37	...	3	21	...	6	13	...	8	8	...	8
Philippines	2002/03	68	55	...	9	25	...	...	11	...	...	4	...	...	4	...	...
	1995/96	50	52	...	n	33	...	51	10	...	37	n	...	28	n	...	22
Russian Federation	2002/03	73	58	...	...	15	...	...	1	...	...	...	...	...	...	...	...
Thailand	2003/04	70	72	...	...	56	...	...	47	...	8	3	...	42	n	...	48
	1995/96	54	30	...	...	21	...	...	13	...	...	3	...	26	...	...	...
Uruguay	2002	89	86	n	n	75	n	n	51	n	8	29	n	16	21	1	19
	1996	75	65	a	n	52	a	4	35	a	13	23	a	13	12	a	10
Zimbabwe	2003	46	45	n	n	33	...	...	17	...	...	10	...	...	n	...	...
	1995	...	...	n	n	...	...	...	...	...	...	...	...	...	n	...	...
WEI mean	2003	73	64	n	1	45	2	...	25	...	...	12	...	...	6	...	...
OECD mean	2003	95	90	n	n	81	1	1	52	3	16	27	4	27	14	3	32

1. Excluding adult education for all ages.

Note: Data for OECD countries are available at *www.oecd.org/edu/eag2005*, Table C1.4.

Source: OECD/UNESCO WEI.

Please refer to the Reader's Guide for information concerning the symbols replacing missing data. Data for ages 3 to 15 are available at *www.uis.unesco.org/wei2005*.

Table 1.9
Index of change in enrolment numbers at different levels of education (base year = 100)
Enrolment in current year expressed as a percentage of enrolment in base year, by level

	Current year	Base year	Total	Pre-primary education	Primary education	Lower secondary education	Upper secondary education	All secondary education	Post-secondary non-tertiary education	All tertiary education	Tertiary (type B) education	Tertiary (type A) & advanced research programmes
			1	**2**	**3**	**4**	**5**	**6**	**7**	**8**	**9**	**10**
WEI participants												
Brazil	2002	1995	118	97	99	124	163	135	a	201	...	201
Chile	2003	1995	121	103	106	123	141	134	a	164	...	...
China	2002/03	1995/96	125	...	94	142	158	146	47	223	157	367
Egypt[1]	2002/03	1994/95	118	173	98	125	121	123	53	273	...	273
India	2002/03	1995/96	124	264	107	126	146	134	120	151	136	151
Indonesia	2002/03	1995/96	107	112	99	118	126	121	a	128	163	119
Jamaica	2002/03	1995/96	99	102	103	96	118	102	141	...	...	...
Jordan	2002/03	1995/96	121	136	115	111	124	115	a	179	...	...
Malaysia	2002	1995	126	122	107	117	161	132	281	278	259	299
Paraguay	2002	1995	144	200	107	169	201	181	...	...	428	...
Peru	2002	1993	118	125	107	134	135	134	...	127	138	119
Philippines	2002/03	1995/96	118	167	112	128	116	126	103	120	...	...
Russian Federation	2002/03	1995/96	98	76	69	87	120	95	108	181	134	213
Thailand	2003/04	1995/96	100	103	98	74	102	84	250	183	...	...
Tunisia	2002/03	1995/96	112	...	87	130	142	135	742	...	...	171
Uruguay[2]	2002	1996	118	142	106	117	132	123	a	126	106	133
Zimbabwe	2003	1995	114	...	95	107	120	113	139	143	113	242
WEI mean	**2003**	**1995**	**116**	**137**	**101**	**120**	**139**	**126**	**142**	**177**	**...**	**208**
OECD countries												
Austria	2003	1995	...	...	...	...	...	...	...	96	105	96
Belgium	2003	1995	107	94	103	109	117	114	96	116	125	108
Czech Republic	2003	1995	98	84	104	92	85	88	91	170	402	154
Denmark	2003	1995	115	124	127	98	104	101	15	122	27	185
Finland	2003	1995	114	132	102	96	126	112	...	125	1	173
France	2003	1995	98	97	93	94	102	98	137	103	26	...
Germany	2003	1995	103	104	89	108	113	109	108	104	99	105
Greece	2003	1995	106	108	92	79	91	85	...	189	201	175
Hungary	2003	1995	104	83	91	96	96	96	145	229	...	219
Ireland	2003	1995	100	76	92	85	99	91	139	142	...	...
Italy	2003	1995	101	103	99	94	100	98	57	112	70	111
Korea	2003	1995	104	104	106	74	83	78	...	158	181	145
Mexico	2003	1995	115	115	102	134	135	134	a	146	...	141
Norway	2003	1995	111	84	135	112	94	101	134	117	59	121
Poland	2003	1995	104	84	90	x(3)	89	160	184	261	143	262
Portugal	2003	1995	93	135	85	78	81	80	a	133	9	167
Spain	2003	1995	89	117	105	111	43	71	...	121	1023	105
Sweden	2003	1995	120	122	121	107	118	113	171	125	142	125
Turkey	2003	1995	127	216	113	x(2)	162	x(2, 4)	a	163	194	163
United Kingdom	2003	1995	125	96	99	109	164	146	...	126	152	115
OECD mean	**2003**	**1995**	**106**	**109**	**103**	**99**	**105**	**104**	**91**	**143**	**174**	**148**

1. For school year 2002/03, excludes enrolment in Al-Azhar institutions.
2. Post-secondary non-tertiary education programme is new and was introduced between 1995 and 2003.
Note: Change in enrolment refers to different reference periods. Table 1.10 provides the index of change expressed as annual growth rate to facilitate comparisons.
Source: OECD/UNESCO WEI.
Please refer to the Reader's Guide for information concerning the symbols replacing missing data. Data by gender are available at *www.uis.unesco.org/wei2005*.

Table 1.10

Average annual growth rates in enrolment numbers at different levels of education

	Current year	Base year	Total	Pre-primary education	Primary education	Lower secondary education	Upper secondary education	All secondary education	Post-secondary non-tertiary education	All tertiary education	Tertiary (type B) education	Tertiary (type A) & advanced research programmes
			1	**2**	**3**	**4**	**5**	**6**	**7**	**8**	**9**	**10**
WEI participants												
Brazil	2002	1995	2.3	−0.4	−0.1	3.1	7.2	4.4	a	10.5	...	10.5
Chile	2003	1995	2.4	0.4	0.8	2.7	4.4	3.7	a	6.4	...	...
China	2002/03	1995/96	3.2	...	−0.8	5.1	6.8	5.6	−10.2	12.1	6.7	20.4
Egypt[1]	2002/03	1994/95	2.1	7.1	−0.3	2.8	2.4	2.6	−7.6	13.4	...	13.4
India	2002/03	1995/96	3.1	14.9	0.9	3.4	5.5	4.2	2.7	6.1	4.5	6.1
Indonesia	2002/03	1995/96	1.0	1.6	−0.2	2.3	3.4	2.7	a	3.6	7.2	2.6
Jamaica	2002/03	1995/96	−0.2	0.3	0.4	−0.6	2.4	0.3	5.1	...	...	...
Jordan	2002/03	1995/96	2.7	4.5	2.0	1.5	3.2	2.0	a	8.7	...	...
Malaysia	2002	1995	3.3	2.9	0.9	2.2	7.1	4.0	15.9	15.7	14.6	16.9
Paraguay	2002	1995	5.3	10.4	1.0	7.8	10.5	8.8	...	...	23.1	...
Peru	2002	1993	1.9	2.5	0.8	3.3	3.4	3.3	...	2.7	3.6	1.9
Philippines	2002/03	1995/96	2.3	7.6	1.7	3.6	2.1	3.3	0.5	2.7	...	...
Russian Federation	2002/03	1995/96	−0.3	−3.8	−5.3	−2.0	2.7	−0.7	1.1	8.9	4.3	11.4
Thailand	2003/04	1995/96	0.0	0.4	−0.3	−3.7	0.3	−2.2	12.1	7.9	...	...
Tunisia	2002/03	1995/96	1.6	...	−2.0	3.8	5.1	4.4	33.1	...	...	8.0
Uruguay[2]	2002	1996	2.8	6.1	0.9	2.6	4.7	3.5	...	3.9	1.0	4.9
Zimbabwe	2003	1995	1.6	...	−0.6	0.9	2.3	1.6	4.2	4.6	1.6	11.7
WEI mean			*2.08*	*3.90*	*−0.01*	*2.28*	*4.32*	*3.04*	*4.06*	*7.64*	*...*	*9.80*
OECD mean			*0.65*	*0.75*	*0.23*	*−0.28*	*0.24*	*0.26*	*0.15*	*4.16*	*−0.85*	*4.15*

1. For school year 2002/03, excludes enrolment in Al-Azhar institutions.
2. Post-secondary non-tertiary education programme is new and was introduced between 1995 and 2003.
Note: See also Table 1.9.
Source: OECD/UNESCO WEI.
Please refer to the Reader's Guide for information concerning the symbols replacing missing data. Data by gender and for OECD countries are available at *www.uis.unesco.org/wei2005*.

ANNEX A4

Table 1.11
Female participation in education
Female enrolment as a percentage of total enrolment, by level of education

	Year	Pre-primary education	Primary education	Lower secondary education	Upper secondary education	All secondary education	All tertiary education	Tertiary (type B) education	Tertiary (type A) & advanced research programmes
		1	2	3	4	5	6	7	8
WEI participants									
Argentina	2002	50	49	50	52	51	59	70	56
Brazil	2002	49	48	50	54	52	55	…	…
	1995	57	46	56	56	56	54	…	54
Chile	2003	49	48	49	49	49	48	46	48
	1995	49	48	49	51	50	46	…	…
China	2002/03	45	47	47	46	47	44	44	44
	1995/96	…	47	46	41	44	47	51	36
Egypt	2002/03	48	48	47	48	48	…	…	42
	1994/95	48	46	45	50	47	…	…	…
India	2002/03	49	47	43	39	42	38	35	38
	1995/96	49	45	39	36	38	35	30	35
Indonesia	2002/03	51	49	50	48	49	44	49	42
	1995/96	51	48	48	47	48	37	46	34
Jamaica	2002/03	50	49	50	51	50	…	…	…
	1995/96	50	49	51	53	51	…	…	…
Jordan	2002/03	47	49	49	50	49	51	63	49
	1995/96	46	49	49	50	49	…	…	…
Malaysia	2002	51	49	50	54	51	55	52	58
	1995	50	49	50	54	51	52	52	51
Paraguay	2002	49	48	49	50	50	58	69	55
	1995	50	48	50	52	51	…	70	…
Peru	2002	50	49	47	48	48	51	56	47
	1993	50	49	47	48	48	50	54	47
Philippines	2002/03	50	49	51	53	51	55	53	55
	1995/96	50	48	49	53	50	57	…	…
Russian Federation	2002/03	47	49	49	49	49	56	53	57
	1995/96	47	49	50	49	50	…	…	54
Sri Lanka	2003	…	49	49	52	51	…	…	…
Thailand	2003/04	49	48	49	50	50	54	50	54
	1995/96	49	48	49	50	49	51	…	…
Tunisia	2002/03	48	48	49	53	51	55	…	…
	1995/96	…	47	…	…	…	…	…	…
Uruguay	2002	49	48	50	54	52	65	83	60
	1996	50	49	51	56	53	65	x(6)	x(6)
Zimbabwe	2003	…	49	49	46	48	39	44	32
	1995	…	49	47	43	45	36	39	28
WEI mean	**2003**	**49**	**48**	**49**	**50**	**49**	**52**	**55**	**49**
OECD countries									
Australia	2003	49	49	49	47	48	54	50	55
Austria	2003	49	49	49	46	47	53	66	52
Belgium	2003	49	49	52	51	51	53	56	50
Czech Republic	2003	49	48	49	50	49	51	67	50
Denmark	2003	49	49	49	51	50	58	42	60
Finland	2003	49	49	49	53	51	53	40	54
France	2003	49	49	49	50	49	55	55	56
Germany	2003	48	49	49	47	48	49	62	47
Greece	2003	49	48	48	49	49	51	49	53
Hungary	2003	48	48	48	50	49	57	61	57
Iceland	2003	49	48	48	52	50	64	51	64
Ireland	2003	50	48	50	52	51	56	54	57
Italy	2003	48	48	47	49	48	56	66	56
Japan	2003	…	49	49	49	49	46	64	40
Korea	2003	48	47	47	48	47	36	36	37
Luxembourg	2003	49	49	50	51	50	53	52	54
Mexico	2003	50	49	52	51	51	50	41	50
Netherlands	2003	48	48	47	50	49	51	60	51
New Zealand	2003	49	48	49	54	51	59	59	59
Norway	2003	…	49	49	50	49	60	51	60
Poland	2003	49	49	48	48	48	58	80	58
Portugal	2003	49	48	49	53	51	57	53	57
Slovakia	2003	48	48	49	50	49	53	81	53
Spain	2003	49	48	49	52	50	53	50	54
Sweden	2003	49	49	50	55	53	60	47	61
Switzerland	2003	49	49	49	45	47	44	41	46
Turkey	2003	48	47	a	37	37	42	43	42
United Kingdom	2003	49	49	49	56	54	56	61	54
United States	2003	46	49	49	49	49	57	56	57
OECD mean	**2003**	**48**	**48**	**47**	**50**	**49**	**53**	**55**	**53**

Source: OECD / UNESCO WEI.
Please refer to the Reader's Guide for information concerning the symbols replacing missing data.

Table 1.12

Upper secondary enrolment patterns

Distribution of enrolment in public and private institutions by programme destination and programme orientation

	Year	Programme destination			Programme orientation		
		ISCED 3A	ISCED 3B	ISCED 3C	General	Pre-vocational	Vocational
		1	**2**	**3**	**4**	**5**	**6**
WEI participants							
Argentina	2002	100.0	a	a	19.3	a	80.7
Brazil	2002	...	...	...	95.3	a	4.7
	1995	...	...	...	58.4	a	41.6
Chile	2003	100.0	a	a	63.1	a	36.9
China	2002/03	60.3	a	39.7	60.3	x(4)	39.7
	1995/96	41.6	a	58.4	41.6	x(4)	58.4
Egypt	2002/03	36.1	a	63.9	36.1	a	63.9
	1994/95	29.5	a	70.5	29.5	a	70.5
India	2002/03	99.9	a	0.1	99.9	a	0.1
	1995/96	99.9	a	0.1	99.9	a	0.1
Indonesia	2002/03	64.7	35.3	a	64.7	a	35.3
	1995/96	64.9	35.1	a	64.9	a	35.1
Jamaica	2002/03	99.5	0.5	a	99.5	a	0.5
	1995/96	98.7	a	1.3	98.7	a	1.3
Jordan	2002/03	94.7	a	5.3	75.1	5.3	19.6
	1995/96	91.6	a	8.4	85.2	a	14.8
Malaysia	2002	14.4	a	85.6	85.1	a	14.9
	1995	20.0	a	80.0	86.8	a	13.2
Paraguay	2002	99.5	a	0.5	79.6	a	20.4
Peru	2002	100.0	a	a	100.0	a	a
	1993	100.0	a	a	100.0	a	a
Philippines	2002/03	100.0	a	a	100.0	a	a
	1995/96	100.0	a	a	100.0	a	a
Russian Federation	2002/03	59.5	11.6	28.8	59.5	11.6	28.8
	1995/96	52.2	12.0	35.8	52.2	12.0	35.8
Thailand	2003/04	70.6	29.4	0.1	70.6	a	29.4
	1995/96	...	...	...	71.0	a	28.4
Tunisia	2002/03	94.6	2.3	3.0	94.6	2.3	3.0
	1995/96	97.3	1.7	1.0	...	1.7	1.0
Uruguay	2002	88.8	a	11.2	81.3	a	18.7
	1996	92.1	a	7.9	81.6	a	18.4
Zimbabwe	2003	10.2	a	89.8	100.0	a	a
	1995	6.5	a	93.5	...	...	...
WEI mean	***2003***	*76.1*	*4.7*	*19.3*	*76.9*	*1.1*	*22.0*
	*2003**	*71.0*	*3.8*	*25.2*	*79.0*	*1.4*	*19.7*
	1995	*68.8*	*3.8*	*27.5*	*74.6*	*1.0*	*24.4*
OECD countries							
Australia	2003	...	...	...	35.8	a	64.2
Austria	2003	44.6	46.7	8.7	20.8	7.4	71.8
Belgium	2003	48.5	a	51.5	29.7	a	70.3
Czech Republic	2003	68.0	0.4	31.6	20.5	0.2	79.3
Denmark	2003	46.7	a	53.3	46.4	0.3	53.3
Finland	2003	100.0	a	a	41.2	a	58.8
France	2003	67.9	a	32.1	43.6	a	56.4
Germany	2003	37.8	61.6	0.6	37.8	a	62.2
Greece	2003	64.0	a	36.0	64.0	a	36.0
Hungary	2003	73.4	2.5	24.1	50.2	37.0	12.8
Iceland	2003	48.2	0.4	51.4	64.9	1.1	34.0
Ireland	2003	75.6	a	24.4	71.7	28.3	a
Italy	2003	79.8	3.3	16.9	36.2	37.8	26.0
Japan	2003	74.5	0.8	24.7	74.5	0.8	24.7
Korea. Rep.	2003	...	...	...	69.3	a	30.7
Luxembourg	2003	59.6	16.1	24.4	35.3	a	64.7
Mexico	2003	89.1	a	10.9	89.1	a	10.9
Netherlands	2003	60.3	a	39.7	30.9	a	69.1
New Zealand	2003	60.0	11.6	28.4	100.0	a	a
Norway	2003	40.8	a	59.2	40.8	a	59.2
Poland	2003	87.3	a	12.7	45.7	a	54.3
Portugal	2003	71.9	19.1	9.0	71.5	0.4	28.1
Slovakia	2003	76.8	a	23.2	24.6	a	75.4
Spain	2003	62.8	n	37.2	62.8	n	37.2
Sweden	2003	...	...	...	47.1	a	52.9
Switzerland	2003	30.8	61.4	7.8	35.0	a	65.0
Turkey	2003	91.6	a	8.4	62.0	a	38.0
United States	2003	100.0	a	a	100.0	a	a
United Kingdom	2003	...	...	...	30.8	x(4)	69.2
OECD mean	***2003***	*63.6*	*8.0*	*27.3*	*51.0*	*4.0*	*45.1*
	*2003**	*–*	*–*	*–*	*56.7*	*x(4)*	*43.8*
	1995	*–*	*–*	*–*	*49.9*	*x(4)*	*50.1*

* Countries providing 1995 data.
Note: Comparisons of country averages between 1995 and 2003 must be based on the same group of countries. The second average for 2003 must be used.
Source: OECD/UNESCO WEI.
Please refer to the Reader's Guide for information concerning the symbols replacing missing data. Data for 1995 for OECD countries are available at *www.uis.unesco.org/wei2005*.

Table 1.13

Students enrolled in public and private institutions by type of institution and level of education

Distribution of students, by type of institution

	Year	Primary education			Lower secondary education			Upper secondary education		
		Type of institution			Type of institution			Type of institution		
		Public	Government-dependent private	Independent private	Public	Government-dependent private	Independent private	Public	Government-dependent private	Independent private
		1	2	3	4	5	6	7	8	9
WEI participants										
Argentina	2002	80.2	16.3	3.5	78.0	18.8	3.2	71.0	23.4	5.7
Brazil	2002	91.8	a	8.2	90.6	a	9.4	86.1	a	13.9
	1995	88.4	a	11.6	88.4	a	11.6	76.6	a	23.4
Chile	2003	51.6	41.4	7.0	55.2	37.9	6.9	48.8	43.2	7.9
	1995	59.2	33.1	7.7	60.2	31.7	8.1	53.7	36.0	10.2
Egypt	2002/03	...	...	...	94.6	1.0	4.4	...	...	...
India	2002/03	80.8	6.0	10.7	67.0	14.4	18.6	45.4	36.3	18.2
	1995/96	...	...	...	66.6	14.5	18.8	45.2	36.4	18.2
Indonesia	2002/03	83.9	a	16.1	63.8	a	36.2	45.7	a	54.3
	1995/96	82.8	a	17.2	60.0	a	40.0	45.4	a	54.6
Jamaica	2002/03	95.2	a	4.8	99.0	a	1.0	97.1	a	2.9
	1995/96	95.2	a	4.8	98.5	a	1.5	97.1	a	2.9
Jordan	2002/03	70.8	a	29.2	80.8	a	19.2	90.8	a	9.2
	1995/96	72.4	a	27.6	80.0	a	20.0	92.2	a	7.8
Malaysia	2002	99.1	a	0.9	97.0	a	3.0	95.9	a	4.1
	1995	99.1	a	0.9	96.9	a	3.1	94.3	a	5.7
Paraguay	2002	84.4	10.3	5.3	79.4	12.2	8.4	67.4	10.3	22.3
	1995	86.5	13.5	x(2)	73.7	26.3	x(5)	73.2	26.8	x(8)
Peru	2002	86.3	3.4	10.3	83.1	4.8	12.1	81.8	4.9	13.3
	1993	87.8	3.3	8.9	84.0	4.9	11.1	81.9	5.1	13.0
Philippines	2002/03	92.9	a	7.1	80.3	a	19.7	76.5	a	23.5
	1995/96	92.6	a	7.4	70.3	a	29.7	64.8	a	35.2
Russian Federation	2002/03	99.6	a	0.4	99.7	a	0.3	99.4	a	0.6
	1995/96	99.7	a	0.3	99.8	a	0.2	99.9	a	0.1
Thailand	2003/04	85.0	15.0	x(2)	93.7	6.3	x(5)	87.7	12.3	x(8)
	1995/96	88.2	11.8	n	95.9	4.1	n	84.6	15.4	n
Tunisia	2002/03	99.1	a	0.9	98.6	a	1.4	93.0	a	7.0
	1995/96	99.4	a	0.6	96.4	a	3.6	86.1	a	13.9
Uruguay	2002	87.1	a	12.9	88.3	a	11.7	89.5	a	10.5
	1996	84.5	a	15.5	86.2	a	13.8	88.3	a	11.7
Zimbabwe	2003	13.1	86.9	a	...	...	a	30.6	69.4	a
	1995	11.7	88.4	a	29.9	70.1	a	33.6	66.4	a
WEI mean	**2003**	**81.4**	**11.1**	**7.9**	**81.0**	**9.8**	**9.8**	**75.5**	**12.0**	**13.3**
OECD countries										
Australia	2003	71.7	28.3	a	65.7	34.3	a	73.3	26.7	a
Austria	2003	95.6	4.4	x(2)	92.3	7.7	x(5)	90.0	10.0	x(8)
Belgium	2003	45.4	54.6	...	43.2	56.8	...	42.1	57.9	...
Czech Republic	2003	98.9	1.1	a	98.2	1.8	a	87.4	12.6	a
Denmark	2003	88.0	12.0	a	76.9	23.1	a	97.5	2.5	a
Finland	2003	98.8	1.2	a	95.8	4.2	a	89.6	10.4	a
France	2003	85.4	14.3	0.2	78.8	21.0	0.2	69.5	29.7	0.8
Germany	2003	97.3	2.7	x(2)	92.9	7.1	x(5)	92.5	7.5	x(8)
Greece	2003	92.4	a	7.6	94.5	a	5.5	93.7	a	6.3
Hungary	2003	94.7	5.3	a	93.7	6.3	a	85.9	14.1	a
Iceland	2003	98.9	1.1	n	99.1	0.9	n	93.9	6.0	0.1
Ireland	2003	99.1	a	0.9	100.0	a	n	98.5	a	1.5
Italy	2003	93.2	a	6.8	96.6	a	3.4	93.9	0.7	5.4
Japan	2003	99.1	a	0.9	94.0	a	6.0	69.8	a	30.2
Korea. Rep.	2003	98.7	a	1.3	79.4	20.6	a	48.2	51.8	a
Luxembourg	2003	93.2	0.7	6.1	79.3	13.1	7.6	84.1	8.2	7.7
Mexico	2003	92.0	a	8.0	87.4	a	12.6	78.4	a	21.6
Netherlands	2003	31.3	68.7	a	23.8	76.2	a	7.8	92.2	a
New Zealand	2003	97.9	a	2.1	95.5	a	4.5	84.1	10.4	5.5
Norway	2003	98.2	1.8	x(2)	97.8	2.2	x(5)	90.1	9.9	x(8)
Poland	2003	98.7	0.3	1.0	98.1	0.4	1.4	91.4	0.5	8.1
Portugal	2003	89.5	a	10.5	88.7	a	11.3	81.8	a	18.2
Slovakia	2003	95.8	4.2	n	94.9	5.1	n	92.0	8.0	n
Spain	2003	66.6	30.1	3.3	67.2	29.7	3.1	76.9	12.0	11.1
Sweden	2003	94.9	5.1	a	94.6	5.4	a	96.6	3.4	a
Switzerland	2003	96.3	1.3	2.4	93.0	2.5	4.5	93.1	3.2	3.7
Turkey	2003	98.5	a	1.5	a	a	a	98.3	a	1.7
United Kingdom	2003	95.1	a	4.9	93.2	0.4	6.4	26.9	70.4	2.7
United States	2003	89.2	a	10.8	90.8	a	9.2	90.9	a	9.1
OECD mean	**2003**	**89.5**	**8.2**	**2.4**	**85.9**	**11.4**	**2.7**	**79.9**	**15.5**	**4.6**

Source: OECD / UNESCO WEI.

Please refer to the Reader's Guide for information concerning the symbols replacing missing data.

Table 1.14

Students enrolled in public and private institutions and full–time and part–time programmes in tertiary education

Distribution of students, by type of institution and mode of study

| | Year | Tertiary (type B) education — Type of institution | | | Tertiary (type A) and advanced research programmes — Type of institution | | | Total tertiary — Type of institution | | | Mode of study — Tertiary (type B) education | | Mode of study — Tertiary (type A) and advanced research programmes | |
| | | Public | Government-dependent private | Independent private | Public | Government-dependent private | Independent private | Public | Government-dependent private | Independent private | Full-time | Part-time | Full-time | Part-time |
		1	2	3	4	5	6	7	8	9	10	11	12	13
WEI participants														
Argentina	2002	58.9	29.6	11.5	...	a	...	78.9	7.6	13.5	...	...	a	100.0
Brazil	2002	x(7)	a	x(9)	x(7)	a	x(9)	31.7	a	68.3	...	...	100.0	a
	1995	x(7)	a	x(9)	x(7)	a	x(9)	40.4	a	59.6	...	...	...	...
Chile	2003	7.2	5.0	87.8	29.5	20.3	50.2	25.8	17.7	56.5	100.0	a	100.0	a
	1995	...	...	...	...	...	...	27.7	19.2	53.1	...	...	...	...
China	2002/03	...	...	...	...	...	...	...	...	...	58.5	41.5	75.3	24.7
Egypt	2002/03	...	...	...	...	...	...	82.4	17.6	x(8)	...	...	...	...
India	2002/03	...	...	...	...	...	...	99.4	0.6	x(8)	100.0	a	84.1	15.9
	1995/96	...	...	...	...	...	...	...	...	...	100.0	a	87.9	12.1
Indonesia	2002/03	57.7	a	42.3	32.4	a	67.6	39.0	a	61.0	100.0	a	100.0	a
	1995/96	50.5	a	49.5	40.9	a	59.1	42.9	a	57.1	100.0	a	100.0	a
Jordan	2002/03	43.8	a	56.2	66.2	a	33.8	62.9	a	37.1	100.0	a	100.0	a
Malaysia	2002	59.3	a	40.7	77.2	a	22.8	68.2	a	31.8	99.0	1.0	94.5	5.5
	1995	...	a	...	...	a	...	66.4	a	33.6	67.9	32.1	29.1	70.9
Paraguay	2002	37.1	6.1	56.9	42.9	a	57.1	41.7	1.3	57.0	100.0	a	...	...
	1995	72.4	x(3)	27.6	...	...	...	...	...	...	...	...	...	...
Peru	2002	45.8	0.6	53.7	59.3	a	40.7	53.1	0.3	46.6	100.0	a	...	...
	1993	63.3	0.8	35.9	...	...	...	63.0	0.3	36.7	...	a	...	...
Philippines	2002/03	36.2	a	63.8	33.3	a	66.7	33.6	a	66.4	100.0	a	100.0	a
	1995/96	...	a	...	...	a	...	24.2	a	75.8	...	...	...	...
Russian Federation	2002/03	96.0	a	4.0	88.2	a	11.8	90.2	a	9.8	68.7	31.3	...	...
	1995/96	99.6	a	0.4	95.3	a	4.7	96.7	a	3.3	68.5	31.5	...	...
Thailand	2003/04	57.8	a	42.2	86.4	a	13.6	81.5	a	18.5	...	...	...	...
	1995/96	...	a	...	...	a	...	77.7	a	22.3	...	...	...	...
Tunisia	2002/03	...	a	...	99.6	a	0.4	99.7	a	0.3	100.0	a	100.0	a
	1995/96	...	a	...	...	a	...	100.0	a	...	100.0	a	100.0	a
Uruguay	2002	98.7	a	1.3	87.0	a	13.0	89.8	a	10.2	100.0	a	100.0	a
	1996	88.4	a	11.6	95.8	a	4.2	93.7	a	6.3	100.0	a	100.0	a
Zimbabwe	2003	90.7	9.3	a	88.1	12.0	a	89.7	10.3	a	86.4	13.6	...	...
	1995	94.2	9.4	...	...	...	...	94.5	7.3	1.1	88.4	11.6	...	...
WEI mean	**2003**	**57.5**	**4.2**	**38.3**	**63.2**	**2.5**	**34.3**	**66.7**	**3.5**	**29.8**	**95.3**	**4.7**	**86.7**	**13.3**
OECD countries														
Australia	2003	98.5	1.5	n	99.8	n	0.2	99.8	0.2	n	33.7	66.3	65.5	34.5
Austria	2003	64.9	35.1	n	91.5	8.5	n	88.4	11.6	n	62.5	37.5	100.0	n
Belgium	2003	46.6	53.4	a	41.9	58.1	a	44.9	55.2	a	70.4	29.7	95.4	4.6
Czech Republic	2003	67.8	31.2	1.0	95.8	n	4.2	93.0	3.2	3.8	97.1	2.9	96.6	3.4
Denmark	2003	99.8	0.2	a	99.3	0.7	a	99.4	0.6	a	100.0	a	100.0	a
Finland	2003	83.4	16.6	a	89.4	10.6	a	89.4	10.6	a	100.0	a	57.0	43.0
France	2003	72.4	8.5	19.1	87.6	0.8	11.7	83.9	2.6	13.5	100.0	a	100.0	a
Gemany	2003	64.8	35.2	x(2)	100.0	a	a	94.7	5.3	x(8)	83.4	16.6	100.0	a
Greece	2003	100.0	a	a	100.0	a	a	100.0	a	a	100.0	a	100.0	a
Hungary	2003	65.4	34.6	a	85.8	14.2	a	85.0	15.0	a	83.1	16.9	52.8	47.2
Iceland	2003	58.6	41.4	a	87.8	11.9	0.4	86.2	13.5	0.3	48.0	52.0	73.9	26.1
Ireland	2003	94.1	a	5.9	93.6	a	6.4	93.8	a	6.2	60.3	39.8	84.1	15.8
Italy	2003	84.4	a	15.6	93.6	a	6.4	93.5	a	6.5	100.0	n	100.0	n
Japan	2003	9.3	a	90.7	27.4	a	72.6	23.0	a	77.0	97.1	2.9	90.5	9.5
Korea. Rep.	2003	14.7	a	85.3	22.6	a	77.4	19.2	a	80.8	100.0	a	100.0	a
Luxembourg	2003	100.0	a	a	100.0	a	a	100.0	a	a	100.0	n	100.0	n
Mexico	2003	95.7	a	4.3	65.9	a	34.1	66.8	a	33.2	100.0	a	100.0	a
Netherlands	2003	n	100.0	a	n	100.0	a	n	100.0	a	49.1	50.9	81.5	18.5
New Zealand	2003	77.8	22.1	n	98.4	1.5	0.1	93.1	6.9	0.1	52.4	48.8	56.1	43.9
Norway	2003	78.3	21.7	x(2)	85.0	15.0	x(5)	84.8	15.2	x(8)	87.0	13.0	67.3	32.7
Poland	2003	82.4	0.4	17.2	71.6	a	28.4	71.7	n	28.3	100.0	a	57.7	42.3
Portugal	2003	43.5	a	56.5	72.9	a	27.1	72.5	a	27.5	...	...	...	...
Slovakia	2003	89.9	10.1	a	99.6	n	0.4	99.2	0.4	0.4	56.7	43.3	68.2	31.8
Spain	2003	76.4	16.3	7.3	88.0	n	12.0	86.4	2.2	11.4	99.4	0.6	89.5	10.5
Sweden	2003	66.3	0.9	32.8	93.6	6.4	a	92.7	6.2	1.2	92.3	7.7	51.2	48.8
Switzerland	2003	32.6	38.1	29.3	90.2	6.9	2.9	78.3	13.3	8.3	25.2	74.8	90.4	9.6
Turkey	2003	98.6	a	1.4	95.8	a	4.2	96.7	a	3.3	100.0	a	100.0	a
United Kingdom	2003	a	100.0	n	a	100.0	n	a	100.0	n	...	...	73.8	26.2
United States	2003	88.9	a	11.1	73.1	a	26.9	76.8	a	23.2	45.7	54.3	64.2	35.8
OECD mean	**2003**	**67.5**	**19.5**	**13.1**	**77.6**	**11.5**	**10.9**	**76.3**	**12.7**	**12.0**	**80.8**	**22.6**	**83.3**	**17.3**

Source: OECD/UNESCO WEI.
Please refer to the Reader's Guide for information concerning the symbols replacing missing data.

Table 1.15

Entry rates into lower and upper secondary and tertiary education

Gross entry rates into secondary education and sum of net entry rate for each year of age for tertiary education, by gender

	Year	Lower secondary education			Upper secondary education			Tertiary (type B) education			Tertiary (type A) education		
		M + F	Males	Females	M + F	Males	Females	M + F	Males	Females	M + F	Males	Females
		1	2	3	4	5	6	7	8	9	10	11	12
WEI participants													
Argentina	2002	99	97	101	80	76	84	41	26	55	62	55	69
Brazil[1]	2002	108	x(1)	x(1)	66	x(4)	x(4)	x(10)	x(10)	x(10)	35	x(10)	x(10)
Chile[1]	2003	102	103	102	98	99	98	17	19	16	53	55	52
Egypt[1]	2002/03	99	101	97	79	80	78	x(10)	x(11)	x(12)	31	32	29
India	2002/03	58	61	54	42	46	39	...	...	...	...	...	...
Indonesia	2002/03	79	79	79	50	50	50	6	7	5	15	17	13
Jordan	2002/03	85	84	86	70	66	74	22	15	29	...	...	...
Malaysia	2002	93	93	92	...	...	...	41	40	42	32	27	36
Paraguay	2002	85	85	85	72	70	74	7	5	9	...	...	...
Peru	2002	95	98	92	77	79	76	19	17	21	...	...	...
Philippines	2002/03	92	89	94	62	54	72	...	...	...	12	10	13
Russian Federation	2002/03	87	x(1)	x(1)	...	...	...	37	x(7)	x(7)	61	x(10)	x(10)
Thailand[1]	2003/04	73	72	75	99	98	99	19	19	20	50	46	54
Uruguay	2002	116	112	121	92	82	103	23	8	39	32	24	41
Zimbabwe[1]	2003	62	65	59	6	7	5	4	5	4	2	3	2
WEI mean	*2003*	*89*	*89*	*89*	*65*	*64*	*67*	*18*	*15*	*21*	*26*	*...*	*...*
OECD countries													
Australia	2003	–	–	–	–	–	–	...	...	...	68	63	73
Austria*	2003	–	–	–	–	–	–	9	8	10	35	32	38
Belgium	2003	–	–	–	–	–	–	33	27	39	34	31	34
Czech Republic	2003	–	–	–	–	–	–	9	7	12	33	31	35
Denmark	2003	–	–	–	–	–	–	11	12	10	53	42	65
Finland	2003	–	–	–	–	–	–	a	a	a	73	66	81
France	2003	–	–	–	–	–	–	34	25	44	39	31	46
Germany*	2003	–	–	–	–	–	–	16	11	21	36	35	37
Hungary	2003	–	–	–	–	–	–	7	6	9	69	61	77
Iceland	2003	–	–	–	–	–	–	9	9	8	83	60	107
Ireland*	2003	–	–	–	–	–	–	17	17	16	41	37	46
Italy*	2003	–	–	–	–	–	–	1	1	1	54	47	60
Japan*	2003	–	–	–	–	–	–	31	22	40	42	48	35
Korea*	2003	–	–	–	–	–	–	51	49	54	50	53	47
Mexico	2003	–	–	–	–	–	–	2	2	1	28	28	28
Netherlands	2003	–	–	–	–	–	–	1	1	1	52	48	55
New Zealand	2003	–	–	–	–	–	–	53	46	59	81	66	95
Norway	2003	–	–	–	–	–	–	1	1	1	68	56	82
Poland*	2003	–	–	–	–	–	–	1	n	1	70	x(10)	x(10)
Slovak Republic	2003	–	–	–	–	–	–	3	1	6	40	39	41
Spain	2003	–	–	–	–	–	–	21	20	22	46	39	54
Sweden	2003	–	–	–	–	–	–	7	7	6	80	64	97
Switzerland	2003	–	–	–	–	–	–	17	19	15	38	39	36
Turkey	2003	–	–	–	–	–	–	24	30	18	23	26	20
United Kingdom	2003	–	–	–	–	–	–	30	26	34	48	45	52
United States	2003	–	–	–	–	–	–	...	...	...	63	56	70
OECD mean	*2003*	*–*	*–*	*–*	*–*	*–*	*–*	*16*	*14*	*17*	*53*	*47*	*57*

1. Tertiary rates as gross rates.
* See Table C2.2 of *Education at a Glance*, 2005, for notes on OECD countries (*www.oecd.org/edu/eag2005*).
Source: OECD/UNESCO WEI.
Please refer to the Reader's Guide for information concerning the symbols replacing missing data.

Table 1.16

Upper secondary graduation rates

Upper secondary graduates as a percentage of the population at the typical age of graduation (gross rates), by programme destination, orientation and gender

	Year	Total M+F	Total Males	Total Females	ISCED 3A [designed to prepare for direct entry to tertiary (type A) education] M+F	ISCED 3A Females	ISCED 3B [designed to prepare for direct entry to tertiary (type B) education] M+F	ISCED 3B Females	ISCED 3C (long) similar to duration of typical 3A or 3B programmes M+F	ISCED 3C (long) Females	ISCED 3C (short) shorter than duration of typical 3A or 3B programmes M+F	ISCED 3C (short) Females	General pro-grammes M+F	Pre-vocational/vocational pro-grammes M+F
		1	**2**	**3**	**4**	**5**	**6**	**7**	**8**	**9**	**10**	**11**	**12**	**13**
WEI participants														
Argentina	2002	48.4	42.0	55.1	48.4	55.1	a	a	a	a	a	a	11.8	36.6
Brazil	2002	66.7	58.8	74.8	66.7	74.8	...	...	a	a	a	a	...	...
	1995	26.1	29.5	22.7	26.1	22.7	a	a	a	a	a	a	15.5	10.6
Chile	2003	67.4	64.4	70.5	67.4	70.5	a	a	a	a	a	a	33.1	32.7
	1995	43.4	40.0	46.8	43.4	46.8	a	a	a	a	a	a	...	...
China	2001/02	30.9	33.0	28.7	15.7	13.5	a	a	12.5	13.4	3.0	2.0	15.7	15.0
Egypt	2002/03	62.2	59.8	64.8	22.1	24.0	a	a	40.3	41.0	a	a	22.1	40.3
	1994/95	78.9	76.6	81.2	25.7	28.4	a	a	54.3	54.6	a	a	25.7	54.3
India	2002/03	21.2	22.3	20.0	21.2	19.9	a	a	n	n	a	a	...	...
	1995/96	15.4	17.9	12.6	15.3	12.5	a	a	0.1	0.1	a	a	...	...
Indonesia	2002/03	41.0	42.5	39.4	26.8	26.6	14.2	12.8	a	a	a	a	26.7	14.1
	1995/96	31.0	32.6	29.3	20.5	20.2	10.5	9.2	a	a	a	a	20.5	10.5
Jamaica	2001/02	73.4	70.2	76.6	4.0	5.0	...	...	73.4	76.6	a	a	73.4	...
Jordan	2001/02	64.5	57.7	72.5	50.1	60.6	11.6	11.6	a	a	2.8	0.3	50.1	14.4
	1995/96	69.3	66.2	72.7	53.8	61.7	a	a	15.5	11.0	a	a	53.8	15.5
Malaysia	2002	83.6	77.1	90.0	15.5	20.1	a	a	83.6	90.0	2.2	0.9	83.6	2.2
	1995	66.9	59.4	74.6	12.6	16.1	a	a	53.1	57.1	...	...	66.9	...
Paraguay	2002	46.9	44.0	50.0	46.9	50.0	a	a	...	...	a	a	37.1	9.9
	1995	19.4	17.8	21.1	19.4	21.1	a	a	...	...	a	a	14.8	4.6
Peru	2002	63.8	64.2	63.5	63.8	63.5	a	a	a	...	a	a	63.8	a
	1993	51.7	52.0	51.3	51.7	51.3	a	a	a	a	a	a	51.7	a
Philippines	2002/03	60.1	51.9	69.3	60.1	69.3	a	a	a	a	a	a	61.0	...
	1995/96	65.2	x(1)	x(1)	65.2	x(4)	a	a	a	a	a	a	65.2	a
Russian Federation	2002/03	87.3	x(1)	x(1)	54.0	x(4)	10.8	x(6)	18.5	10.8	a	a	54.0	33.4
	1995/96	83.9	x(1)	x(1)	43.2	x(4)	11.0	x(6)	22.0	13.1	a	a	43.2	41.5
Thailand	2002/03	59.0	53.0	65.0	36.0	42.0	23.0	x(6)	a	a	a	a	36.0	23.0
	1995/96	35.3	35.2	35.5	22.1	23.2	13.2	12.3	a	a	a	a	22.1	13.2
WEI mean	**2003**	**58.4**	**53.9**	**59.1**	**39.9**	**42.5**	**4.8**	**3.1**	**15.5**	**17.2**	**0.5**	**0.2**	**43.7**	**20.1**
OECD countries														
Australia	2003	...	...	...	69	75	x(8)	x(9)	47	47	x(8)	x(9)	69	47
Austria	2003	...	...	...	15	18	54	41	n	n	...	...	15	41
Belgium	2003	...	...	...	60	65	a	a	19	18	19	25	36	66
Czech Republic	2003	88	86	90	54	65	n	n	33	25	a	a	18	67
Denmark	2002	86	81	91	54	65	a	a	54	59	a	a	54	59
Finland	2002	84	77	92	84	92	a	a	a	a	a	a	52	79
France	2003	81	78	84	52	60	11	9	38	33	3	2	34	64
Germany	2003	97	95	99	35	38	61	60	a	a	a	a	35	60
Greece	2003	96	87	105	58	67	a	a	38	38	x(8)	x(9)	58	40
Hungary	2003	87	84	91	57	65	7	7	22	17	x(8)	x(9)	33	49
Iceland	2003	79	68	90	57	73	1	1	31	22	17	18	59	39
Ireland	2003	91	85	97	90	97	a	a	5	5	a	a	66	33
Italy	2002	81	79	83	73	76	3	4	a	a	19	17	29	59
Japan	2003	91	90	93	67	71	1	n	23	21	x(8)	x(9)	67	22
Korea	2003	...	...	...	63	62	a	a	30	30	a	a	63	30
Luxembourg	2003	71	66	75	41	50	8	7	19	17	a	a	27	44
Mexico	2003	36	33	39	32	35	a	a	4	4	x(8)	x(9)	32	4
Netherlands	2003	...	...	...	55	62	a	a	19	21	19	16	32	64
New Zealand	2003	...	...	...	63	68	22	25	42	50	x(8)	x(9)	...	a
Norway	2003	92	82	102	59	71	a	a	43	41	...	...	59	41
Poland	2003	86	86	85	74	76	a	a	a	a	22	15	40	42
Slovak Republic	2003	56	57	55	42	45	a	a	23	16	1	2	11	51
Spain	2003	67	59	75	46	54	a	a	17	17	8	9	46	27
Sweden	2003	76	73	79	75	78	a	a	n	n	a	a	38	35
Switzerland	2003	90	90	91	30	32	49	41	14	18	...	...	33	54
Turkey	2003	41	44	37	41	38	a	a	...	...	a	a	27	11
United States	2003	73	72	75	73	75	...	...	...	...	...	...	73	...
OECD mean	**2003**	**78**	**75**	**82**	**56**	**62**	**9**	**8**	**19**	**19**	**8**	**8**	**45**	**43**

Source: OECD/UNESCO WEI.
Please refer to the Reader's Guide for information concerning the symbols replacing missing data.

Table 1.17

Graduation rates in tertiary education

Tertiary graduates as a percentage of the population at the typical age of graduation (gross rates), by programme destination and gender

	Year	First 5B degrees			First 5A degrees			Advanced research programmes		
		Total	Male	Female	Total	Male	Female	Total	Male	Female
		1	**2**	**3**	**4**	**5**	**6**	**7**	**8**	**9**
WEI participants										
Argentina	2002	13.5	8.3	18.6	8.1	7.3	8.9	0.1	n	0.1
Brazil	2002	x(4)	x(5)	x(6)	14.0	10.5	17.6	0.9	0.9	0.9
	1995	...	...	...	9.9	7.8	12.0	0.5	0.5	0.5
Chile	2003	7.6	7.0	8.3	16.3	15.5	17.1	0.1	0.1	0.1
	1995	6.6	7.3	6.0	8.5	9.0	7.9	n	n	n
China	2001/02	5.2	x(1)	x(1)	4.8	...	...	0.1	0.1	n
Egypt	2001/02	x(4)	x(5)	x(6)	21.9	22.7	21.0	...	...	...
	1994/95	...	...	...	...	...	...	...	...	...
Indonesia	2002/03	4.0	3.8	4.1	9.4	11.0	8.0	0.2	0.3	0.2
	1995/96	3.8	3.9	3.8	7.5	8.9	6.1	0.1	0.1	0.1
Jordan	2002/03	10.0	4.6	16.8	23.5	19.9	27.9	0.1	0.2	0.1
Malaysia	2002	25.0	24.8	25.2	14.3	12.7	15.9	0.1	0.2	0.1
	1995	5.9	6.1	5.7	3.6	3.3	4.0	n	n	n
Philippines	2002/03	3.2	2.7	3.7	21.5	15.8	28.0	0.1	0.1	0.1
	1995/96	5.3	x(1)	x(1)	14.8	x(4)	x(4)	n	n	n
Russian Federation	2002/03	29.1	x(1)	x(1)	33.1	x(4)	x(4)	1.3	1.5	1.1
	1995/96	...	...	...	...	...	...	...	...	...
Thailand	2002/03	15.8	20.7	10.8	27.0	20.8	33.5	0.1	0.1	0.1
	1995/96	8.5	8.2	8.8	11.0	10.6	11.4	n	n	n
Uruguay	2002	5.0	1.9	8.1	9.0	7.2	10.9	...	...	...
WEI mean	**2003**	**11.1**	...	...	**16.2**	...	...	**0.5**	...	...
OECD countries										
Australia	2003	...	...	...	49.0	...	...	1.5	...	...
Austria	2003	...	...	...	19.0	...	...	1.9	...	...
Czech Republic*	2003	3.6	...	...	17.0	...	...	1.0	...	...
Denmark*	2003	9.7	...	...	42.2	...	...	1.1	...	...
Finland*	2003	1.6	...	...	48.7	...	...	1.9	...	...
France	2003	18.6	...	...	26.7	...	...	1.2	...	...
Germany	2003	10.0	...	...	19.5	...	...	2.0	...	...
Hungary*	2003	2.3	...	...	35.2	...	...	0.8	...	...
Iceland	2003	7.0	...	...	43.1	...	...	0.1	...	...
Ireland	2003	19.3	...	...	36.8	...	...	1.1	...	...
Italy*	2003	1.1	...	...	26.7	...	...	0.5	...	...
Japan	2003	26.4	...	...	34.2	...	...	0.8	...	...
Norway	2003	4.5	...	...	39.8	...	...	1.0	...	...
Poland	2003	n	...	...	44.1	...	...	1.0	...	...
Slovak Republic*	2003	2.4	...	...	25.2	...	...	2.5	...	...
Spain	2003	15.7	...	...	32.1	...	...	1.1	...	...
Sweden	2003	4.0	...	...	35.4	...	...	2.8	...	...
Switzerland	2003	18.7	...	...	21.6	...	...	2.5	...	...
Turkey	2003	...	...	...	10.5	...	...	0.2	...	...
United Kingdom	2003	13.8	...	...	38.2	...	...	1.8	...	...
United States	2003	8.8	...	...	32.9	...	...	1.2	...	...
OECD mean	**2003**	**9.3**	...	...	**32.2**	...	...	**1.3**	...	...

* See Table A3.1 of *Education at a Glance*, 2005, for notes on OECD countries (*www.oecd.org/edu/eag2005*).
Source: OECD/UNESCO WEI.
Please refer to the Reader's Guide for information concerning the symbols replacing missing data.

Table 1.18

Grade repetition at primary and secondary levels of education

Percentage of students repeating current grade, by level and gender, and expected years repeating grades in primary and secondary education

	Year	Primary education			Lower secondary education			Upper secondary education			Expected years repeating grades
		M + F	Males	Females	M + F	Males	Females	M + F	Males	Females	M + F
		1	2	3	4	5	6	7	8	9	10
WEI participants											
Argentina	2002	5.9	7.0	4.8	6.5	7.8	5.2	4.3	5.5	3.2	0.7
Brazil	2002	19.2	x(1)	x(1)	17.2	x(4)	x(4)	16.9	x(7)	x(7)	2.0
Chile	2002	2.2	2.6	1.7	1.8	2.2	1.3	1.6	1.8	1.4	0.2
China	2002/03	0.3	0.4	0.3	0.2	0.2	0.1	0.4	0.5	0.4	0.0
Egypt	2002/03	4.5	5.6	3.3	8.8	10.0	7.5	1.0	1.3	0.6	0.5
India	2002/03	3.5	3.5	3.5	4.8	5.0	4.6	4.7	5.2	4.1	0.3
Indonesia	2002/03	3.8	3.8	3.8	0.4	0.7	0.2	0.2	0.3	0.1	0.3
Jamaica	2002/03	2.8	x(1)	x(1)	0.7	x(4)	x(4)	3.2	x(7)	x(7)	0.2
Jordan	2002/03	0.5	0.5	0.4	1.0	1.1	0.9	0.6	0.9	0.4	0.1
Malaysia	2002	a	a	a	a	a	a	...	...	...	...
Paraguay	2002	7.6	8.8	6.3	1.4	1.8	1.0	0.4	0.5	0.2	0.6
Peru	2002	9.9	10.2	9.7	6.5	7.4	5.4	3.8	4.4	3.1	0.9
Philippines	2002/03	2.1	2.7	1.4	2.6	4.1	1.2	1.0	1.6	0.6	0.2
Russian Federation	2002/03	0.8	x(1)	x(1)	0.9	x(4)	x(4)	0.1	x(7)	x(7)	0.1
Sri Lanka	2002	0.9	1.0	0.7	0.9	1.1	0.6	0.1	0.1	0.1	0.0
Tunisia	2002/03	9.2	10.8	7.3	14.6	18.2	10.8	13.1	14.3	12.1	1.0
Uruguay	2002	8.4	9.7	6.9	13.3	14.7	12.0	4.9	5.5	4.4	1.0
Zimbabwe	2002	a	a	a	a	a	a	a	a	a	a
WEI mean	**2003**	**4.5**	**4.4**	**3.3**	**4.5**	**5.0**	**3.4**	**3.3**	**3.0**	**2.2**	**0.5**

Source: OECD/UNESCO WEI.

Please refer to the Reader's Guide for information concerning the symbols replacing missing data. Data for OECD countries are available at *www.uis.unesco.org/wei2005*.

Table 2.1

Changes in population, 1995 and 2003 and in main economic agregates, 1995 and 2002

	Population		Gross Domestic Product			
	2003		2002	2002	1995	Index change at constant prices (1995 = 100)
	Thousands	Index change (1995=100)	Millions USD PPP converted	Millions, local currency units at constant prices	Millions, local currency units at constant prices	
	1	**2**	**3**	**4**	**5**	**6**
WEI participants						
Argentina[1]	36 480	103	411 290	235 235	243 186	97
Brazil[1,2]	172 879	112	1 318 748	745 437	646 192	115
Chile	15 773	111	153 087	8 840 300	6 800 952	130
China	1 280 400	m	5 854 223	5 654 424	3 266 480	173
Egypt	66 372	113	253 294	215 173	155 700	138
India[1]	1 048 641	113	2 799 959	14 406 300	9 939 460	145
Indonesia	211 716	109	682 874	426 943 000	384 417 700	111
Jamaica	2 617	106	10 420	229 536	224 565	102
Jordan	5 171	119	21 982	5 911	4 628	128
Malaysia[1]	24 305	119	221 263	219 988	166 625	132
Paraguay[1]	5 510	110	25 386	1 130 190	1 087 400	104
Peru[1]	26 749	124	134 079	126 980	107 039	119
Philippines	79 944	118	333 557	1 046 083	802 224	130
Russian Federation	144 071	98	1 185 961	8 036 600	6 743 054	119
Sri Lanka	18 968	m	67 671	968 358	739 981	131
Thailand	61 613	109	432 001	3 237 559	2 941 736	110
Tunisia	9 781	174	66 422	18 319	13 085	140
Uruguay[1]	3 361	107	26 330	246	258	95
Zimbabwe	13 001	118	...	21 726	22 817	95

	GDP per capita			Total public expenditure		Comparison tools	
	2002	1995		2002	1995	2002	
	USD PPP converted at constant prices	USD PPP converted at constant prices	Index change at constant prices (1995 = 100)	As a % of GDP	As a % of GDP	Purchasing Power Parity exchange rate (local currency unit to international PPP USD)	2002 GDP deflator (1995 = 100)
	7	**8**	**9**	**10**	**11**	**12**	**13**
WEI participants							
Argentina[1]	10 664	11 240	95	12.2	13.3	0.76	1.25
Brazil[1,2]	7 480	6 930	108	20.1	19.6	0.91	1.64
Chile	9 432	7 993	118	12.0	9.8	288.71	1.32
China	4 379	2 702	162	11.4	13.2	1.79	1.04
Egypt	3 669	3 025	121	10.5	10.3	1.53	1.37
India[1]	2 572	1 994	129	12.5	10.8	8.82	1.43
Indonesia	3 057	3 011	102	8.2	7.8	2357.7	3.19
Jamaica	3 800	3 812	100	16.3	11.1	36.57	1.98
Jordan	4 063	4 056	100	23.6	22.7	0.3	1.10
Malaysia[1]	8 811	7 683	115	13.8	12.4	1.63	1.23
Paraguay[1]	4 431	4 933	90	7.7	7.2	1240.22	1.71
Peru[1]	4 820	4 590	105	10.3	9.8	1.48	1.38
Philippines	4 013	3 737	107	12.1	11.4	12.06	1.62
Russian Federation	7 993	6 453	124	17.0	19.1	9.16	6.37
Sri Lanka	3 426	2 866	120	11.5	8.8	23.42	1.82
Thailand	6 740	6 438	105	11.2	9.9	12.62	1.18
Tunisia	6 508	5 083	128	16.5	16.9	0.45	1.25
Uruguay[1]	7 474	8 228	91	12.9	11.8	9.95	2.23
Zimbabwe	...	2 611	...	18.0	16.9	...	16.65

1. Year of reference in columns 1 is 2002.
2. Year of reference in columns 4 and 7 is 2001.
Source: OECD/UNESCO WEI (columns 1 and 2); World Bank, World Development Indicators 2004 edition (columns 3 to 13).

Table 2.2

Expenditure on educational institutions as a percentage of GDP

Expenditure from public and private sources, by level of education, source of fund and year

	Year	Primary, secondary and post-secondary non-tertiary education			Tertiary education			All levels of education		
		Public[1]	Private[2]	Total	Public[1]	Private[2]	Total	Public[1]	Private[2]	Total
		1	**2**	**3**	**4**	**5**	**6**	**7**	**8**	**9**
WEI participants										
Argentina[3]	2002	2.9	0.4	3.3	0.7	0.4	1.1	3.9	0.8	4.7
Brazil[3]	2001	3.0	…	…	0.8	…	…	4.1	…	…
	1995	2.3	…	…	0.6	…	…	3.3	…	…
Chile	2002	3.4	1.4	4.8	0.5	1.7	2.2	4.3	3.2	7.5
	1995	2.2	0.8	3.1	0.4	1.2	1.6	2.9	2.2	5.1
India	2001/02	2.7	1.1	3.8	0.7	0.2	0.8	3.4	1.4	4.8
	1995/96	2.6	0.1	2.8	0.7	n	0.7	3.3	0.2	3.5
Indonesia[3]	2002	0.9	0.3	1.2	0.3	0.4	0.7	1.2	0.6	1.9
Jamaica	2002/03	4.7	4.1	8.7	1.1	1.5	2.6	6.1	5.9	12.1
	1995/96	2.3	…	…	0.8	…	…	3.3	…	…
Jordan	2002	4.4	…	…	…	…	…	…	…	…
Malaysia[3]	2002	5.3	…	…	2.7	…	…	8.1	…	…
	1995	3.4	…	…	1.1	…	…	4.5	…	…
Paraguay	2002	3.5	1.1	4.6	0.7	0.9	1.6	4.5	2.1	6.6
	1995	2.5	0.9	3.4	0.6	…	…	3.1	…	…
Peru[3]	2002	1.9	1.3	3.1	0.3	0.6	0.9	2.7	1.9	4.6
Philippines	2002	2.6	…	…	0.4	…	…	3.1	2.0	5.2
	1995	2.4	…	…	0.4	…	…	3.0	…	…
Russian Federation	2002	2.2	…	…	0.6	…	…	3.7	…	…
Thailand[3]	2002/03	2.8	…	…	0.6	…	…	4.6	…	…
	1995	2.5	…	…	0.8	…	…	4.0	…	…
Tunisia[3]	2002	4.9	…	…	1.5	…	…	6.4	…	…
	1995	5.2	…	…	1.3	…	…	6.6	…	…
Uruguay[3, 4]	2002	1.8	0.2	1.9	0.6	n	0.6	2.6	0.2	2.8
	1995	2.9	…	…	1.0	…	…	3.3	…	…
WEI mean	**2002**	*3.1*	*1.2*	*3.9*	*0.8*	*0.8*	*1.3*	*4.2*	*2.0*	*5.6*
	1995	*2.8*	*0.6*	*3.1*	*0.8*	*…*	*1.2*	*3.7*	*1.2*	*4.3*
OECD countries										
Australia	2002	3.6	0.7	4.2	0.8	0.8	1.6	4.4	1.5	6.0
Austria	2002	3.7	0.1	3.8	1.1	n	1.1	5.4	0.3	5.7
Belgium[4]	2002	4.1	0.2	4.3	1.2	0.1	1.4	6.1	0.3	6.4
Czech Republic	2002	2.8	0.1	2.9	0.8	0.1	0.9	4.2	0.2	4.4
Denmark[3, 5]	2002	4.1	0.1	4.2	1.9	n	1.9	6.8	0.3	7.1
Finland	2002	3.8	n	3.9	1.7	n	1.8	5.9	0.1	6.0
France	2002	4.0	0.2	4.2	1.0	0.1	1.1	5.7	0.4	6.1
Germany	2002	3.0	0.7	3.6	1.0	0.1	1.1	4.4	0.9	5.3
Greece[3]	2002	2.5	0.2	2.7	1.2	n	1.2	3.9	0.2	4.1
Hungary	2002	3.1	0.2	3.3	1.0	0.3	1.2	5.0	0.6	5.6
Iceland[3, 5]	2002	5.4	0.3	5.7	1.0	n	1.1	6.8	0.6	7.4
Ireland[4]	2002	3.0	0.1	3.1	1.1	0.2	1.3	4.1	0.3	4.4
Italy	2002	3.4	0.1	3.5	0.8	0.2	0.9	4.6	0.3	4.9
Japan[5]	2002	2.7	0.2	3.0	0.4	0.6	1.1	3.5	1.2	4.7
Korea	2002	3.3	0.9	4.1	0.3	1.9	2.2	4.2	2.9	7.1
Luxembourg[3]	2002	3.9	n	3.9	…	…	…	…	…	…
Mexico	2002	3.5	0.7	4.1	1.0	0.4	1.4	5.1	1.1	6.3
Netherlands	2002	3.3	0.2	3.4	1.0	0.3	1.3	4.6	0.5	5.1
New Zealand	2002	4.4	0.5	4.9	0.9	0.6	1.5	5.6	1.2	6.8
Norway	2002	4.2	n	4.3	1.4	0.1	1.5	6.7	0.3	6.9
Poland[3]	2002	4.0	0.1	4.1	1.1	0.5	1.5	5.5	0.7	6.1
Portugal[3]	2002	4.2	n	4.2	0.9	0.1	1.0	5.7	0.1	5.8
Slovak Republic[3]	2002	2.7	0.1	2.8	0.7	0.1	0.9	4.0	0.2	4.2
Spain	2002	2.9	0.2	3.2	1.0	0.3	1.2	4.3	0.5	4.9
Sweden[4]	2002	4.6	n	4.6	1.6	0.2	1.8	6.7	0.2	6.9
Switzerland	2002	4.0	0.6	4.6	1.4	…	…	5.7	…	…
Turkey[3]	2002	2.3	0.3	2.6	1.0	0.1	1.1	3.4	0.4	3.8
United Kingdom	2002	3.7	0.6	4.3	0.8	0.3	1.1	5.0	0.9	5.9
United States	2002	3.8	0.3	4.1	1.2	1.4	2.6	5.3	1.9	7.2
OECD mean	**2002**	*3.6*	*0.3*	*3.8*	*1.1*	*0.3*	*1.4*	*5.1*	*0.7*	*5.8*

1. Including public subsidies to households attributable for educational institutions. Including direct expenditure on educational institutions from international sources.
2. Net of public subsidies attributable for educational institutions.
3. Public subsidies to households not included in public expenditure but in private expenditure.
4. Direct expenditure on tertiary-level educational institutions from international sources exceeds 1.5% of all public expenditure. International sources at primary and secondary levels exceed 1.5% in Uruguay.
5. Post-secondary non-tertiary included in both upper secondary and tertiary education.
Source: OECD/UNESCO WEI.
Please refer to the Reader's Guide for information concerning the symbols replacing missing data.

Table 2.3

Change in expenditure on educational institutions

Index of change in public and private expenditure on educational institutions, by level of education (Base year = 100)

	Current year	Base year	Primary, secondary and post-secondary non-tertiary education			Tertiary education			All levels of education		
			Public expenditure on educational institutions	Private expenditure on educational institutions	Total expenditure on educational institutions from both public and private sources	Public expenditure on educational institutions	Private expenditure on educational institutions	Total expenditure on educational institutions from both public and private sources	Public expenditure on educational institutions	Private expenditure on educational institutions	Total expenditure on educational institutions from both public and private sources
			1	2	3	4	5	6	7	8	9
WEI participants											
Brazil	2001	1995	122	...	...	125	...	...	129	...	...
Chile	2002	1995	200	202	200	137	189	176	193	195	194
India	2001/02	1995/96	201	...	...	204	...	...	205	...	...
Jamaica	2001/02	1995/96	120	...	...	...	...	...	...	...	...
Malaysia	2002	1995	233	...	...	360	...	...	264	...	...
Paraguay	2002	1995	216	212	215	187	...	...	229	...	...
Philippines	2002	1995	160	...	...	158	...	...	158	...	...
Thailand	2002/03	1995/96	122	...	...	...	...	...	...	...	...
Tunisia	2001/02	1995/96	131	...	...	146	...	...	134	...	...
WEI mean	*2002*	*1995*	*167*	...	...	*188*	...	...	*187*	...	...
OECD countries											
Australia	2002	1995	141	160	144	92	178	122	129	168	137
Austria	2002	1995	106	112	107	106	239	111	109	110	109
Czech Republic	2002	1995	100	27	93	144	52	118	106	43	98
Denmark*	2002	1995	125	113	125	134	482	136	132	150	132
Finland	2002	1995	124	...	125	116	...	118	123	...	124
France	2002	1995	114	106	114	115	103	114	115	105	114
Germany	2002	1995	109	104	108	108	129	110	109	107	108
Greece*	2002	1995	144	...	...	243	...	...	174	...	...
Hungary	2002	1995	123	89	120	158	174	161	134	123	133
Ireland	2002	1995	142	140	142	212	81	169	156	97	149
Italy	2002	1995	103	...	...	131	174	139	107	...	...
Japan*	2002	1995	107	106	107	119	121	120	109	114	110
Mexico	2002	1995	133	140	135	158	221	172	145	161	147
Netherlands	2002	1995	137	...	137	106	...	110	128	127	128
New Zealand	2002	1995	148	...	...	106	...	...	142	...	...
Norway*	2002	1995	122	77	121	110	62	103	121	87	115
Poland	2002	1995	144	...	...	166	...	...	135	...	...
Portugal	2002	1995	137	...	...	128	337	135	134	...	...
Slovak Republic	2002	1995	115	284	117	132	406	149	114	200	117
Spain	2002	1995	109	...	...	155	140	151	121	...	...
Sweden	2002	1995	...	...	112	...	...	115	111	168	113
Switzerland	2002	1995	113	...	...	149	...	...	120	...	...
Turkey	2002	1995	171	...	...	191	...	...	176	...	...
United Kingdom	2002	1995	133	160	136	106	165	118	127	161	131
United States	2002	1995	129	...	...	...	...	...	...	...	...
OECD mean	*2002*	*1995*	*126*	*124*	*121*	*138*	*191*	*130*	*128*	*128*	*123*

* See Table B2.2 of *Education at a Glance*, 2005, for notes (www.oecd.org/edu/eag2005).
Source: OECD/UNESCO WEI.
Please refer to the Reader's Guide for information concerning the symbols replacing missing data.

Table 2.4

Relative proportions of public and private expenditure on educational institutions

Distribution of public and private sources of funds for educational institutions after transfers from public sources, by level of education and year

	Year	Pre-primary education		Primary, secondary and post-secondary non-tertiary education		Tertiary education	
		Public sources	Private sources[1]	Public sources	Private sources[1]	Public sources	Private sources[1]
		1	**2**	**3**	**4**	**5**	**6**
WEI participants							
Argentina	2002	100.0	n	87.7	12.3	64.3	35.7
Chile	2002	73.1	26.9	71.6	28.4	19.6	80.4
	1995	71.1	28.9	71.8	28.2	25.1	74.9
India	2001/02	70.9	29.1	70.7	29.3	77.8	22.2
	1995/96	92.3	7.7	94.6	5.4	99.7	0.3
Indonesia	2002	5.3	94.7	76.2	23.8	43.8	56.2
Jamaica	2002/03	49.8	50.2	52.4	47.6	40.1	59.9
	1995/96	59.0	41.0	61.0	39.0	93.4	6.6
Malaysia	2002	89.6	10.4	100.0	a	100.0	a
	1995	79.9	20.1	100.0	a	100.0	a
Paraguay	2002	81.6	18.4	74.3	25.7	45.7	54.3
	1995	x(3)	x(4)	73.9	26.1	90.1	9.9
Peru	2002	87.1	12.9	59.3	40.7	36.4	63.6
Tunisia	2002	...	...	100.0	a	100.0	a
	1995	...	...	100.0	a	100.0	a
Uruguay	2002	86.2	13.8	92.0	8.0	96.9	3.1
	1995	83.1	16.9	100.0	a	100.0	a
WEI mean	***2002***	***71.5***	***28.5***	***78.4***	***21.6***	***62.5***	***37.5***
	1995	***77.1***	***22.9***	***85.9***	***14.1***	***86.9***	***13.1***
OECD countries							
Australia	2002	70.5	29.5	83.9	16.1	48.7	51.3
Austria	2002	76.2	23.8	96.0	4.0	91.6	8.4
Belgium	2002	97.4	...	96.1	...	86.0	14.0
Czech Republic	2002	92.7	7.3	97.4	2.6	87.5	12.5
Denmark*	2002	81.1	18.9	98.0	2.0	97.9	2.1
Finland	2002	90.9	9.1	99.2	0.8	96.3	3.7
France	2002	95.9	4.1	93.0	7.0	85.7	14.3
Germany	2002	74.6	25.4	81.7	18.3	91.6	8.4
Greece	2002	x(3)	x(4)	93.1	6.9	99.6	0.4
Hungary	2002	91.7	8.3	93.8	6.2	78.7	21.3
Iceland*	2002	...	...	95.1	4.9	95.6	4.4
Ireland	2002	...	...	96.5	3.5	85.8	14.2
Italy	2002	88.8	11.2	96.9	3.1	78.6	21.4
Japan*	2002	50.1	49.9	91.7	8.3	41.5	58.5
Korea	2002	31.8	68.2	77.4	22.6	14.9	85.1
Mexico	2002	86.1	13.9	83.1	16.9	71.0	29.0
Netherlands	2002	96.7	3.3	94.1	5.9	78.1	21.9
New Zealand	2002	60.6	39.4	89.6	10.4	62.5	37.5
Norway	2002	82.7	17.3	99.4	0.6	96.3	3.7
Poland	2002	82.8	17.2	97.1	2.9	69.7	30.3
Portugal	2002	...	...	99.9	0.1	91.3	8.7
Slovak Republic	2002	97.1	2.9	97.9	2.1	85.2	14.8
Spain	2002	85.8	14.2	93.5	6.5	76.3	23.7
Sweden	2002	100.0	a	99.9	0.1	90.0	10.0
Switzerland	2002	...	...	86.6	13.4	...	...
Turkey	2002	...	...	89.6	10.4	90.1	9.9
United Kingdom	2002	95.8	4.2	86.5	13.5	72.0	28.0
United States	2002	77.6	22.4	91.6	8.4	45.1	54.9
OECD mean	***2002***	***82.1***	***17.9***	***92.8***	***7.2***	***78.1***	***21.9***

1. Including subsides attributable to payments to educational institutions received from public sources.
* See Table B3.2a of *Education at a Glance*, 2005, for notes (*www.oecd.org/edu/eag2005*).
Source: OECD/UNESCO WEI.
Please refer to the Reader's Guide for information concerning the symbols replacing missing data.

Table 2.5

Total public expenditure on education

Public expenditure on educational institutions plus public subsidies to households (which include subsidies for living costs and other private entities)
as a percentage of GDP and as a percentage of total public expenditure, by level of education and year

	Year	Public expenditure[1] on education as a percentage of total public expenditure			Public expenditure[1] on education as a percentage of GDP		
		Primary, secondary and post-secondary non-tertiary education	Tertiary education	All levels of education	Primary, secondary and post-secondary non-tertiary education	Tertiary education	All levels of education
		1	2	3	4	5	6
WEI participants							
Argentina	2002	10.3	2.4	13.8	3.0	0.7	4.0
Brazil	2001	8.4	2.6	12.0	3.0	0.9	4.2
	1995	7.7	2.3	11.2	2.3	0.7	3.4
Chile	2002	14.5	2.6	18.7	3.4	0.6	4.4
	1995	10.9	2.5	14.5	2.2	0.5	3.0
India	2001/02	9.0	2.2	11.4	2.7	0.7	3.4
	1995/96	8.9	2.2	11.2	2.7	0.7	3.4
Indonesia	2002	4.6	1.4	5.9	0.9	0.3	1.2
Jamaica	2002/03	8.5	2.1	11.3	4.7	1.2	6.3
	1995/96	5.7	2.1	8.2	2.3	0.8	3.3
Malaysia	2002	18.4	9.4	28.1	5.3	2.7	8.1
	1995	13.6	4.6	18.5	3.4	1.1	4.6
Paraguay	2002	8.6	1.9	11.4	3.3	0.7	4.5
	1995	6.0	1.5	7.6	2.5	0.6	3.2
Peru	2002	10.6	1.9	15.7	1.9	0.3	2.7
Philippines	2002	11.8	1.8	14.0	2.6	0.4	3.1
	1995	10.0	1.7	12.3	2.4	0.4	3.0
Russian Federation	2002	6.1	1.7	10.4	2.2	0.6	3.7
Thailand	2002/03	15.4	5.3	27.5	2.8	1.0	5.0
	1995/96	12.3	4.0	20.2	2.5	0.8	4.1
Tunisia	2002	14.2	4.0	18.2	4.9	1.5	6.4
	1995	…	…	…	5.3	1.4	6.7
Uruguay	2002	6.5	2.1	9.6	1.7	0.6	2.6
	1995	…	…	…	3.0	1.0	4.1
WEI mean	**2002**	**10.5**	**3.0**	**14.9**	**3.0**	**0.9**	**4.3**
	1995	**9.4**	**2.6**	**12.9**	**2.9**	**0.8**	**3.9**
OECD countries							
Australia	2002	10.6	3.5	14.3	3.7	1.2	5.0
Austria	2002	7.6	2.6	11.5	3.8	1.3	5.7
Belgium	2002	8.3	2.7	12.5	4.2	1.4	6.3
Czech Republic	2002	6.5	1.9	9.6	3.0	0.9	4.4
Denmark*	2002	8.7	4.9	15.3	4.8	2.7	8.5
Finland	2002	7.9	4.1	12.7	4.0	2.1	6.4
France	2002	7.7	1.9	11.0	4.1	1.0	5.8
Germany	2002	6.4	2.4	9.8	3.1	1.2	4.8
Greece	2002	5.3	2.7	8.4	2.5	1.3	4.0
Hungary	2002	6.2	2.3	10.3	3.3	1.3	5.5
Iceland*	2002	12.0	2.9	15.6	5.5	1.3	7.1
Ireland	2002	9.2	3.6	13.0	3.1	1.2	4.4
Italy	2002	7.2	1.8	9.9	3.5	0.9	4.7
Japan*	2002	8.0	1.6	10.6	2.7	0.5	3.6
Korea	2002	13.2	1.4	17.0	3.3	0.3	4.2
Luxembourg	2002	9.2	…	…	4.0	…	…
Mexico	2002	16.2	4.7	23.9	3.6	1.0	5.3
Netherlands	2002	7.2	2.7	10.6	3.4	1.3	5.1
New Zealand	2002	14.7	5.2	20.8	4.7	1.7	6.7
Norway	2002	9.4	4.4	16.1	4.5	2.1	7.6
Poland	2002	…	…	…	4.1	1.1	5.6
Portugal	2002	9.2	2.2	12.6	4.3	1.0	5.8
Slovak Republic	2002	5.5	1.7	8.3	2.9	0.9	4.3
Spain	2002	7.5	2.5	11.1	3.0	1.0	4.4
Sweden	2002	8.5	3.7	13.1	5.0	2.2	7.6
Switzerland	2002	9.1	3.1	12.9	4.1	1.4	5.8
Turkey	2002	…	…	…	2.4	1.2	3.6
United Kingdom	2002	9.0	2.6	12.7	3.7	1.1	5.3
United States	2002	10.3	3.8	15.2	3.8	1.4	5.6
OECD mean	**2002**	**8.9**	**3.0**	**12.9**	**3.7**	**1.3**	**5.4**
	1995	**x(3)**	**x(3)**	**11.9**	**x(6)**	**x(6)**	**5.3**

1. Public expenditure presented in this table includes public subsidies to households for living costs, which are not spent on educational institutions. Thus the figures presented here exceed those on public spending on institutions found in Table 2.2.
* See Table B4.1 of *Education at a Glance*, 2005, for notes (www.oecd.org/edu/eag2005).
Source: OECD/UNESCO WEI.
Please refer to the Reader's Guide for information concerning the symbols replacing missing data.

Table 2.6

Distribution of total public expenditure on education

Public expenditure on education transferred to educational institutions and public transfers to the private sector as a percentage
of total public expenditure on education, by level of education and year

	Year	Primary, secondary and post-secondary non-tertiary education			Tertiary education		
		Direct public expenditure on public institutions	Direct public expenditure on private institutions	Indirect public transfers and payments to the private sector	Direct public expenditure on public institutions	Direct public expenditure on private institutions	Indirect public transfers and payments to the private sector
		1	2	3	4	5	6
WEI participants							
Argentina	2002	85.1	12.4	2.5	96.2	3.4	0.4
Brazil	2001	96.8	a	3.2	88.1	a	11.9
	1995	96.3	a	3.7	88.0	a	12.0
Chile	2002	63.6	36.0	0.4	37.2	33.3	29.5
	1995	71.2	28.6	0.2	46.3	34.5	19.2
India	2001/02	72.9	27.0	0.1	77.9	21.9	0.3
	1995/96	70.7	29.1	0.2	78.5	21.2	0.3
Indonesia	2002	90.1	6.6	3.4	100.0	n	n
Jamaica	2002/03	97.5	0.1	2.4	87.3	n	12.7
	1995/96	98.9	n	1.0	99.3	n	0.7
Jordan	2002	100.0	a	a	...	...	...
Malaysia	2002	99.6	a	0.4	97.8	a	2.2
	1995	99.6	a	0.3	95.9	a	4.1
Paraguay	2002	93.5	6.5	n	100.0	a	n
	1995	96.2	3.7	n	99.0	a	1.0
Philippines	2002	99.3	a	0.7	97.9	a	2.1
	1995	100.0	a	n	100.0	a	n
Thailand	2002/03	93.8	3.7	2.6	63.2	n	36.8
	1995/96	100.0	n	n	100.0	n	n
Tunisia	2002	100.0	a	a	100.0	a	a
	1995	100.0	a	a	100.0	a	a
Uruguay	2002	99.9	a	0.1	100.0	a	n
	1995	100.0	a	n	100.0	a	n
WEI mean	**2002**	**91.7**	**7.1**	**1.2**	**87.1**	**4.9**	**8.0**
	1995	**93.3**	**6.1**	**0.5**	**90.7**	**5.6**	**3.7**
OECD countries							
Australia	2002	77.8	18.9	3.2	65.2	n	34.8
Austria	2002	97.6	0.4	2.0	79.4	0.5	20.2
Belgium	2002	44.3	53.5	2.2	34.3	50.6	15.1
Canada	2002	...	...	...	...	...	...
Czech Republic	2002	91.4	3.3	5.3	92.1	0.9	7.0
Denmark*	2002	78.4	7.2	14.3	68.7	n	31.3
Finland	2002	90.6	6.0	3.4	74.2	7.2	18.5
France	2002	83.2	13.5	3.3	88.1	3.3	8.7
Germany	2002	83.8	11.2	5.0	81.3	2.1	16.6
Greece	2002	99.7	a	0.3	94.5	a	5.5
Hungary	2002	86.1	7.5	6.5	74.3	3.3	22.4
Iceland*	2002	97.5	1.3	1.2	71.1	7.9	21.0
Ireland	2002	95.5	n	4.5	87.7	n	12.3
Italy	2002	96.2	2.4	1.4	76.0	8.2	15.8
Japan*	2002	96.3	3.5	0.2	69.9	13.8	16.3
Korea	2002	82.6	15.2	2.2	70.4	26.1	3.5
Luxembourg	2002	...	...	...	...	...	...
Mexico	2002	95.1	n	4.9	94.9	n	5.1
Netherlands	2002	23.6	70.6	5.8	n	77.7	22.3
New Zealand	2002	88.3	4.0	7.7	52.9	2.8	44.2
Norway	2002	88.1	6.6	5.4	62.6	4.5	32.9
Poland	2002	...	...	...	...	...	...
Portugal	2002	93.1	5.7	1.2	92.8	a	7.2
Slovak Republic	2002	88.7	4.5	6.8	82.4	a	17.5
Spain	2002	84.5	14.3	1.1	90.5	1.6	7.9
Sweden	2002	87.9	4.5	7.6	66.0	4.7	29.3
Switzerland	2002	90.0	7.5	2.5	91.0	6.3	2.6
Turkey	2002	99.0	...	1.0	87.1	0.3	12.6
United Kingdom	2002	78.2	21.7	0.2	a	76.1	23.9
United States	2002	99.8	0.2	...	72.9	11.6	15.5
OECD mean	**2002**	**85.8**	**10.9**	**3.8**	**71.1**	**11.5**	**17.4**

* See Table B4.1 of *Education at a Glance*, 2005, for notes (*www.oecd.org/edu/eag2005*).
Source: OECD/UNESCO WEI.
Please refer to the Reader's Guide for information concerning the symbols replacing missing data.

ANNEX A4

Table 2.7

Expenditure on educational institutions by resource category

Distribution of total and current expenditure on educational institutions from public and private sources, by level of education and year

		Primary, secondary and post-secondary non-tertiary education						Tertiary education					
		Percentage of total expenditure		Percentage of current expenditure				Percentage of total expenditure		Percentage of current expenditure			
		Current	Capital	Compensation of teachers	Compensation of other staff	Compensation of all staff	Other current	Current	Capital	Compensation of teachers	Compensation of other staff	Compensation of all staff	Other current
		1	2	3	4	5	6	7	8	9	10	11	12
WEI participants													
Argentina[1]	2002	99.1	0.9	73.5	16.3	89.8	10.2	99.1	0.9	54.4	34.9	89.3	10.7
Brazil[1]	2001	92.2	7.8	x(5)	x(5)	80.5	19.5	92.9	7.1	x(11)	x(11)	80.1	19.9
	1995	90.0	10.0	x(5)	x(5)	78.2	21.8	93.1	6.9	x(11)	x(11)	82.6	17.4
Chile[1]	2002	83.5	16.5	...	...	...	...	90.2	9.8	x(11)	x(11)	66.4	33.6
	1995	95.0	5.0	...	...	...	...	92.0	8.0	x(11)	x(11)	72.1	27.9
India[1]	2001/02	94.4	5.6	80.5	8.0	88.5	11.5	98.9	1.1	x(11)	x(11)	99.7	0.3
	1995/96	93.5	6.5	81.4	7.6	89.0	11.0	95.1	4.8	x(11)	x(11)	99.6	0.4
Indonesia[1]	2002	93.9	6.1	78.0	7.8	85.8	14.2	82.0	18.0	87.2	11.8	99.0	1.0
Jamaica[1]	2002/03	94.5	5.5	70.9	14.9	85.8	14.2	94.4	5.6	57.6	24.4	82.1	17.9
	1995/96	82.2	17.8	73.2	12.2	85.4	14.6	99.8	0.2	56.6	12.6	69.2	30.8
Jordan[1]	2002	95.4	4.6	89.3	6.4	95.6	4.4	..	..	..	..	..	..
Malaysia[1]	2002	60.4	39.6	69.4	12.3	81.8	18.2	53.0	47.0	24.6	10.5	35.1	64.9
	1995	87.1	12.9	64.8	11.4	76.2	23.8	65.5	34.5	47.9	8.4	56.3	43.7
Paraguay[1]	2002	95.5	4.5	73.4	12.9	86.3	13.7	98.7	1.3	76.0	16.4	92.4	7.6
	1995	93.3	6.7	x(5)	x(5)	81.4	18.6	89.0	11.0	x(11)	x(11)	80.6	19.4
Peru[1]	2002	97.7	2.3	x(5)	x(5)	94.8	5.2	93.5	6.5	x(11)	x(11)	63.9	36.1
Philippines[1]	2002	96.5	3.5	x(5)	x(5)	90.6	9.4	97.8	2.2	x(11)	x(11)	83.5	16.5
Tunisia[1]	2002	92.3	7.7	...	...	...	...	75.2	24.8	...	...	...	...
	1995	88.9	11.1	...	...	...	...	80.0	20.0				
Uruguay[1]	2002	91.0	9.0	44.6	13.9	58.5	41.5	94.3	5.7	55.9	25.9	81.7	18.3
	1995	87.1	12.9	64.8	11.4	76.2	23.8	65.5	34.5	47.9	8.4	56.3	43.7
WEI mean	*2002*	*91.3*	*8.7*	*72.4*	*11.6*	*84.0*	*16.0*	*89.2*	*10.8*	*59.3*	*20.7*	*79.4*	*20.6*
	1995	*89.6*	*10.4*	*71.0*	*10.7*	*81.7*	*18.3*	*85.0*	*15.0*	*50.8*	*9.8*	*73.8*	*26.2*
OECD countries													
Australia	2002	92.0	8.0	59.8	16.9	76.7	23.3	90.4	9.6	32.0	27.6	59.6	40.4
Austria	2002	95.9	4.1	70.3	8.1	78.4	21.6	95.0	5.0	42.9	19.6	62.5	37.5
Belgium	2002	98.0	2.0	70.3	17.9	88.2	11.8	97.1	2.9	56.3	15.7	72.1	27.9
Czech Republic	2002	89.8	10.2	51.1	16.8	67.9	32.1	88.3	11.7	27.7	20.6	48.3	51.7
Denmark*	2002	92.0	8.0	51.9	26.3	78.2	21.8	94.3	5.7	52.1	25.1	77.2	22.8
Finland	2002	90.1	9.9	54.1	11.9	66.0	34.1	94.7	5.3	34.7	27.1	61.8	38.2
France	2002	91.7	8.3	x(5)	x(5)	79.0	21.0	89.8	10.2	x(11)	x(11)	70.1	29.9
Germany[1]	2002	92.3	7.7	x(5)	x(5)	85.4	14.6	90.3	9.7	x(11)	x(11)	71.9	28.1
Greece[1]	2002	93.5	6.5	x(5)	x(5)	92.0	8.0	59.9	40.1	x(11)	x(11)	46.7	53.3
Hungary[1]	2002	92.2	7.8	x(5)	x(5)	77.6	22.4	82.7	17.3	x(11)	x(11)	65.7	34.3
Iceland*	2002	89.0	11.0	...	...	...	...	90.1	9.9	x(11)	x(11)	80.4	19.6
Ireland[1]	2002	90.4	9.6	78.3	7.6	85.9	14.1	86.9	13.1	45.4	22.9	68.3	31.7
Italy[1]	2002	94.1	5.9	65.6	15.8	81.5	18.5	83.4	16.6	42.4	20.8	63.1	36.9
Japan*	2002	89.2	10.8	x(5)	x(5)	87.7	12.3	84.3	15.7	x(11)	x(11)	68.2	31.8
Korea	2002	82.7	17.3	63.3	8.9	72.2	27.8	78.8	21.2	38.7	12.4	51.2	48.8
Luxembourg	2002	84.0	16.0	74.8	12.2	87.0	13.0	...	...	...	...	...	...
Mexico[1]	2002	97.3	2.7	82.4	12.0	94.4	5.6	97.3	2.7	59.0	18.3	77.3	22.7
Netherlands	2002	94.6	5.5	x(5)	x(5)	76.7	23.3	95.1	4.9	x(11)	x(11)	75.2	24.8
Norway	2002	89.0	11.0	x(5)	x(5)	80.4	19.6	90.2	9.8	x(11)	x(11)	62.7	37.3
Poland	2002	92.7	7.3	x(5)	x(5)	71.0	29.0	94.9	5.1	x(11)	x(11)	57.5	42.5
Portugal	2002	96.6	3.4	x(5)	x(5)	96.7	3.3	88.5	11.5	x(11)	x(11)	90.3	9.7
Slovak Republic[1]	2002	95.1	5.0	61.5	13.6	75.1	24.9	90.1	9.9	31.9	24.2	56.1	43.9
Spain	2002	92.7	7.4	75.2	9.4	84.6	15.4	81.2	18.8	57.6	21.3	78.9	21.1
Sweden	2002	92.7	7.3	50.7	16.9	67.8	32.2	...	...	x(11)	x(11)	58.7	41.3
Switzerland[1]	2002	90.0	10.0	71.6	13.2	84.8	15.2	89.3	10.7	53.9	23.3	77.2	22.8
Turkey[1]	2002	93.5	6.5	x(5)	x(5)	95.5	4.5	78.0	22.0	x(11)	x(11)	71.0	29.0
United Kingdom	2002	91.4	8.6	53.2	21.9	75.0	25.0	95.7	4.3	32.7	25.0	57.7	42.3
United States	2002	88.1	11.9	55.5	25.6	81.1	18.9	90.8	9.2	27.0	29.0	56.1	43.9
OECD mean	*2002*	*91.8*	*8.2*	*64.1*	*15.0*	*81.0*	*19.0*	*88.4*	*11.6*	*42.3*	*22.2*	*66.1*	*33.9*

1. Public institutions only.
* See Table B6.3 of *Education at a Glance*, 2005, for notes (*www.oecd.org/edu/eag2005*).
Source: OECD/UNESCO WEI.
Please refer to the Reader's Guide for information concerning the symbols replacing missing data.

Table 2.8
Student to teaching staff ratio and changes in underlying factors
Index of change in student-teacher ratio, enrolment aligned to personnel data and teaching staff, by level of education (Base year = 100)

	Current year	Base year	Primary education					Lower secondary education				
			Student-teacher ratio		Index change in STR (BaseYear = 100)	enrolment aligned to personnel data (BaseYear=100)	Index change in teaching staff (BaseYear = 100)	Student-teacher ratio		Index change in STR (BaseYear = 100)	enrolment aligned to personnel data (BaseYear=100)	Index change in teaching staff (BaseYear = 100)
			2003	1995				2003	1995			
			[1]	[2]	[3]	[4]	[5]	[6]	[7]	[8]	[9]	[10]
WEI participants												
Argentina	2002		19.1	...	...	...	...	21.3	...	...	...	...
Brazil	2002	1995	24.0	25.8	93	96	103	19.5	21.9	89	124	139
Chile	2003	1995	33.9	...	...	...	...	33.5	...	...	...	...
China[1]	2002/03	1995/96	21.9	...	...	...	...	20.0	...	...	...	...
Egypt	2002/03	1994/95	22.2	...	...	...	...	20.2	...	...	...	...
India	2002/03	1995/96	40.2	40.4	99	114	115	37.2	29.4	127	157	124
Indonesia	2002/03	1995/96	23.4	21.9	107	99	92	18.8	18.9	100	118	118
Jamaica	2002/03	1995/96	29.7	34.1	87	103	118	x(11)	x(12)	x(13)	x(14)	x(15)
Jordan	2002/03	1995/96	19.9	20.8	96	114	118	x(1)	x(2)	x(3)	x(4)	x(5)
Malaysia	2002	1995	18.8	20.0	94	107	114	x(11)	x(12)	x(13)	x(14)	x(15)
Paraguay	2002	1995	17.3	24.2	71	100	140	14.2	...	...	...	...
Peru	2002	1993	25.1	...	...	...	...	18.9	...	...	...	...
Philippines	2002/03	1995/96	34.9	36.4	96	112	117	37.2	33.3	112	128	115
Russian Federation	2002/03	1995/96	17.0	19.7	86	68	79	x(11)	x(12)	x(13)	x(14)	x(15)
Sri Lanka	2002		23.4	...	...	...	...	22.0	...	...	...	...
Thailand	2003/04	1995/96	18.5	...	...	...	...	19.5	...	...	...	...
Tunisia	2002/03	1995/96	21.5	24.5	88	87	99	17.9	...	...	...	143
Uruguay	2002	1996	21.2	19.4	109	106	97	x(11)	x(12)	x(13)	x(14)	x(15)
Zimbabwe	2003	1995	38.6	39.0	99	95	96	22.1	24.4	91	112	124
WEI mean	**2003**	**1995**	**24.8**	**27.2**	**94**	**100**	**107**	**23.0**	**23.1**	**114**	**129**	**117**
OECD mean	**2003**	**1995**	**16.5**	...	...	...	...	**14.3**	...	...	...	...

	Current year	Base year	Upper secondary education					Tertiary education				
			Student-teacher ratio		Index change in STR (BaseYear = 100)	enrolment aligned to personnel data (BaseYear = 100)	Index change in teaching staff (BaseYear = 100)	Student-teacher ratio		Index change in STR (BaseYear = 100)	enrolment aligned to personnel data (BaseYear = 100)	Index change in teaching staff (BaseYear = 100)
			2003	1995				2003	1995			
			[11]	[12]	[13]	[14]	[15]	[16]	[17]	[18]	[19]	[20]
WEI participants												
Argentina	2002		17.9	...	...	...	...	16.0	...	...	...	...
Brazil	2002	1995	18.4	16.8	109	163	149	15.7	11.0	143	201	150
Chile	2003	1995	32.3	...	...	...	...	...	...	...	...	...
China[1]	2002/03	1995/96	16.3	...	...	...	...	...	...	...	...	...
Egypt	2002/03	1994/95	14.5	...	...	...	...	...	...	...	...	...
India	2002/03	1995/96	27.5	31.5	87	145	166	22.2	20.4	109	136	125
Indonesia	2002/03	1995/96	16.8	15.3	110	123	112	18.7	17.9	104	128	123
Jamaica	2002/03	1995/96	20.3	20.3	100	102	102	...	21.4	...	...	...
Jordan	2002/03	1995/96	15.5	16.6	93	135	145	...	...	...	...	...
Malaysia[2]	2002	1995	16.9	18.6	91	132	145	18.8	12.6	150	263	176
Paraguay	2002	1995	14.8	...	...	...	...	15.4	...	...	...	...
Peru	2002	1993	x(6)	...	...	...	...	14.8	...	...	...	...
Philippines	2002/03	1995/96	36.7	39.0	94	99	106	22.1	37.8	58	120	206
Russian Federation	2002/03	1995/96	10.8	11.7	92	96	103	13.0	9.8	133	179	135
Sri Lanka	2002		17.1	...	...	...	...	...	...	...	...	...
Thailand	2003/04	1995/96	19.9	...	...	...	...	35.0	...	...	...	...
Tunisia	2002/03	1995/96	18.0	...	...	...	x(10)	20.4	17.4	117	234	200
Uruguay	2002	1996	19.8	15.2	130	138	106	8.2	...	...	...	...
Zimbabwe	2003	1995	x(6)	x(7)	x(8)	x(9)	x(10)	...	17.4	...	...	...
WEI mean	**2003**	**1995**	**19.6**	**20.6**	**101**	**126**	**126**	**18.4**	**18.4**	**116**	**180**	**159**
OECD mean	**2003**		**13.0**	...	...	...	...	**14.9**	...	...	...	...

1. Ratio calculated with full-time personnel only.
2. Ratio calculated at upper secondary level is for public institutions only.
3. Ratio calculated at tertiary level is for public institutions only.
Source: OECD/UNESCO WEI.
Please refer to the Reader's Guide for information concerning the symbols replacing missing data.

ANNEX A4

Table 2.9

Average class size

Average class size by type of institution, level of education and year, calculations based on number of students and number of classes

	Year	Primary education				Lower secondary education			
		Public institutions	Government-dependent private institutions	Independent private institutions	**Total public and private institutions**	Public institutions	Government-dependent private institutions	Independent private institutions	**Total public and private institutions**
		1	**2**	**3**	**4**	**5**	**6**	**7**	**8**
WEI participants									
Argentina	2002	28.0	26.7	26.7	27.8	28.8	27.9	27.9	28.6
Brazil	2002	32.6	a	18.8	30.6	34.3	a	25.9	33.2
	1995	28.5	a	27.3	28.3	37.3	a	34.8	37.0
Chile	2003	31.4	34.5	23.4	31.7	32.0	34.7	24.8	32.2
	1995	34.8	34.8	34.8	34.8	30.5	28.9	32.4	30.1
China	2002/03	34.4	a	36.2	34.5	57.1	a	47.1	56.7
	1995/96	x(4)	x(4)	x(4)	32.7	x(8)	x(8)	x(8)	51.8
Egypt	2002/03	41.5	36.9	35.0	40.8	43.2	39.6	30.9	42.4
	1994/95	44.7	x(3)	38.9	44.2	41.8	x(7)	33.2	41.5
India	2002/03	40.0	…	…	…	39.0	…	…	…
	1995/96	40.1	…	…	…	38.0	…	…	…
Jamaica	2002/03	42.0	…	…	…	32.0	…	…	…
Jordan	2002/03	28.8	a	27.8	28.5	30.7	a	30.2	30.6
	1995/96	28.6	a	31.3	29.3	30.6	a	34.0	31.2
Malaysia	2002	31.7	a	…	…	34.0	a	…	…
	1995	33.2	a	…	…	34.0	a	…	…
Paraguay	2002	17.9	21.7	16.2	18.1	26.2	26.4	19.6	25.5
	1995	20.4	…	…	…	31.8	…	…	…
Peru	2002	…	…	…	…	32.0	33.0	20.0	29.9
	1993	…	…	…	…	32.2	37.6	24.4	31.3
Philippines	2002/03	43.9	a	32.5	42.9	56.1	a	55.7	56.0
	1995/96	38.4	a	36.0	38.2	40.3	a	45.7	41.8
Russian Federation	2002/03	15.8	a	9.8	15.8	20.2	a	10.2	20.1
	1995/96	18.6	a	12.0	18.6	21.0	a	11.8	21.0
Sri Lanka	2002	x(4)	x(4)	x(4)	25.8	x(8)	x(8)	x(8)	29.8
Thailand	2003/04	22.9	36.9	a	24.3	41.5	39.0	a	41.3
	1995/96	22.0	…	…	…	37.2	…	…	…
Tunisia	2002/03	27.1	a	24.4	27.1	33.1	a	19.0	32.7
	1995/96	30.8	…	…	…	36.3	…	…	…
Uruguay	2002	19.3	a	…	…	29.7	a	25.9	29.2
	1996	27.0	a	…	…	31.0	a	…	…
WEI Mean	**2003**	**30.5**	**31.3**	**25.1**	**29.0**	**35.6**	**33.4**	**28.1**	**34.9**
	1995	**30.6**	**34.8**	**30.0**	**32.3**	**34.0**	**33.3**	**30.9**	**35.7**
OECD countries									
Australia	2003	22.7	26.0	a	23.8	22.2	26.2	a	24.7
Austria	2003	20.0	20.5	x(2)	20.1	24.0	26.2	x(6)	24.0
Belgium (Fr.)	2003	19.9	20.8	a	20.3	21.1	21.8	a	21.5
Czech Republic	2003	20.8	16.8	a	20.8	23.3	21.2	a	23.2
Denmark	2003	19.7	17.4	a	19.4	19.4	18.1	a	19.2
France	2003	22.3	23.9	n	22.6	24.1	25.0	13.4	24.2
Germany	2003	22.0	23.4	x(2)	22.0	24.6	25.9	x(6)	24.7
Greece	2003	17.1	a	18.8	17.2	22.7	a	24.9	22.8
Hungary	2003	20.5	19.1	a	20.4	21.5	22.1	a	21.6
Iceland	2003	18.2	15.2	n	18.1	19.4	13.1	n	19.3
Ireland	2003	24.0	a	…	…	20.4	a	…	…
Italy	2003	18.0	a	20.0	18.1	20.9	a	21.3	20.9
Japan	2003	28.6	a	33.9	28.6	33.9	a	36.0	34.0
Korea	2003	34.7	a	34.1	34.7	35.4	34.6	a	35.2
Luxembourg	2003	15.5	21.2	20.4	15.7	20.2	20.8	20.7	20.3
Mexico	2003	20.0	a	23.3	20.2	30.1	a	28.1	30.0
Netherlands	2003	x(4)	x(4)	a	22.2	…	…	a	…
Poland	2003	20.8	11.9	11.8	20.6	24.6	25.7	14.3	24.3
Portugal	2003	18.6	a	22.4	18.9	22.1	a	23.9	22.3
Slovak Republic	2003	20.2	19.9	n	20.2	23.0	23.3	n	23.0
Spain	2003	19.4	24.7	20.9	20.8	23.4	27.8	21.7	24.5
Switzerland	2003	19.5	14.4	16.7	19.3	18.8	18.1	15.9	18.7
Turkey	2003	26.9	a	17.8	26.7	a	a	a	a
United Kingdom	2003	x(4)	x(4)	x(4)	26.0	x(8)	x(8)	x(8)	24.2
United States	2003	22.0	a	19.6	21.7	23.2	a	18.8	22.6
OECD mean	**2003**	**21.4**	**19.7**	**21.6**	**21.6**	**23.6**	**23.2**	**21.7**	**23.9**

Source: OECD/UNESCO WEI.

Please refer to the Reader's Guide for information concerning the symbols replacing missing data.

Table 2.10

Age distribution of teachers

Percentage of teachers in public and private institutions, by level of education and age group, based on head counts

	Year	Primary education					Lower secondary education					Upper secondary education				
		< 30 years	30-39 years	40-49 years	50-59 years	≥ 60 years	< 30 years	30-39 years	40-49 years	50-59 years	≥ 60 years	< 30 years	30-39 years	40-49 years	50-59 years	≥ 60 years
		1	2	3	4	5	6	7	8	9	10	11	12	13	14	15
WEI participants																
Argentina	2002	30.5	31.4	27.2	10.0	0.9	x(11)	x(12)	x(13)	x(14)	x(15)	24.5	34.6	26.8	11.7	2.4
Brazil	2002	33.6	33.5	23.6	8.4	0.9	22.4	37.7	28.1	10.0	1.7	22.0	35.8	28.4	12.4	1.3
	1995	39.2	33.7	21.0	5.7	0.4	30.6	37.4	27.1	4.3	0.6	25.1	31.5	35.1	6.6	1.6
Chile	2003	4.9	19.4	29.0	34.2	12.4	4.9	19.4	29.0	34.2	12.4	5.4	24.8	34.2	26.4	9.1
China	2002/03	34.1	25.4	26.3	14.1	0.1	45.6	33.4	13.4	7.5	0.1	36.0	41.0	13.0	8.5	1.4
Indonesia	2002/03	51.6	34.9	9.8	3.7	a	14.2	50.2	21.5	12.6	1.4	16.5	48.5	24.7	8.9	1.5
	1995	51.6	34.9	9.8	3.7	x(4)	14.1	50.2	21.6	12.7	1.4	16.5	48.4	24.8	8.9	1.4
Jamaica	2002/03	17.5	20.1	23.1	24.1	3.3	x(11)	x(12)	x(13)	x(14)	x(15)	22.3	30.2	27.2	16.9	2.3
Jordan	2002/03	57.7	30.5	9.9	1.9	x(4)	x(11)	x(12)	x(13)	x(14)	x(15)	52.9	33.9	10.1	3.0	x(14)
Malaysia	2002	26.9	46.5	22.0	4.5	x(4)	x(11)	x(12)	x(13)	x(14)	x(15)	15.4	46.5	30.4	7.6	x(14)
	1995	26.5	46.7	22.4	4.4	x(4)	x(11)	x(12)	x(13)	x(14)	x(15)	14.2	46.3	31.4	8.0	n
Paraguay	2002	38.4	43.9	12.0	4.5	1.0	34.5	38.5	19.8	5.6	1.1	31.4	41.0	20.6	5.4	1.3
Philippines	2002/03	7.6	24.1	24.7	27.5	16.0	x(11)	x(12)	x(13)	x(14)	x(15)	13.5	35.9	28.2	18.8	3.5
WEI mean	*2003*	*30.3*	*31.0*	*20.8*	*13.3*	*4.9*	*22.8*	*35.7*	*23.9*	*14.4*	*3.2*	*24.0*	*37.2*	*24.4*	*12.0*	*2.9*
	1995	*39.1*	*38.4*	*17.7*	*4.6*	*0.1*	*22.4*	*43.8*	*24.3*	*8.5*	*1.0*	*18.6*	*42.1*	*30.4*	*7.9*	*1.0*

Source: OECD/UNESCO WEI.

Please refer to the Reader's Guide for information concerning the symbols replacing missing data. Data for OECD countries are available at *www.uis.unesco.org/wei2005*.

Table 2.11

The organization of teachers' teaching time

Teaching time and weeks per year in public institutions, by level of education and year

	Year	Teaching hours per year			Teaching weeks per year		
		Primary education	Lower secondary education	Upper secondary education (general)	Primary education	Lower secondary education	Upper secondary education (general)
		1	2	3	4	5	6
WEI participants							
Argentina	2002	810	900	900	38	38	38
	1996	788	875	875	37	37	37
Brazil	2002	800	800	800	40	40	40
	1995	800	800	800	40	40	40
Chile	2003	864	864	864	40	40	40
	1995	864	864	864	40	40	40
Egypt	2002/03	748	748	748	36	36	36
India	2002/03	1 013	1 125	1 125	52	52	52
	1995/96	1 013	1 125	1 125	52	52	52
Indonesia	2002/03	1 260	738	738	44	44	44
	1995/96	1 260	738	738	44	44	44
Jamaica	2002/03	950	950	950	38	38	38
	1995/96	950	950	950	38	38	38
Jordan	2002/03	810	810	810	36	36	36
	1995/96	833	833	694	41	41	41
Malaysia	2002	782	798	798	41	41	41
	1995	782	798	798	41	41	41
Paraguay	2002	732	814	915	38	38	38
	1995	720	895	895	37	37	37
Peru	2002	1 000	1 169	1 169	36	36	36
	1993	1 007	1 007	1 007	38	38	38
Philippines	2002/03	1 176	1 176	1 176	40	40	40
	1995/96	1 296	1 296	1 296	44	44	44
Russian Federation	2002/03	656	946	946	34	35	35
	1995/96	860	774	774	45	45	45
Sri Lanka	2002	987	1 260	1 260	42	42	42
Thailand	2001/02	760	652	652	40	40	40
Tunisia	2002/03	735	548	548	32	30	30
	1995/96	730	544	544	32	30	30
Uruguay	2002	660	427	427	37	36	36
	1996	732	712	712	38	37	37
Zimbabwe	2003	954	954	954	37	37	37
WEI Mean	**2003**	**872**	**871**	**877**	**39**	**39**	**39**
	1995	**902**	**872**	**862**	**41**	**40**	**40**
OECD countries							
Australia	2003	885	825	813	40	40	40
Austria	2003	792	622	602	38	38	38
Belgium (Fl.)	2003	797	712	668	37	37	37
Belgium (Fr.)	2003	717	720	661	37	37	37
Czech Republic	2003	772	614	586	38	38	38
Denmark	2003	640	640	560	42	42	42
England	2003	…	…	…	38	38	38
Finland	2003	684	599	556	38	38	38
France	2003	900	626	602	35	35	35
Germany	2003	782	735	684	40	40	40
Greece	2003	780	629	629	40	38	38
Hungary	2003	777	555	555	37	37	37
Iceland	2003	653	653	560	36	36	36
Ireland	2003	915	735	735	37	33	33
Italy	2003	792	594	594	33	33	33
Japan	2003	648	535	467	35	35	35
Korea	2003	809	560	544	37	37	37
Luxembourg	2003	774	642	642	36	36	36
Mexico	2003	800	1047	848	42	42	36
Netherlands	2003	930	750	750	40	37	37
New Zealand	2003	985	968	950	39	39	38
Norway	2003	741	656	524	38	38	37
Poland	2003	637	637	637	37	37	37
Portugal	2003	783	626	580	36	36	36
Scotland	2003	950	893	893	38	38	38
Slovak Republic	2003	656	656	627	38	38	38
Spain	2003	880	564	548	37	36	35
Turkey	2003	639	a	567	38	a	38
United States	2003	1 139	1 127	1 121	36	36	36
OECD mean	**2003**	**795**	**701**	**661**	**38**	**37**	**37**

Source: OECD/UNESCO WEI.

Please refer to the Reader's Guide for information concerning the symbols replacing missing data.

Table 2.12a

Teachers' salaries

Teachers' salaries in US$ PPP converted at starting salary, after 15 years of experience and at the top of the salary scale, minimum training, by level of education

	Year	Primary education			Lower secondary education			Upper secondary education, general programmes		
		Starting salary	Salary after 15 years of experience	Salary at top of scale	Starting salary	Salary after 15 years of experience	Salary at top of scale	Starting salary	Salary after 15 years of experience	Salary at top of scale
		1	**2**	**3**	**4**	**5**	**6**	**7**	**8**	**9**
WEI participants										
Argentina	2002	6 901	9 670	11 612	9 459	13 264	15 929	9 459	13 264	15 929
Brazil	2002	8 888	12 005	13 292	12 138	14 380	17 444	15 494	17 669	17 908
Chile	2003	11 709	13 671	18 437	11 709	13 671	18 437	11 709	14 306	19 302
Egypt	2002/03	1 046	2 184	…	1 046	2 184	…	…	…	…
Indonesia	2002/03	1 002	1 586	3 022	1 002	1 586	3 022	1 042	1 910	3 022
Jamaica	2002/03	13 354	16 520	16 520	13 354	16 520	16 520	13 354	16 520	16 520
Jordan	2002/03	8 828	12 250	30 830	8 828	12 250	30 830	8 828	12 250	30 830
Malaysia	2002	9 230	14 490	17 470	13 480	23 029	29 151	13 480	23 029	29 151
Paraguay	2002	7 950	7 950	7 950	12 400	12 400	12 400	12 400	12 400	12 400
Peru	2002	5 669	5 669	5 669	5 606	5 606	5 606	5 606	5 606	5 606
Philippines	2002/03	9 890	10 916	11 756	9 890	10 916	11 756	9 890	10 916	11 756
Sri Lanka	2002	3 100	3 945	3 945	3 100	4 509	4 509	3 945	5 073	5 073
Thailand	2003/04	6 048	14 862	28 345	6 048	14 862	28 345	6 048	14 862	28 345
Tunisia	2002/03	13 120	13 262	15 067	16 693	16 853	19 067	20 320	20 511	22 960
Uruguay	2002	4 850	5 812	7 017	4 850	5 812	7 017	5 278	6 241	7 444
WEI mean	*2003*	*7 439*	*9 653*	*13 638*	*8 640*	*11 190*	*15 717*	*9 775*	*12 468*	*16 161*
OECD countries										
Australia	2003	28 642	42 057	42 057	28 865	42 078	42 078	28 865	42 078	42 078
Austria	2003	24 475	32 384	48 977	25 439	34 666	51 269	25 776	35 670	54 139
Belgium (Fl.)	2003	27 070	37 128	44 626	27 070	37 913	46 223	33 588	48 485	58 279
Belgium (Fr.)	2003	25 684	35 474	42 884	25 995	36 690	44 945	32 395	47 193	56 925
Czech Republic	2003	13 808	18 265	23 435	13 808	18 265	23 435	16 817	20 259	25 988
Denmark	2003	32 939	37 076	37 076	32 939	37 076	37 076	32 331	45 425	45 425
England	2003	28 608	41 807	41 807	28 608	41 807	41 807	28 608	41 807	41 807
Finland	2003	27 023	31 785	31 785	30 336	36 444	36 444	34 374	42 139	42 139
France	2003	23 106	31 082	45 861	25 564	33 540	48 440	26 035	34 010	48 957
Germany	2003	38 216	46 223	49 586	39 650	48 804	50 949	42 881	52 570	54 928
Greece	2003	22 990	28 006	33 859	22 990	28 006	33 859	22 990	28 006	33 859
Hungary	2003	11 701	14 923	19 886	11 701	14 923	19 886	13 286	18 463	24 185
Iceland	2003	18 742	21 692	24 164	18 742	21 692	24 164	24 159	29 641	31 433
Ireland	2003	24 458	40 514	45 910	25 295	40 514	45 910	25 295	40 514	45 910
Italy	2003	23 751	28 731	34 869	25 602	31 304	38 306	25 602	32 186	40 058
Japan	2003	24 514	45 515	57 327	24 514	45 515	57 327	24 514	45 543	59 055
Korea	2003	27 214	46 640	74 965	27 092	46 518	74 843	27 092	46 518	74 843
Luxembourg	2003	44 712	61 574	91 131	64 416	80 520	111 910	64 416	80 520	111 910
Mexico	2003	12 688	16 720	27 696	16 268	21 242	35 056	…	…	…
Netherlands	2003	30 071	39 108	43 713	31 188	43 054	47 977	31 492	57 647	63 586
New Zealand	2003	18 132	35 078	35 078	18 132	35 078	35 078	18 132	35 078	35 078
Norway	2003	29 719	35 541	36 806	29 719	35 541	36 806	29 719	35 541	36 806
Poland	2003	6 257	9 462	10 354	6 257	9 462	10 354	6 257	9 462	10 354
Portugal	2003	20 150	33 815	53 085	20 150	33 815	53 085	20 150	33 815	53 085
Scotland	2003	27 223	43 363	43 363	27 223	43 363	43 363	27 223	43 363	43 363
Slovak Republic	2003	5 771	7 309	9 570	5 771	7 309	9 570	5 771	7 309	9 570
Spain	2003	29 973	34 890	43 816	33 702	39 019	48 352	34 614	40 231	49 712
Sweden	2003	24 488	28 743	32 956	25 278	29 617	33 567	26 278	30 934	35 610
Switzerland	2003	37 544	49 932	59 667	44 563	58 520	69 645	52 572	67 355	80 706
Turkey	2003	12 903	14 580	16 851	a	a	a	11 952	13 630	15 900
United States	2003	30 339	43 999	53 563	30 352	43 999	52 603	30 471	44 120	52 745
OECD mean	*2003*	*24 287*	*33 336*	*40 539*	*26 241*	*35 876*	*43 477*	*27 455*	*38 317*	*45 948*

Source: OECD/UNESCO WEI.

Please refer to the Reader's Guide for information concerning the symbols replacing missing data.

Table 2.12b

Index of change in teachers' salaries

Index of change in teachers' salaries at starting salary, after 15 years of experience and at the top of the salary scale,
minimum training, by level of education, adjusted for inflation (Base year = 100)

	Current year	Base year	Primary education			Lower secondary education			Upper secondary education, general programmes		
			Starting salary	Salary after 15 years of experience	Salary at top of scale	Starting salary	Salary after 15 years of experience	Salary at top of scale	Starting salary	Salary after 15 years of experience	Salary at top of scale
			1	2	3	4	5	6	7	8	9
WEI participants											
Argentina	2002	1996	78	83	84	73	74	75	73	74	75
Brazil	2002	1995	125	114	103	119	132	114	112	97	109
Chile	2003	1995	160	145	146	160	145	146	160	152	152
Indonesia	2002/03	1995/96	48	42	48	48	42	48	43	40	41
Jamaica	2002/03	1995/96	148	154	154	148	154	154	148	154	154
Paraguay	2002	1995	91	91	91	87	87	87	87	87	87
Philippines	2002/03	1995/96	125	134	143	125	134	143	125	134	143
WEI mean	**2003**	**1995**	**111**	**109**	**110**	**109**	**110**	**110**	**107**	**105**	**109**

Source: OECD/UNESCO WEI.

Table 2.13

Annual expenditure on educational institutions per student, 2002

In US$ PPP converted, by level of education, based on full-time equivalents

	Pre-primary education	Primary education	Secondary education			Post-secondary non-tertiary education	Tertiary education (incl. R&D activities)			Primary to tertiary education
			Lower secondary education	Upper secondary education	All secondary education		All tertiary education	Tertiary (type B) education	Tertiary (type A) and advanced research programmes	
	1	**2**	**3**	**4**	**5**	**6**	**7**	**8**	**9**	**10**
WEI participants										
Argentina	1 305	1 241	1 286	2 883	1 918	a	3 235	3 891	2 777	1 755
Brazil[1,2]	965	842	913	1 008	944	a	10 361	x(7)	x(7)	1 121
Chile	1 766	2 110	2 070	2 094	2 085	a	6 901	3 486	7 611	2 732
India[2]	79	396	397	1 155	712	571	2 486	x(7)	x(7)	606
Indonesia	64	110	278	379	315	a	1 296	x(7)	x(7)	262
Jamaica[1,2]	707	640	909	1 029	950	...	...	...	...	...
Jordan[1]	393	805	830	852	837	...	...	...	...	...
Malaysia[1]	552	1 897	x(5)	x(5)	2 923	10 520	14 405	10 769	15 276	3 239
Paraguay	800	676	747	1 168	919	...	2 791	2 109	2 966	...
Peru	357	354	x(5)	x(5)	503	...	1 346	739	1 749	1 473
Philippines[1]	62	491	452	452	452	2 452	1 730	x(7)	x(7)	548
Russian Federation[1]	1 582	x(5)	x(5)	x(5)	1 327	x(5)	...	1547	...	...
Tunisia[1]	...	x(5)	x(5)	x(5)	2 583	x(5)	3 674	x(7)	x(7)	...
Uruguay[1]	1 038	844	921	544	732	a	1 721	x(7)	x(7)	898
WEI mean	*744*	*867*	*880*	*1 157*	*1 229*	*4 514*	*4 541*	*...*	*...*	*1 404*
OECD countries										
Australia	...	5 169	7 063	7 908	7 375	7 121	12 416	7 544	13 410	7 209
Austria	6 169	7 015	8 683	9 125	8 887	12 471	12 448	9 584	12 701	8 943
Belgium	4 420	5 665	x(5)	x(5)	8 272	x(5)	12 019	x(7)	x(7)	7 933
Czech Republic	2 724	2 077	3 601	3 657	3 628	1 623	6 236	2 703	6 671	3 449
Denmark	4 673	7 727	7 949	8 054	8 003	x(4.7)	15 183	x(7)	x(7)	9 261
Finland	3 929	5 087	8 197	6 455	7 121	x(5)	11 768	3 185	11 833	7 304
France	4 512	5 033	7 820	9 291	8 472	6 897	9 276	9 801	9 132	7 467
Germany	4 999	4 537	5 667	9 835	7 025	9 896	10 999	5 739	11 860	7 129
Greece	x(2)	3 803	x(5)	x(5)	4 058	2 958	4 731	2 840	5 646	4 136
Hungary[1]	3 475	3 016	2 836	3 573	3 184	5 383	8 205	8 691	8 187	3 872
Iceland	...	7 171	7 532	7 001	7 229	x(4.7)	8 251	12 869	8 232	7 548
Ireland	...	4 180	5 698	5 758	5 725	5 978	9 809	x(7)	x(7)	5 711
Italy[1]	5 445	7 231	8 073	7 221	7 568	...	8 636	7 429	8 649	7 708
Japan	3691	6 117	6 607	7 274	6 952	x(4.7)	11 716	9 580	11 984	7 438
Korea	2497	3 553	5 036	6 747	5 882	a	6 047	3 772	7 630	5 053
Luxembourg	x(2)	10 611	x(5)	x(5)	15 195	x(5)	...	...	...	...
Mexico	1643	1 467	1 477	2 378	1 768	a	6 074	x(7)	x(7)	1 950
Netherlands	4923	5 558	7 257	6 256	6 823	5 872	13 101	7 622	13 163	7 241
New Zealand	4650	4 536	4 540	7 330	5 698	...	...	...	...	...
Norway	...	7 508	8 536	11 510	10 154	x(5)	13 739	x(7)	x(7)	9 560
Poland	2691	2 585	x(2)	2 599	...	2 896	4 834	x(7)	x(7)	2 962
Portugal[1]	4158	4 940	6 727	7 155	6 921	a	6 960	x(7)	x(7)	6 080
Slovak Republic	2 125	1 471	1 806	2 694	2 193	x(4)	4 756	x(4)	4 756	2300
Spain	3845	4 592	x(5)	x(5)	6 010	x(5)	8 020	7 718	8 074	5 914
Sweden	4107	7 143	7 075	7 670	7 400	3 952	15 715	x(7)	x(7)	8 520
Switzerland[1]	3450	7 776	9 200	14 693	11 900	8 591	23 714	7 286	25 524	11 334
United Kingdom	8 452	5 150	x(5)	x(5)	6 505	x(5)	11 822	x(7)	x(7)	6691
United States	7881	8 049	8 669	9 607	9 098	...	20 545	x(7)	x(7)	11 152
OECD mean	*4294*	*5 313*	*6 089*	*7 121*	*7 002*	*4 602*	*10 655*	*...*	*...*	*6 687*

1. Public institutions only.
2. Year of reference is 2001 in Brazil, 2001/02 in India and 2002/03 in Jamaica.
Source: OECD/UNESCO WEI.
Please refer to the Reader's Guide for information concerning the symbols replacing missing data.

Table 2.14

Change in expenditure on educational institutions per student relative to different factors

Index of change in expenditure per student at constant prices, by level of education (Base year = 100)

	Current year	Base year	Primary, secondary and post-secondary non-tertiary education			Tertiary education		
			Change in expenditure	Change in the number of students	Change in expenditure per student	Change in expenditure	Change in the number of students	Change in expenditure per student
			1	2	3	4	5	6
WEI participants								
Brazil[1,2]	2001	1995	122	117	104	125	142	88
Chile	2002	1995	200	117	171	176	151	116
India[1,2]	2001/02	1995/96	201	138	146	204	136	150
Jamaica	2001/02	1995/96	137	98	140	...	152	...
Malaysia[2]	2002	1995	233	113	206	360	238	151
Paraguay	2002	1995	215	122	176	...	...	..
Philippines[2]	2002	1995	160	127	126	158	167	94
Thailand	2002/03	1995/96	122	79	154	...	314	...
Tunisia[2]	2002/03	1995/96	131	105	125	146	189	77
WEI mean	*2002*	*1995*	*169*	*113*	*150*	*195*	*186*	*113*
OECD countries								
Australia	2002	1995	144	108	132	122	131	93
Austria	2002	1995	107	...	...	111	94	118
Czech Republic	2002	1995	93	93	100	118	170	69
Denmark[1]	2002	1995	125	105	118	136	105	129
Finland	2002	1995	125	108	115	118	113	104
France	2002	1995	114	97	118	114	97	117
Germany	2002	1995	108	103	104	110	100	110
Greece[2,3]	2002	1995	144	92	156	243	181	134
Hungary[4]	2002	1995	120	93	129	161	161	100
Ireland	2002	1995	142	93	152	169	131	129
Italy[2,4]	2002	1995	103	98	106	131	108	121
Japan[1]	2002	1995	107	85	125	120	102	118
Korea	2002	1995	...	91	...	...	158	...
Mexico	2002	1995	135	111	121	172	142	121
Netherlands	2002	1995	137	104	131	110	107	103
New Zealand[2]	2002	1995	148	...	...	106	...	...
Norway[3]	2002	1995	121	116	105	110	104	105
Poland[2]	2002	1995	144	87	165	166	197	84
Portugal[2,4]	2002	1995	137	81	170	135	132	102
Slovak Republic	2002	1995	117	92	127	149	177	84
Spain[2]	2002	1995	109	81	134	151	115	132
Sweden	2002	1995	112	117	96	115	135	85
Switzerland[2,4]	2002	1995	113	107	106	149	106	141
Turkey[2,4]	2002	1995	171	115	148	191	110	174
United Kingdom	2002	1995	136	121	112	118	118	100
United States[2]	2002	1995	129	106	122	...	117	...
OECD mean	*2002*	*1995*	*126*	*100*	*126*	*138*	*128*	*112*

1. Post-secondary non-tertiary included in both upper secondary and tertiary education.
2. Public expenditure only.
3. Pre-primary included in primary. secondary and post-secondary non-tertiary education.
4. Public institutions only.
Source: OECD/UNESCO WEI.
Please refer to the Reader's Guide for information concerning the symbols replacing missing data.

■ ANNEX A5*a* –
INTERNATIONAL STANDARD CLASSIFICATION OF EDUCATION (ISCED97)

■ ANNEX A5*b* –
ALLOCATION OF NATIONAL EDUCATION PROGRAMMES TO ISCED97

- Argentina
- Brazil
- Chile
- China
- Egypt
- India
- Indonesia
- Jamaica
- Jordan
- Malaysia
- Paraguay
- Peru
- Philippines
- Russian Federation
- Sri Lanka
- Thailand
- Tunisia
- Uruguay
- Zimbabwe

■ ANNEX A5a
INTERNATIONAL STANDARD CLASSIFICATION OF EDUCATION (ISCED97)

0 PRE-PRIMARY LEVEL	**Main criteria**	**Auxiliary criteria**
Initial stage of organized instruction, designed primarily to introduce very young children to a school-type environment.	Should be centre- or school-based, designed to meet the educational and developmental needs of children at least three years of age, and have staff that are adequately trained (i.e. qualified) to provide an educational programme for the children.	Pedagogical qualifications for the teaching staff; implementation of a curriculum with educational elements.

1 PRIMARY LEVEL	**Main criteria**	**Auxiliary criteria**
Normally designed to give students a sound basic education in reading, writing and mathematics.	Beginning of systematic studies characteristic of primary education, e.g. reading, writing and mathematics. Entry into the nationally designated primary institutions or programmes. The commencement of reading activities alone is not a sufficient criterion for classification of an educational programme at ISCED 1.	In countries where the age of compulsory attendance (or at least the age at which virtually all students begin their education) comes after the beginning of systematic study in the subjects noted, the first year of compulsory attendance should be used to determine the boundary between ISCED 0 and ISCED 1.

2 LOWER SECONDARY LEVEL	**Main criteria**	**Auxiliary criteria**
The lower secondary level of education generally continues the basic programmes of the primary level, although teaching is typically more subject-focused, often employing more specialized teachers who conduct classes in their field of specialization. The end of compulsory education in most WEI countries.	Programmes at the start of Level 2 should correspond to the point where programmes are beginning to be organized in a more subject-oriented pattern, using more specialized teachers conducting classes in their field of specialization. If this organizational transition point does not correspond with a natural split in the boundaries between national educational programmes, then programmes should be split at the point where national programmes begin to reflect this organizational change.	If there is no clear break point for this organizational change, countries should artificially split national programmes into ISCED 1 and 2 at the end of six years of primary education. In countries with no system break between lower secondary and upper secondary education, and where lower secondary education lasts for more than three years, only the first three years following primary education should be counted as lower secondary education.

3 UPPER SECONDARY LEVEL	**Main criteria**	**Modular programmes**
Instruction is often more organized along subject-matter lines than at ISCED 2 and teachers typically need to have a higher level or more subject-specific qualification than at ISCED 2.	National boundaries between lower secondary and upper secondary education should be the dominant factor for splitting Levels 2 and 3. Admission into educational programmes usually require the completion of ISCED 2 for admission, or a combination of basic education and life experience that demonstrates the ability to handle ISCED 3 subject matter.	An educational qualification is earned in a modular programme by combining blocks of courses, or modules, into a programme meeting specific curricular requirements. A single module, however, may not have a specific educational or labour market destination or a particular programme orientation. Modular programmes should be classified at Level 3 only, without reference to the educational or labour market destination of the programme.

4 POST-SECONDARY NON-TERTIARY	**Main criteria**	**Types of programmes which can fit into Level 4**
These programmes straddle the boundary between upper secondary and post-secondary education from an international point of view, even though they might clearly be considered as upper secondary or post-secondary programmes in a national context. They are often not significantly more advanced than programmes at ISCED 3 but they serve to broaden the knowledge of participants who have already completed a programme at Level 3. The students are typically older than those in ISCED 3 programmes. ISCED 4 programmes typically have a full-time-equivalent (FTE) duration of between six months and two years.	Students entering ISCED 4 programmes will typically have completed ISCED 3. As described above, successful completion of any programme at Level 3A or 3B counts as a Level 3 completion. For 3C programmes, a cumulative theoretical duration of three years is specified in ISCED97 as the minimum programme length in order meet the requirements for a Level 3 completion.	Short vocational programmes where either the content is not considered 'tertiary' in many OECD countries or the programme does not meet the duration requirement for ISCED 5B – at least two years FTE since the start of Level 5. These programmes are often designed for students who have completed Level 3, although a formal ISCED 3 qualification may not be required for entry. Also, programmes are nationally considered as upper secondary programmes, even though entrants to these programmes will have typically already completed another upper secondary programme (i.e. second-cycle programmes).

5 FIRST STAGE OF TERTIARY EDUCATION	**Classification criteria for level and sub-categories (5A and 5B)**	
ISCED 5 programmes have an educational content more advanced than those offered at Levels 3 and 4.	Entry to these programmes normally requires the successful completion of ISCED 3A or 3B or a similar qualification at ISCED 4A or 4B (see next page). Programmes at Level 5 must have a cumulative theoretical duration of at least two years from the beginning of the first programme.	
5A ISCED 5A programmes are largely theoretically based and intended to provide sufficient qualifications for gaining entry into advanced research programmes and professions with high skills requirements.	1. A minimum cumulative theoretical duration (at tertiary level) of three years (FTE). 2. Typically requires that the faculty have advanced research credentials. 3. May involve completion of a research project or thesis. 4. Provides the level of education required for entry into a profession with high skills requirements or an advanced research programme.	
5B ISCED 5B programmes are generally more practical/technical/occupationally specific than ISCED 5A programmes.	1. More practically oriented and occupationally specific than programmes at ISCED 5A and does not prepare students for direct access to advanced research programmes. 2. A minimum of two years' FTE duration. 3. Programme content is typically designed to prepare students to enter a particular occupation.	

6 SECONDARY STAGE OF TERTIARY EDUCATION (Leading to an advanced research qualification)		
This level is reserved for tertiary programmes that lead to the award of an advanced research qualification. The programmes are devoted to advanced study and original research.	1. Requires the submission of a thesis or dissertation of publishable quality that is the product of original research and represents a significant contribution to knowledge. 2. Not solely based on course work. 3. Prepares recipients for faculty posts in institutions offering ISCED 5A programmes as well as research posts in government and industry.	

Destination for which the programmes have been designed to prepare students	Programme orientation
2A Programmes designed to prepare students for direct access to Level 3 in a sequence which would ultimately lead to tertiary education, i.e. entrance to ISCED 3A or 3B.	G General
2B Programmes designed to prepare students for direct access to programmes at Level 3C.	P Pre-vocational or pre-technical
2C Programmes primarily designed for direct access to the labour market at the end of this level (sometimes referred to as 'terminal' programmes).	V Vocational or Technical

Destination for which the programmes have been designed to prepare students	Programme orientation
3A Programmes at Level 3 designed to provide direct access to ISCED 5A.	G General
3B Programmes at Level 3 designed to provide direct access to ISCED 5B.	P Pre-vocational or pre-technical
3C Programmes at Level 3 not designed to lead directly to ISCED 5A or 5B. These programmes lead to other ISCED 3 programmes, ISCED 4 programmes or the labour market.	V Vocational or Technical

Destination for which the programmes have been designed to prepare students	Programme orientation
4A Programmes at Level 4, designed to provide direct access to ISCED 5A.	G General
4B Programmes at Level 4, designed to provide direct access to ISCED 5B.	P Pre-vocational or pre-technical
4C Programmes at Level 4 not designed to lead directly to ISCED 5A or 5B. These programmes lead directly to other ISCED 4 programmes or the labour market.	V Vocational or Technical

Cumulative theoretical duration at ISCED Level 5A*	Position in the national degree and qualification structure
5A Short: three years or less Medium: more than three years to five years Long: more than five years	5A Intermediate; First; Second; Third.
* ISCED97 duration categories have been modified slightly to suit programmes in WEI countries.	5B Intermediate; First; Second; Third and further.

LEGEND

PROGRAMME ORIENTATION

G *Type 1: General education*
Education which is not designed explicitly to prepare participants for a specific class of occupations or trades or for entry into further vocational / technical education programmes. Less than 25 % of the programme content is vocational or technical.

P *Type 2: Pre-vocational or pre-technical*
Education mainly designed as an introduction to the world of work and as preparation for further vocational or technical education. Does not lead to a labour-market relevant qualification. Content is at least 25 per cent vocational or technical.

V *Type 3: Vocational or technical*
Education which prepares participants for direct entry, without further training, into specific occupations. Successful completion of such programmes leads to a labour-market relevant vocational qualification.

ANNEX A5*b*
ALLOCATION OF NATIONAL EDUCATION PROGRAMMES TO ISCED97

ARGENTINA

ISCED97 level for WEI data collection	Programme orientation	Country description of programme	Entrance requirements	Qualifications awarded	Theoretical starting age (in years)	Theoretical ending age (in years)	Theoretical duration of the programme (in years)	Theoretical cumulative years of education at the end of the programme	Notes	ISCED97 Flows
0		Pre-primary (*Inicial*)			3	5	2	...		0
0		Pre-primary, compulsory (*Inicial*)			5	6	1	...	Compulsory for 5-year-olds, and 4-year-olds in some provinces.	
1		General basic, 1st and 2nd cycles (*Educación general básica 1er y 2do ciclo*)	Compulsory pre-primary		6	12	6	6	Typically a five-hour school day.	1
2A	General	General Basic, 3rd cycle (*Educación General Básica 3er ciclo*)	General basic, 2nd cycle	Lower secondary diploma	12	15	3	9	Separate schools for youths with severe disabilities.	2A
3A	General/ Vocational	Upper secondary (*Polimodal*)	Lower secondary diploma	Upper secondary diploma	15	18	3	12	General and technical education. It is possible to earn a technical qualification through combined work and study.	3A
5B		Tertiary Non-University (*Superior no universitario*)	Upper secondary diploma	Primary and secondary teacher's diploma; technician diploma	18	21–22	3–4	15–16	Training for primary and secondary school teachers. Occupational training for laboratory technicians, radio operators, mechanics, librarians, social workers, *etc.*	5B
5A (1st, medium)		Tertiary-university (*Superior universitario*)	Upper secondary diploma	*Licenciatura* or professional qualification.	18	23–24	5–6	17–18	Professional qualifications can be earned at the same time as the licenciatura (*e.g.* engineering or economic degrees). Medical programmes are six years in duration, fine arts programmes are seven years.	5A
5A (2nd)		Master's, post-graduate courses (*Posgrados*)	University degree (*e.g.* Licenciatura, Accountant, Lawyer)	Master's degree, specialisation diploma	...	...	...	...	ISCED 5A, second-degree programmes were recently introduced and do not have uniform curricular organisation and entrance requirements. Thus, it is difficult to indicate typical starting and completion ages, duration, *etc.*	
6		Doctorate programmes (*Doctorado*)	Tertiary university diploma (*e.g.* Licenciatura, Accountant, Lawyer)	Doctorate	...	...	...	...	ISCED 6 programmes were recently introduced and do not have uniform curricular organisation and entrance requirements. Thus, it is difficult to indicate typical starting and completion ages, duration, *etc.*	6

BRAZIL

ISCED97 level for WEI data collection	Programme orientation	Country description of programme	Entrance requirements	Qualifications awarded	Theoretical starting age (in years)	Theoretical ending age (in years)	Theoretical duration of the programme (in years)	Theoretical cumulative years of education at the end of the programme	Notes	ISCED97 Flows
–		Nursery schools/ day care centres (*Creche*)			<3	4	…	…	Nursery schools/day care centres – children aged 3 years and less.	**0**
0		Pre-school (*Pré-escola*)			4	7	3	…	Pre-school - children aged 4-6 years.	
0		Literacy classrooms for children (*Classe de Alfabetização*)			6	7	1	…	Literacy classrooms for children aged 6 years.	
1		Primary education: Grades 1-4 (*Ensino Fundamental de 1ª a 4ª série*)			7	11	4	4	Beginning of compulsory schooling.	**1**
1		Youth and adult education – EJA literacy programs. Grades 1-4 (*Educação de Jovens e Adultos- EJA Alfabetização 1ª a 4ª série*)	14 years old and above		14+	…	4	…	Duration of the programme: flexible, up to 4 years. Schools offering this modality of education may assess students to assign them to a grade-level if they do not have a record of previous formal schooling. EJA programmes do not have uniform curricular organisation (cycles, phases, graded system, *etc.*).	
2A	General	Elementary education Grades 5-8 (*Ensino fundamental de 5ª a 8ª série*)	Primary education	Elementary education certificate – Grades 1-8 (*Certificado de Conclusão do Ensino Fundamental*)	11	15	4	8	Ending of compulsory schooling	
2A	General	Youth and adult education – EJA (*EJA*)	Primary education + age of 14 years-old and above	Elementary education certificate – Grades 1-8 (*Certificado de Conclusão do Ensino Fundamental*)	14+	…	4	…	Duration of the programme: flexible, up to 4 years. EJA programmes do not have uniform curricular organisation (cycles, phases, graded system, *etc.*).	**2A**
3A	General	Secondary education (*Ensino Médio*)	Elementary education certificate	Secondary education certificate (*Certificado de Conclusão do Ensino Médio*)	15	18	3	11	Enrolments in teacher education courses at the secondary level (normal) included.	**3A**
3A	General	Youth and adult education at the secondary level (*Educação de jovens e adultos- EJA ensino médio*)	Elementary education certificate + age of 17 years-old and above	Secondary education certificate (*Certificado de Conclusão do Ensino Médio*)	14+	…	3	…	Duration of the programme: flexible. EJA programmes do not have uniform curricular organisation (cycles, phase, graded system, *etc.*).	
3C	Vocational	Teacher education in the modality normal at the secondary level (*Formação de professores na modalidade normal em nível médio*)	Elementary education certificate	Teaching Certificate (*Certicado de Magistério*)	15	18	3	11	Teacher education at the secondary level (in the modality normal) programmes prepare teachers to teach at Early childhood and primary (Grades 1-4) Education programmes. According to the National Education Guidelines and Framework Law (LDB) of 1996, these teachers should earn Teacher education at the tertiary level (non-university) by the end of 2006.	**3C**

…

BRAZIL *(continued)*

ISCED97 level for WEI data collection	Programme orientation	Country description of programme	Entrance requirements	Qualifications awarded	Theoretical starting age (in years)	Theoretical ending age (in years)	Theoretical duration of the programme (in years)	Theoretical cumulative years of education at the end of the programme	Notes	ISCED97 Flows
3C	Vocational	Professional education -technical level at secondary level (*Educação Profissional de Nível Técnico*)	Secondary education certificate	Technical Diploma, including the name of the occupation (*Diploma de Técnico nome da ocupação*)	18+	...	...	...	According to the National Education Guidelines and Framework Law (LDB) of 1996, to enroll in the Professional Technical Education programmes (at the secondary level) students should be enrolled in the secondary education programme (general) or have earned the Secondary Education Certificate. However, it is required that students complete secondary education in order to receive the Diploma de Técnico (Technical Diploma at the Secondary-Level). These programmes prepare participants for direct entry into specific occupations, without further training. The programme content focuses on labour market curricular requirements. Successful completion of such programmes leads to a labour-market relevant vocational qualification (Technical Diploma at the Secondary-Level).	
5A and 5B		Higher education (tertiary university) (*Educação Superior*)	Secondary education certificate	Teacher´s Diploma (*Diploma de Licenciatura Plena*), Bachelor´s Diploma (*Diploma de Bacharel*) and Professional´s Diploma (*Diploma Específico da Profissão*)	18	22–24	4-6	15-17	Professional qualifications can be earned at the same time as the bachelor or teacher's diploma. Medical programmes are six years in duration. Data on 5A and 5B are aggregated (for the WEI tables).	**5A** **5B**
6		Master's programmes [*Mestrado (Pós-graduação stricto sensu)*]	University tertiary education diploma	Master's degree (*Diploma de Mestrado*)	24	26	2	17	Submission of thesis required. Prepares for research position.	
6		Doctorate programmes (*Doutorado (Pós-Graduação stricto sensu)*)	Tertiary university diploma or Masters degree	Doctorate´s Degree (*Diploma de Doutorado*)	30–40	...	4	21	Submission of thesis required.	**6**

CHILE

ISCED97 level for WEI data collection	Programme orientation	Country description of programme	Entrance requirements	Qualifications awarded	Theoretical starting age (in years)	Theoretical ending age (in years)	Theoretical duration of the programme (in years)	Theoretical cumulative years of education at the end of the programme	Notes	ISCED97 Flows
0		Pre-primary			3	6	3	…		0
1		Basic education (Grades 1-6)			6	12	6	6	For the purposes of ISCED, the last two grades (7-8) are reported as ISCED 2A.	1
2A	General	Basic education (Grades 7-8)	Grade 6 basic education	Basic Education Diploma	12	14	2	8		2A
3A	General	Secondary education (Grades 9-12)	Basic education diploma	Middle Education Diploma	14	18	4	12		3A
3A	Vocational	Secondary education	Basic education diploma		14	18	4	12		
5B		Tertiary, technical	Secondary education diploma	Technical Diploma with specific specialisation	18	22	4	16	Some institutions require passing a national examination for entrance.	5B
5A (1st, medium)		Tertiary, professional (mostly university)	Secondary education diploma	Bachelor's degree or other professional qualification	18	23	5	17	The first degree in most universities. Most institutions require passing a national examination for entrance.	5A
5A (2nd, short)		Tertiary, professional	Bachelor's degree or other professional qualification	Post-graduate diploma	24	25	1	18		
5A (2nd)		Master's	Bachelor's degree or other professional qualification	Master's degree	24	26	2	19		
6		Doctorate	Master's degree	Doctorate	26	29	3	22		6

CHINA

ISCED97 level for WEI data collection	Programme orientation	Country description of programme	Entrance requirements	Qualifications awarded	Theoretical starting age (in years)	Theoretical ending age (in years)	Theoretical duration of the programme (in years)	Theoretical cumulative years of education at the end of the programme (in years)	Notes
0		Pre-primary			4	7	3	…	Mostly full-time.
1		Primary			7	12–13	5–6	5–6	
2A		Lower secondary (junior secondary school)	Primary		12	15–16	3–4	8–10	
2C		Lower secondary	Primary		12	15	3	8–9	Programme offered in special schools in rural areas, aims at training workers, peasants and employees in other sectors with basic professional knowledge and certain professional skills.
3A	General/ Pre-vocational	Upper secondary (senior secondary school)	Junior secondary school		15	18	3	11–13	
3C	Vocational	Upper secondary (senior secondary school)	Junior secondary school		…	…	3	11–13	
4C		Post-secondary, non-tertiary	Secondary		…	…	…	…	Generally, occupationally specific training but at a lower level than programmes reported in 5B.
5B		Tertiary, non-university	Secondary and pass national undergraduate entrance examination	Diploma	18	20–21	2–3	13–16	Generally, occupationally specific training.
5A (1st, medium)		University	Secondary and pass national undergraduate entrance examination	Bachelor's degree	18	22	4	15–17	
5A (1st, medium)		University	Secondary and pass national undergraduate entrance examination	Bachelor's degree	18	23	5	16–18	Engineering and medicine.
5A (2nd)		Master's	Bachelor's degree	Master's degree	22	24–25	2–3	17–20	
6		Doctorate	Master's degree	Doctorate	24	27–28	3–4	20–24	

ISCED97 Flows

EGYPT

ISCED97 level for WEI data collection	Programme orientation	Country description of programme	Entrance requirements	Qualifications awarded	Theoretical starting age (in years)	Theoretical ending age (in years)	Theoretical duration of the programme (in years)	Theoretical cumulative years of education at the end of the programme	Notes
0		Pre-primary			4	6	2	...	
1		Primary			6	11	5	5	
2A	General	Preparatory school	Primary	Basic education certificate	11	14	3	8	
2C		Vocational school	Two repetitions in primary school	Certificate	13	16	3	8	
3A	General	General secondary school	High score on basic education certificate examination	Secondary school leaving certificate (*Thanawiya Amma*)	14	17	3	11	Must pass secondary school leaving examination to graduate.
3C	Vocational	Technical school	Basic education certificate	Middle diploma	14	17–19	3–5	11–13	
4C	Vocational	Industrial, commercial and technical institutes	Secondary school leaving certificate (*Thanawiya Amma*)	Above-middle diploma	17	19–20	2–3	13–14	Some new institutions offer programmes of less than two years in duration.
5B		Community service, non-credit; industrial, commercial and technical institutes or programmes within university	According to field of study	Certificate	17	18–19	0.5–2	11.5–13	Some universities offer two-year, occupationally specific programmes such as accounting, secretarial, computer sciences and electronics.
5A (long)		University	High score on secondary school leaving examination	Bachelor's degree or licence	17	21–23	4–6	15–17	Medical programmes are seven years in duration.
5A (2nd)		Master's	Bachelor's degree or licence	Master's degree	21–23	23–26	2–3	17–20	
6		Doctorate	Master's degree	Doctorate	23–25	25+	2+	19+	

ISCED97 Flows

0
1
2A
2C
3A
3C
4C
5B
5A
6

INDIA

ISCED97 level for WEI data collection	Programme orientation	Country description of programme	Entrance requirements	Qualifications awarded	Theoretical starting age (in years)	Theoretical ending age (in years)	Theoretical duration of the programme (in years)	Theoretical cumulative years of education at the end of the programme	Notes	ISCED97 Flows
0		Pre-primary	Test, age (3-5)	Pre-primary certificate	3	5 or 6	2 or 3	...		**0**
1		Primary	Age 6	Primary certificate	6	11	5	5	In some provinces admission to class 1 is 5+ years, in others it is 6+ years.	**1**
1		Primary – Education Guarantee Scheme and Altenative and Innovative scheme (EGS & AIE)	Age 7	Primary certificate	7	...	...	...	The main objective of this scheme is to enrol children who are not attending schools because the school is too far away from their place of residence, dropouts, older unenroled and children needing flexible norms of education.	
2A	General	Upper primary	Primary certificate	Upper primary certificate	11	14	3	8	In some states, the state school boards conduct public examinations at Grade 8. Candidates must pass a minimum of five subjects.	**2A**
2C	Vocational	Industrial Training Institute (ITI), lower-level technical and vocational	Upper primary certificate	ITI Certificate	14	15	1	9	Examinations are conducted by the State Technical Boards supervised by the National Council for Vocational Training.	**2C**
3A (part-1)	General	High school	Upper primary certificate	Matriculation certificate	14	16	2	10	Matriculation certificate awarded after 10 years of schooling and passing a public examination organised by Secondary School Boards.	**3A**
3A (part-2)	General	Senior secondary/ Intermediate	Matriculation certificate	Senior secondary-school-leaving-certificate	16	18	2	12	Senior certificate awarded after 12 years of schooling and passing a public examination organised by Higher Secondary/Intermediate Boards.	
3C	Vocational	Senior school level cerificate courses in agriculture and forestery/nursing/ music & fine arts/ arts & craft, etc.	Matriculation certificate	Senior school certificate in agriculture & forestery/nursing/ music & fine arts/ arts & crafts, etc.	16	18	2	12	Senior school cerificate awarded in agriculture & forestery/nursing/music & fine arts/arts & crafts.	**3C**
4B	Vocational	Technical education training	Matriculation certificate	Diploma in technical education	16	19	3	13	Diploma is granted in a specific field like electrical, mechanical, agricultural, civil studies, *etc.*	**4B**
4C	Vocational	Junior basic teacher's training/ nursing	Senior secondary school leaving certificate	Junior basic teacher's training/nursing certificate	18	20	2	14	Junior basic teachers training and all other programmes are market oriented and terminal courses.	**4C**
5B		Tertiary, technical	Senior secondary school leaving certificate	Diploma/ certificate equivalent to Bachelor's degree	18	21	3	15	Nursing, paramedical studies, fashion designing, *etc.*	**5B**
5A(1st)		Tertiary, professional	Senior secondary school leaving certificate	Bachelor's degree	18	22	4	16	Agriculture, medical, engineering and architecture.	**5A**
5A (1st, short)		University	Senior secondary pre-university certificate	Bachelor's degree	18	21	3	15		
5A (2nd)		University	Bachelor's degree	Bachelor of Education	21	22	1	16		
5A (2nd)		University	Bachelor's degree	Bachelor of Law	21	24	3	18		
5A (2nd)		Master's degree	Bachelor's degree	Master's degree	21	23	2	17	Master's degree is awarded in the specialised subject/field.	
6(1st)		Master of Philosophy	Master's degree	Master of Philosophy	23	25	2	19	Specialised degree is awarded in a particular field.	**6**
6(1st)		Doctor of Philosophy	Master's/ Master of Philosophy	Doctor of Philosophy	25	28	3	22		
6 (2nd)		Doctor of Letters	Doctor of Philosophy (Ph.D.)	Doctor of Literature/ Doctor of Science	...	...	2	24	Awarded by some universities.	

INDONESIA

ISCED97 level for WEI data collection	Programme orientation	Country description of programme	Entrance requirements	Qualifications awarded	Theoretical starting age (in years)	Theoretical ending age (in years)	Theoretical duration of the programme (in years)	Theoretical cumulative years of education at the end of the programme	Notes	ISCED97 Flows
0		Pre-primary (playgroup) (*Kelompok Bermain*)			3	4–5	1–2	…		
0		Kindergarten (*Taman Kanak-kanak*)			5	6–7	1–2	…		
1		Primary (*Sekolah Dasar*)			7	13	6	6		
2A	General	Junior secondary, general [*Sekolah Menengah Pertama (SMP)*]	Graduation from primary school	Junior secondary certificate	13	16	3	9		
3A	General	Senior secondary, general [*Sekolah Menengah Atas (SMA)*]	Junior secondary certificate	Secondary school leaving certificate	16	19	3	12		
3B	Vocational	Senior secondary, technical/vocational [*Sekolah Menengah Kejuruan (SMK)*]	Junior secondary certificate	Secondary school leaving certificate	16	19–20	3–4	12–13		
5B (1st)		Diploma I programmes	Secondary school leaving certificate and an entrance examination	Diploma (DI)	19	20	1	13–14		
5B (1st)		Diploma II programmes	Secondary school leaving certificate and an entrance examination	Diploma (DII)	19	21	2	14–15		
5B (1st)		Diploma III programmes	Secondary school leaving certificate and an entrance examination	Diploma (DIII)	19	22	3	15–16	Entitles graduates to teach one subject at lower secondary level.	
5B (1st)		Diploma IV programmes	Secondary school leaving certificate and an entrance examination	Diploma (DIV)	19	23	4	16–17	Equivalent to graduate diploma (SI).	
5A (1st, short and long)		Degree stream (*Program Sarjana*)	Secondary school leaving certificate and an entrance examination	Graduate diploma (SI)	19	23–25	4–6	16–18	Most degrees are 4 years, some take longer, *i.e.* law and medicine.	
5B (2nd)		Specialist I programmes	Diploma (DIV) or Graduate diploma (SI)	Specialist I (SpI)	23	26–28	3–5	19–22	Certificate awarded in the non-degree stream equivalent to Master's. Usually requires original research or a special contribution to a field of study.	
5A (2nd)		Master's programmes (*Program Magister*)	Graduate diploma (SI)	Master's degree (SII)	23	25–28	2–5	18–23		
6		Specialist II programmes	Specialist I (SpI)	Specialist II (SpII)	25	28–30	3–5	22–27	Equivalent to a Doctorate. Usually requires original research or a special contribution to a field of study.	
6		Doctorate programmes (*Program Doktor*)	Master's degree (SII)	Doctorate degree (SIII)	25	28–30	3–5	21–28	Includes professional degrees awarded in faculties of medicine, veterinary medicine and dentistry.	

ISCED97 Flows: 0 → 1 → 2A → 3A → 3B → 5B → 5A → 5B → 5A → 6 → 6

JAMAICA

ISCED97 level for WEI data collection	Programme orientation	Country description of programme	Entrance requirements	Qualifications awarded	Theoretical starting age (in years)	Theoretical ending age (in years)	Theoretical duration of the programme (in years)	Theoretical cumulative years of education at the end of the programme	Notes	ISCED97 Flows
0		Pre-primary (Early childhood education)			3-4	5-7	2-3	...		
1		Primary			6	12	6	6		
2A		Lower secondary (1st cycle secondary)	Completion of primary education	Junior high school certificate	12	15	3	9		
3A		Upper secondary (2nd cycle secondary)	Completion of lower secondary	Caribbean Secondary Examination Certificate (CSEC); General Certificate Examination (GCE) Ordinary Level (O-level)	15	17	2	11		
3B		Upper secondary (2nd cycle secondary)	Completion of lower secondary	Caribbean Secondary Examination Certificate (CSEC); General Certificate Examination (GCE) Ordinary Level (O-level); Secondary School Certificate (SSC); Agricultural Certificate	15	17	2	11		
4A*		Post-secondary non-tertiary	Completion of upper secondary with 4 or more CSEC including mathematics and english	Caribbean Advanced Proficiency Examination (CAPE); GCE Advanced Level (A-level)	17	19	2	13		
4B		Post-secondary non-tertiary	Completion of upper secondary with less than 4 CSEC or school leaving certificate including mathematics and english	Technical or other non-tertiary certificate or diploma	17	19	2	13		
5B		Tertiary (Professional/ Diploma/ Certificate/ Associate degree programmes)	Completion of upper secondary or post-secondary with CSEC; GCE (A-level), CAPE, or any equivalent certificate	Professional or technical certificate or diploma (e.g. Teacher's Diploma, Nursing Diploma, etc.)	17	19–21	2-4	13–15		
5A (1st)		Undergraduate programmes (Tertiary undergraduate)	Completion of upper secondary or post-secondary with CSEC; A-level; CAPE or any equivalent certificate or completion of professional certificate or diploma	Bachelor's degree	17	20	3	14		
5A (2nd)		Graduate programmes (Higher education)	First degree	Master's degree, Post-graduate diploma/certificate	21	23–24	1.5-3	16–17		
6		Doctorate (Higher education)	Master's degree	Doctorate	23	25+	2+	18+		

* Upper secondary programmes equivalent to the Anglo-Saxon O-level and
A-level are classified differently in different countries. For comparison reasons,
graduates from 4A programmes in Jamaica are considered as 3A graduates in
this report.

JORDAN

ISCED97 level for WEI data collection	Programme orientation	Country description of programme	Entrance requirements	Qualifications awarded	Theoretical starting age (in years)	Theoretical ending age (in years)	Theoretical duration of the programme (in years)	Theoretical cumulative years of education at the end of the programme	Notes	ISCED97 Flows
0		Pre-primary (Kindergarten)			4	6	2	...	Run almost exclusively by private agencies.	0
1		Primary (Basic education, 1st cycle)			6	12	6	6		1
2A	General	Lower secondary (Basic education, 2nd cycle)	Basic education, 1st cycle		12	16	4	10		2A
3A	General	Upper secondary education (Comprehensive secondary education)	Basic education, 2nd cycle	General Secondary Education Certificate	16	18	2	12		3A
3C	Vocational	Upper secondary (Applied secondary education)	Basic education, 2nd cycle	Completion Certificate	16	18	2	12	Preparation of skilled workers in training centres and formal apprenticeship schemes. Apprenticeships are followed by one year of supervised employment.	3C
5B		Tertiary non-university (Community college programmes)	Passage of General (Academic) Secondary Education Certificate Examination	Diploma; entrance to ISCED 5A university programmes	18	20	2	14	Graduates with highest marks can enter to ISCED 5A programmes. Includes special programmes (theoretically oriented vocational) for teacher training which can lead to the ISCED 5A 1st short university programme.	5B
5B		Tertiary non-university (Community college programmes)	Passage of General (Academic) Secondary Education Certificate Examination	Diploma in technology	18	21	3	15		
5A (1st, short)		Tertiary university programmes	Community college diploma and teaching experience	Bachelor's degree	18	21	3	15	Practising teachers who have community college diplomas can enter university to upgrade their qualifications through a special government programme.	5A
5A (1st, long)		Tertiary university programmes	Passage of General (Academic or Vocational) Secondary Education Certificate Exam, or Community College Diploma with high marks	Bachelor's degree	18	22–24	4–6	16–18	Five year programmes in engineering, pharmacy and dentistry, six year programme in medicine	
5A (2nd)		Education diploma programmes	Bachelor's degree	Diploma in education	23	24	1	18		
5A (2nd)		Master's programmes	Bachelor's degree	Master's degree	23	25–26	2–3	19–20		
6		Doctorate programmes	Master's degree	Doctorate	25	28–29	3–4	22–23		6

MALAYSIA

ISCED97 level for WEI data collection	Programme orientation	Country description of programme	Entrance requirements	Qualifications awarded	Theoretical starting age (in years)	Theoretical ending age (in years)	Theoretical duration of the programme (in years)	Theoretical cumulative years of education at the end of the programme (in years)	Notes	ISCED97 Flows
0		Pre-school			4	5	1	…		**0**
1		Primary	School age	Primary school achievement test	6	12	6	6		**1**
2A	General	'Remove' class	Primary		12	13	1	7	Pupils from Chinese and Tamil primary school spend a year in the Remove class to become proficient in Bahasa Melayu language before the transition to secondary school.	**2A**
2A	General	Lower secondary (Forms 1-3)	Primary	Lower secondary assessment	12	15	3	9	Students who do not pass the lower certificate of education examination enter the labour market.	
3C	General	Upper secondary (Forms 4-5), academic	Lower secondary assessment	Certificate of education	15	17	2	11	Based on performance in the lower certificate of education examination, students are placed in either academic or technical and vocational schools.	**3C**
3C	Vocational	Upper secondary (Forms 4-5), technical and vocational	Lower secondary assessment	Certificate of education	15	17	2	11		
3A	General	Pre-university (Form 6, GCE, A-level)	Certificate of education	Higher school certificate of examination, General Certificate of Education (GCE)	17	19	2	13	Two-year pre-university course that prepares students for the higher school certificate examination.	**3A**
3A	General	Pre-university matriculation	Certificate of education	Matriculation certificate	17	19	2	13		
4C		Post-secondary, teacher training	Certificate of education	Teaching certificate	17	18	1	12	Training of pre-primary teachers.	**4C**
4C		Skills training	Certificate of education	Certificate	17	18–19	1–2	12–13		
5B		Tertiary, teacher training	Certificate of education	Teaching diploma, diploma in education	18	20–21	2–3	13–14	Training of pre-primary and primary teachers.	**5B**
5B		Tertiary, polytechnical	Certificate of education	Certificate or diploma in various engineering fields	18	20–22	2–4	13–15		
5A (1st, short)		University	Higher school certificate of examination, GCE	Bachelor's degree	19	22	3	16		**5A**
5A (1st, long)		University	Higher school certificate of examination, GCE	Bachelor's degree	19	24–25	5–6	18–19	These programmes include medicine, dentistry and veterinary science.	
5A (2nd)		Master's	Bachelor's degree	Master's degree	24	26–27	2–3	18–19		
6		Doctorate	Master's degree	Doctorate	24	26	2	20–21		**6**
6 (2nd)		Doctorate	Master's degree or doctorate	Doctorate of law, literature or science	24+	29+	5–7	23–26		

PARAGUAY

ISCED97 level for WEI data collection	Programme orientation	Country description of programme	Entrance requirements	Qualifications awarded	Theoretical starting age (in years)	Theoretical ending age (in years)	Theoretical duration of the programme (in years)	Theoretical cumulative years of education at the end of the programme	Notes	ISCED97 Flows
0		Nursery school (*Jardín Maternal*)			2	5	3	...		**0**
0		Initial education (pre-primary) (*Educación Inicial*)			4	6	2	...	This level of education is not compulsory. Includes kindergarten for 4-years-olds and pre-school for 5-years-olds.	
1		Basic school education, 1st and 2nd cycles (*Educación Escolar Básica, 1° y 2° ciclo*)			6	12	6	6	1st and 2nd cycle of compulsory education.	**1**
1		Adult basic education (*Educación Básica de Adultos*)			15+	...	3	...	These programmes are designed to give adults who have not completed Basic School Education a second chance to do so.	
1		Special needs education (*Educación Especial*)			...	...	6	6	This programme provides educational services to mentally, physically or emotionally disadvantaged students and others groups with special learning needs.	
2A	General	Basic School Education, 3rd cycle (*Educación Escolar Básica, 3° ciclo*)	Approval of Basic School Education 2nd cycle	Basic School Education-leaving certificate	12	15	3	9	3rd cycle of compulsory education.	**2A**
2C	Vocational	Professional Formation (*Formación Profesional*)	Approval of Basic School Education 2nd cycle	Vocational Certificate	15+	16–18	1 or 3	7 or 9	Occupationally specific training courses. Length of programmes varies from 1 year to 3 years and are organised in a modular system.	**2C**
3A	General/ Vocational	Humanistic-scientist baccalaureate (*Educación Media – Bachillerato Humanístico / Bachillerato Técnico*)	Approval of Basic School Education 3rd cycle	Humanistic or technical diploma	15	18	3	12	General and technical education. Entrance requirement for technical education are aptitude tests + entrance examination.	**3A**
3C	Vocational	Technical baccalaureate (*Programas Técnicos*)	Approval of Basic School Education 3rd cycle	Technical Diploma	15	17	2	11	Occupational training for auxiliary or technical professions.	**3C**
4B	Vocational	Professional education (*Educación Profesional*)	Completion of ISCED 3A	Diploma	18	19–20	1–2	13–14	These programmes are designed to help students get jobs quickly. The courses are organised in a modular system. Qualifications awarded are according to duration of the programme.	**4B**
5B		Non-university tertiary level	Completion of ISCED 3A + aptitude tests + entrance examination	Teachers of initial education, basic school education, secondary education or title of technician superior	18	21–22	3–4	15–16	Teacher training schools and occupational training for computer science technicians, business administration, social workers, *etc*.	**5B**
5B		Specialisation programmes (*Programas de Especialización*)	Completion of 5B (1st)	Specialisation diploma	21–22	23–24	2	17–18		
5A (1st)		University education (*Educación terciaria universitaria*)	Completion of ISCED 3A + entrance examination or probationary course	Licentiate or degree title	18	22–24	4–6	16–18	Length of programme varies by field of study. Includes courses of medicine, dentistry, economics, *etc*.	**5A**
5A (2nd)		Master's, Post-graduate Courses (*Programas de Post-grados: Master y Especialización*)	Completion of 5A (1st) programme	Master's degree, specialisation diploma	...	...	1–2	17–20		
6		Doctoral programme (*Doctorados*)	Degree title	Doctorate degree	...	...	3–4	19–22	Requires submission of a thesis.	**6**

PERU

ISCED97 level for WEI data collection	Programme orientation	Country description of programme	Entrance requirements	Qualifications awarded	Theoretical starting age (in years)	Theoretical ending age (in years)	Theoretical duration of the programme (in years)	Theoretical cumulative years of education at the end of the programme	Notes	ISCED97 Flows
–		Nursery (*Educación Inicial 0 a 2 años*)			0	2	2	…		**0**
0		Pre-primary, school-based (*Educación Inicial 3 a 5 años, escolarizada*)			3	6	3	…	Compulsory for 5-year-olds.	
0		Pre-primary, not school-based (*Educación Inicial 3 a 5 años, no escolarizada*)			3	6	3	…	Centre-based programmes designed for rural areas. Teaching staff without formal teaching education, but supervised by qualified staff.	
0		Pre-primary for those with special needs (*Educación Especial- Inicial 3 a 5 años*)			3	6	3	…	The content of the instruction is broadly similar to that of other ISCED 0 programmes.	
1		Primary for minors (*Educación Primaria de Menores*)		Primary certificate	6	12	6	6		**1**
1		Primary for adults (*Primaria para Adultos*)		Primary certificate	…	…	6	6	The content of the instruction is broadly similar to that of other ISCED 1 programmes.	
1		Primary for those with special needs (*Educación Especial- Primaria*)		Primary certificate	6	12	6	6	The content of the instruction is broadly similar to that of other ISCED 1 programmes.	
2A	General	Secondary- 3 first grades (*Educación Secundaria de Menores*)	Completion of primary education		12	15	3	9	Includes the modality called "technical secondary for minors", because less than 25 per cent of the programme content is vocational or technical.	**2A**
2A	General	Secondary 3 first grades for adults (*Secundaria para Adultos*)	Completion of primary education		…	…	3	9	The content of the instruction is broadly similar to that of other ISCED 2 programmes.	
2A	General	Secondary 3 first grades for those with special needs (*Educación Especial- Secundaria*)	Completion of primary education		12	15	3	9	The content of the instruction is broadly similar to that of other ISCED 2 programmes.	
3A	General	Secondary last 2 grades for minors (*Educación Secundaria de Menores*)	Secondary- 3 first grades	Secondary certificate	15	17	2	11	Includes the modality called "technical secondary for minors", because less than 25 per cent of the programme content is vocational or technical.	**3A**
3A	General	Secondary last 2 grades for adults (*Secundaria para Adultos*)	Secondary- 3 first grades	Secondary certificate	…	…	2	11	The content of the instruction is broadly similar to that of other ISCED 3 programmes.	
3A	General	Secondary last 2 grades for those with special needs (*Educación Especial- Secundaria*)	Secondary- 3 first grades	Secondary certificate	15	17	2	11	The content of the instruction is broadly similar to that of other ISCED 3 programmes.	
4C	General	Short courses offered by universities and other tertiary institutions (*Extensión universitaria*)	Secondary certificate	Certificate with mention of the course	…	…	…	…		**4C**
5B		Tertiary non-university-technical; military and policy programmes (*Superior No-universitaria Técnica; Escuelas de Sub Oficiales*)	Secondary certificate	Technical certificates	17	20	3	14	No data available for military and policy programmes.	**5B**
5B		Tertiary non-university pedagogical and artistic (*Superior no-universitaria pedeógogica y artistica*)	Secondary certificate	Pedagogical and artistic certificates	17	21-22	4-5	15-16		
5A (1st)		Tertiary university; military and policy programmes (*Superior universitaria; Escuelas de Oficiales*)	Secondary certificate	Bachelor's degree	17	22	5	16		**5A**
5A (2nd)		Master's programmes (*Maestría*)	Bachelor's degree	Master's degree	22	24	2	18		
6		Doctorate programmes (*Doctorado*)	Master's degree	Doctorate degree	24	29	5	23		**6**

PHILIPPINES

ISCED97 level for WEI data collection	Programme orientation	Country description of programme	Entrance requirements	Qualifications awarded	Theoretical starting age (in years)	Theoretical ending age (in years)	Theoretical duration of the programme (in years)	Theoretical cumulative years of education at the end of the programme	Notes
0		Pre-primary		Certificate	3	6	3	...	
1		Elementary		Elementary school leaving certificate	6	12	6	6	
2A	General	Secondary, general (years 1-3)	Primary/ elementary school leaving certificate		12	15	3	9	
3A	General	Secondary, general (year 4)		Secondary school leaving certificate	15	16	1	10	
4A	General	Post-secondary technical vocational programmes	Secondary school leaving certificate	Certificate of proficiency	16	17–19	1–3	11–13	
4C	Vocational	Post-secondary technical vocational programmes	Secondary school leaving certificate	Certificate of proficiency	16	17	< 2	11	
5B		University	Secondary school leaving certificate	Associate of Arts	16	18	2	12	Agricultural technology, secretarial studies, business studies, fine arts, computer studies, midwifery, marine transportation, etc.
5A (1st, medium)		Tertiary programmes	Secondary school leaving certificate	Bachelor's degree	16	20	4	14	Many tertiary institutions require students to pass an entrance examination. Graduates of teacher training institutions are required to take an exam in order to practise.
5A (1st, long)		Tertiary programmes	Secondary school leaving certificate	Bachelor's degree	16	21	5	15	These programmes include engineering and dentistry. Graduates are required to pass an exam in order to practise their professions.
5A (2nd)		Tertiary programmes second stage – professional	Bachelor's degree	Bachelor's degree (medicine, dentistry, engineering, law)	20	24	4	19	These professional programmes include law and medicine. Graduates are required to pass an exam in order to practise their professions.
5A (2nd)		Tertiary programmes second stage	Bachelor's degree	Master's degree	20	22	2	16	Requires defence of a thesis.
6		Doctorate programmes	Master's degree	Doctorate degree	22	24–25	2–3	18–19	Requires defence of a dissertation.

ISCED97 Flows

0 → 1 → 2A → 3A → 4A, 4C, 5B, 5A, 6

RUSSIAN FEDERATION

ISCED97 level for WEI data collection	Programme orientation	Country description of programme	Entrance requirements	Qualifications awarded	Theoretical starting age (in years)	Theoretical ending age (in years)	Theoretical duration of the programme (in years)	Theoretical cumulative years of education at the end of the programme	Notes	ISCED97 Flows
0		Kindergarten			3	6	3	…		**0**
1		Primary			6–7	9–11	3–4	4		**1**
2A	General	Basic general education		Attestat 1	10	15	5	9	Lower secondary education is compulsory for all pupils (Level 2A).	**2A**
3A	General	Secondary, general		Attestat 2	15	17–18	2–3	11	Upper level of secondary education is feasible in gymnasium, lyceum and secondary school; awarded by Attestat 2 of maturity (*zrelost*).	**3A**
3B	Vocational	Secondary, vocational	Entrance examination, Attestat 1	Attestat 2 + Certificate	15	18	3	12		**3B**
3C	Vocational	Secondary, vocational	Entrance examination, Attestat 1	Certificate (short); Attestat 2 + Certificate (long)	15	16–17	1–2	10–11	Feasible in specialised school (uchilische), awarded by: (a) one-year duration: certificate with worker's qualification; (b) two-year duration: Attestat 2, confirm upper secondary education and certificate with worker's qualification.	**3C**
4C	Vocational	Secondary, vocational	Entrance examination, Attestat 2	Certificate	17	18–19	1–2	12–13	Vocational education based on upper secondary education, duration of one year and awarded by certificate with worker's qualification.	**4C**
3B + 5B	Vocational	Secondary, vocational	Entrance examination, Attestat 1	Specialist's diploma 1	15	19	4	13	Secondary special education is combination of ISCED levels 3B and 5B, duration 4 years, based on lower secondary education, awarded by Specialist's diploma 1, confirmed upper secondary level and first stage tertiary education, technician training, teacher training, *etc*.	**3B + 5B**
5B		Post-secondary special programme	Attestat 2; Entrance examination	Specialist's diploma 1	17	20	3	14	Post-secondary special programme based on upper secondary level (11 years). Feasible in colleges and technicums, awarded by Specialist's diploma 1.	**5B**
5A		Basic higher education	Attestat 2; Entrance examination	Bachelor's degree	17	21	4	15	Basic higher education, duration of 4 years in university or institution, awarded by Bachelor's degree.	
5A		Professional higher education	Attestat 2; Entrance examination	Specialist's diploma 2	17	22–23	5–6	16–17	Professional higher education, duration of 5 years in economics and humanities, 5 to 6 years in engineering and 7 years in medicine; awarded by Specialist's diploma 2.	**5A**
5A		University (*Magistratura*)	Bachelor's degree	Master's degree	20	22	2	17	Educational programme with research elements in certain fields of science. Graduates may work as a scientist or a teacher in secondary school and at tertiary level.	
5A		University internship (*Internatura*)	Bachelor's, Master's degree in Medicine	*Internatura*	24	25	1	19		
6		Post-graduate university (*Aspirantura*)	Master's degree, Specialist's diploma 2	*Kandidat nauk*	22–24	25–27	3	20	Requires public defence of an independently elaborated thesis and by final examinations.	**6**
6		Doctorate (*Doktorantura*)	*Kandidat nauk*	*Doktor nauk*	25–27	27–30	2–3	22–23	Requires defence of thesis offering new solutions to a major scientific/academic problem which is of substantial importance to the field or discipline.	

SRI LANKA

ISCED97 level for WEI data collection	Programme orientation	Country description of programme	Entrance requirements	Qualifications awarded	Theoretical starting age (in years)	Theoretical ending age (in years)	Theoretical duration of the programme (in years)	Theoretical cumulative years of education at the end of the programme	Notes	ISCED97 Flows
0		Early childhood programmes			2.5	5	2.5	...	Provided by private sector and local governing bodies.	0
0		Pre-primary			4	5	1	...	Provided by some local governments and private organisations on a fee-paying basis.	
1		Primary			5	10	5	5		1
2A	General	Junior secondary	Primary	Completion of junior secondary	10	14	4	9		2A
3A	General	Upper secondary, ordinary level (O-level)	Completion of junior secondary	General certificate of education (O-level)	14	16	2	11		3A
3A	General	Senior secondary, advanced level (A-level)	General certificate of education (O-level)	General certificate of education (A-level)	16	18	2	13		
3B	Vocational	Technical and vocational	Completion of junior secondary	Certificate	14	16	2	11		3B
5B		College	General certificate of education (A-level)	Diploma or certificate	18	19–22	1–4	14–17		5B
5A (inter., short)		College	General certificate of education (O-level)	Diploma or certificate, entrance to university	18	20	2	15	Includes primary school teacher training.	5A
5A (1st, long)		University	General certificate of education (A-level)	Bachelor's degree	19	22–25	3–6	16–19	Includes secondary school teacher training.	
5A (2nd)		University	Bachelor's degree	Master's degree	22–25	23–27	1–2	17–21		
6		Doctorate	Master's degree	Doctorate	23–27	25+	2+	19+		6

THAILAND

ISCED97 level for WEI data collection	Programme orientation	Country description of programme	Entrance requirements	Qualifications awarded	Theoretical starting age (in years)	Theoretical ending age (in years)	Theoretical duration of the programme (in years)	Theoretical cumulative years of education at the end of the programme	Notes
0		Pre-primary			3	6	3	…	
0		Early childhood development programme			…	…	…	…	
1		Primary			6	12	6	6	
1		Primary (Basic education for adults)		Adult Basic Education Certificate for Primary	any age	…	variable	…	Non-formal education is organised to provide an opportunity for those who have missed formal schooling to have a second chance in education. Not including vocational training and informal education.
2A	General	Lower secondary	Graduation from primary school (Grade 6)	Lower secondary education certificate	12	15	3	9	
2A	General	Lower secondary (Basic education for adults)		Adult Basic Education Certificate for Lower Secondary.	any age	…	variable	…	
3A	General	Upper secondary, general	Graduation from lower secondary school (Grade 9)	Upper secondary education certificate	15	18	3	12	
3A	General	Upper secondary (Basic education for adults)		Adult Basic Education Certificate for Upper Secondary	any age	…	variable	…	
3B	Vocational	Upper secondary, vocational	Graduation from lower secondary school (Grade 9)	Vocational education certificate	15	18	3	12	
3C	General	Upper secondary, education provided by other agencies for specific purposes	Graduation from lower secondary school (Grade 9)	Upper secondary certificate for specialised education in accordance with their needs and expertise.	any age	…	3	…	All responsible agencies have developed their own curricula.
4C	General	Post-secondary non-tertiary	Graduation from upper secondary school	Post-secondary certificate	18	19–20	1–2	13–14	
4C	General	Post-secondary non-tertiary, education provided by other agencies for specific purposes	Graduation from upper secondary school	Post-secondary certificate for specialised education in accordance with their needs and expertise.	any age	…	1–2	…	All responsible agencies have developed their own curricula.
5B		Diploma programmes	Vocational education certificate and upper secondary education, or equivalent	Diploma in vocational education	18	20	2	14	
5A (1st, short)		University level education	Upper secondary education certificate	Bachelor's degree	18	22	4	16	Some subjects are specifically designed for part-time only.
5A (1st, long)		University level education	Upper secondary education certificate	Bachelor's degree	18	23–24	5–6	17–18	Most professional qualifications, including architecture, painting, sculpture, graphic arts and pharmacy (5 years); medicine, dentistry and veterinary science (6 years). Including in 5A (1st, short) programme.
5A (1st, short)		Education provided by other agencies for special purposes	Upper secondary education certificate or upper secondary certificate for specialised education in accordance with their needs and expertise.	Bachelor's degree for specialised education in accordance with their needs and expertise.	approx. 18	22	4	16	Some subjects are specifically designed for part-time only.

ISCED97 Flows

0 → 1 → 2A → 3A, 3B, 3C → 4C → 5B, 5A

THAILAND *(continued)*

ISCED97 level for WEI data collection	Programme orientation	Country description of programme	Entrance requirements	Qualifications awarded	Theoretical starting age (in years)	Theoretical ending age (in years)	Theoretical duration of the programme (in years)	Theoretical cumulative years of education at the end of the programme	Notes	ISCED97 Flows
5A (2nd)		Master's programmes, Post-graduate courses	Bachelor's degree	Master's degree, Graduate diploma	22	24–25	2–3	19–21	Candidates are usually required to submit a research project and a thesis.	
5A (2nd)		Education provided by other agencies for special purposes	Bachelor's degree	Master's degree, Graduate diploma for specialised education in accordance with their needs and expertise.	22	24–25	2–3	18–19	Candidates are usually required to submit a research project and a thesis.	
6		Doctorate programmes	Master's degree	Doctor's degree (Ph.D.)	25	28–29	3–4	22–25		6

TUNISIA

ISCED97 level for WEI data collection	Programme orientation	Country description of programme	Entrance requirements	Qualifications awarded	Theoretical starting age (in years)	Theoretical ending age (in years)	Theoretical duration of the programme (in years)	Theoretical cumulative years of education at the end of the programme	Notes
0		Kindergarten (*Riadh al Atfaal*)			3	6	3	...	
0		Pre-primary (*Tahdhiry*)			5	6	1	...	Programme first introduced in the school year 2001/02
1		Primary (*Ibtidaaiy*)			6	12	6	6	
2A	General	Lower secondary, general (*Ii'daady*)	Completion of primary	Basic education diploma	12	15	3	9	
2B	Vocational	Lower secondary, professional (*Madaris al Mihan*)	Completion of primary	Diploma of technical qualification schools	15	17	2	8	
2C	Vocational	Lower secondary, technical (*Tadrib mihni*)	Completion of primary	Testimonial of apprenticeship	15	17	2	8	
3A	General	Upper secondary, general (*Thanawy*)	Completion of Basic Education	Baccalauréat (upper secondary leaving certificate)	15	19	4	13	
3B	Vocational	Vocational Training (BTP) (*Takwin mihny*)	CAP or 2 years secondary-general	Certificate of Aptitude Professionnal (CAP)	17	19	2	11	
3C	Vocational	Vocational Training (*CAP*) (*Takwin mihny*)	Completion of Basic Education	Certificate of Aptitude Professionnal (CAP)	17	19	2	13	
4B	Vocational	Vocational Training (*BTS*) (*Takwin mihny*)	*Baccalauréat* or BTP	Brevet of Technician Superior (BTS)	19	21	2	15	
5B		Vocational programmes (*Jaami'y*)	*Baccalauéat* or *Brevet de Technicien Professionnel*	*Brevet de Technicien Supérieur*	19	22	3	16	
5A		University (1st & 2nd cycles) (*Jaami'y*)	*Baccalauréat*	Master's degree, engineering degree, Diploma of specialty	19	23	4	17	
6		Doctorate programmes (*Jaami'y*)	Master's degree	*DEA, DESS,* Doctor's degree, (Ph.D.)	23	25	2	19	

ISCED97 Flows

URUGUAY

ISCED97 level for WEI data collection	Programme orientation	Country description of programme	Entrance requirements	Qualifications awarded	Theoretical starting age (in years)	Theoretical ending age (in years)	Theoretical duration of the programme (in years)	Theoretical cumulative years of education at the end of the programme	Notes	ISCED97 Flows
0		Initial education (*Educación Inicial*)			3	6	3	...	Compulsory for 5-year-olds.	**0**
1		Primary (*Primaria*)			6	12	6	6	Compulsory for 6-year-olds.	**1**
1		Basic adult education		Certificate (*Pase escolar*)	15+	18+	3	...		
2A	General	Lower secondary (*Ciclo Básico de Educación Media*)	Primary	Lower secondary certificate	12	15	3	9		**2A**
2B	Pre-vocational	Lower secondary (*Nivel Básico de Educación Técnica*)	Primary	Lower secondary certificate	12	15	3	9		**2B**
3A	General	Upper secondary general (*Bachillerato Diversificado*)	Lower secondary	Upper secondary certificate	15	18	3	12	The Bachillerato gives the right to enrol in the Faculty which corresponds to the option chosen in the second year of diversified education (humanities, science or biology).	**3A**
3A	Vocational	Upper secondary (*Bachillerato Técnico*)	Lower secondary	Upper secondary certificate	15	18	3	12	The Bachillerato gives the right to enrol in the Faculty which corresponds to the option chosen.	
3C	Vocational	Upper secondary (*Formación Profesional Superior*)	Lower secondary	Diploma	15	18	3	12		**3C**
4C	Vocational	Technical courses (*Cursos técnicos terciario*)	Upper secondary	Title *Técnico Terciario*	18	19–20	1–2	13–14		**4C**
5B		Professional qualification (*Carreras Universitarias*)	Upper secondary	Professional qualification	18	21	3	15	Medical Technology Colleges.	**5B**
5B		Teacher training (primary schools) (*Magisterio*)	Upper secondary	Title Teacher Primary	18	21	3	15	Qualification which entitles the holder to teach in a primary school.	
5B		Teacher training (secondary schools) (*Profesorado*)	Upper secondary	Title Teacher Secondary or Teacher Technical	18	22	4	16	Qualification which entitles the holder to teach in a secondary or technical school.	
5B		Tertiary education (*Carreras Universitarias*)	Upper secondary	Title Professional qualification	18	22	4	16	Programmes to train public administrators, business administrators, textile and industrial design.	
5A (medium)		Licenciate programmes (*Carreras Universitarias*)	Upper secondary	*Licenciatura*	18	22–23	4–5	16–17		**5A**
5A (long)		Professional degree programmes (*Carreras Universitarias*)	Upper secondary	Professional degree	18	23–26	5–8	17–20	Dentistry, Law, Medicine, Economics.	
6		Doctorate programmes (*Postgrado*)	*Licenciatura / Ingeniero*	*Doctorado*	22–24	23–26	1–2	18–22	Requires submission of a thesis	**6**

ZIMBABWE

ISCED97 level for WEI data collection	Programme orientation	Country description of programme	Entrance requirements	Qualifications awarded	Theoretical starting age (in years)	Theoretical ending age (in years)	Theoretical duration of the programme (in years)	Theoretical cumulative years of education at the end of the programme	Notes	ISCED97 Flows
0		Pre-school			3	5	2	...		
1		Primary school		Primary school achievement test (Grade 7 certificate)	6	13	7	7		
2A	General	Lower secondary (Form 2)	7 years of primary education	Junior certificate	13	15	2	9		
3C	General	Senior secondary (O-Level)	Form 2	O-level certificate	15	17	2	11		
3A	General	Upper secondary	O-level	A-level certificate	17–18	19-20	2	13	Minimum entry requirement is 5 Ordinary level subjects.	
4C	Vocational	Vocational training	Grade 7, Form 2 and O-level	certificate	17–18	19-20	2	13	Skill Training courses.	
5B		Teaching courses	Five O-level credits or two A-level credits	Primary and secondary teaching certificate	17–18	20-21	3	14	Courses of teaching either at primary or secondary.	
5B		Technical courses	O-level	Technical diploma	17–18	20-21	3	14	College-based training.	
5B		Apprenticeship programmes	O-level	Technical diploma	17–18	21-22	4	15	Industrial-based training.	
5A (1st)		Academic degree programmes	A-level	Bachelor's degree	19	22-23	3–4	16-17	1st degrees.	
5A (2nd)		Master's courses	Bachelor's degree	Master's degree	22	25	3	19-20	Requires submission of a thesis.	
6		Doctorate medical courses	A-level	Doctor of medicine	19	25	6	19	Medical degrees.	
6		Doctorate courses	Master's degree	Doctorate degree	25	28-29	3–4	22-24	Awarded in philosophy, literature, law, science, etc.	

Acknowledgements

This publication is the result of a collective effort by countries participating in the
OECD/UNESCO World Education Indicators programme, and the OECD and UNESCO.

The WEI team at the UNESCO Institute for Statistics consists of
Aurélie Acoca, Michael Bruneforth, Hugo Castellano, Simon Ellis, Katja Frostell, Tin Nam Ho,
Albert Motivans, John Pacifico and Saïd Ould A. Voffal.
This team was responsible for drafting Chapters 1 and 3 and for the production of the report.

The WEI team from the Indicators and Analysis Division of the
OECD Directorate for Education consists of Annette Panzera and Karine Tremblay.
This team was responsible for drafting Chapter 2 with valuable contributions from Nanno Mulder and Neville Postlethwaite.

The WEI Secretariat acknowledges the contribution of other staff of the UNESCO Institute for Statistics and the OECD
who were involved in the data collection, indicator calculation, publication preparation and other activities in the preparation
of this report, and recognises the important contributions of Fung-Kwan Tam to the design and layout of the report.

The following list of names acknowledges the WEI national coordinators, their staff and experts who have taken part in
the preparatory work for this edition of the World Education Indicators Report. The OECD and UNESCO Institute for Statistics
wish to express gratitude for their collegial spirit and valued advice.

Ms. Irene Beatriz Oiberman (Argentina)
Ms. Carmilva Souza Flores (Brazil)
Ms. Oroslinda Maria Taranto Goulart (Brazil)
Ms. Vivian Heyl (Chile)
Mr. Cesar Muñoz (Chile)
Ms. Zhi Hua Lin (China)
Mr. Mohamed Abdul Salam Ragheb (Egypt)
Mr. C. Balakrishnan (India)
Mr. Chander Kant (India)
Mr. S.S. Shokeen (India)
Mr. Ade Cahyana (Indonesia)
Ms. Barbara Allen (Jamaica)
Mr. Dwight Hamilton (Jamaica)
Ms. Janet McFarlane-Edwards (Jamaica)
Ms. Jehad Jamil Abu El-Shaar (Jordan)
Mrs. Khalijah Mohammad (Malaysia)
Ms. Dalila Noemi Zarza Paredes (Paraguay)
Ms. Hilda Gonzalez Garcete (Paraguay)
Ms. Patricia Valdivia Huaringa (Peru)
Mr. Ramon Bacani (Philippines)
Ms. Lilia Roces (Philippines)
Mr. Mark Agranovitch (Russian Federation)
Mr. P. Dias Amarasinghe (Sri Lanka)
Mr. Prabath Nalaka Ilapperuma (Sri Lanka)
Ms. Sirivarn Svastiwat (Thailand)
Mr. Mohsen Ktari (Tunisia)
Ms. Mara Pérez Torrano (Uruguay)
Mr. Thomas Machingaidze (Zimbabwe)
Mr. Farai Choga (Zimbabwe)

The WEI programme, including the preparation of this report, is supported by a grant from
the World Bank Development Grant Facility and by the financial and material support of OECD Member countries
and UNESCO Member States.

———— ■ ————

UNESCO Institute for Statistics, 5255, avenue Decelles, 7th floor, Montreal, Quebec, Canada H3T 2B1
UIS Ref.: UIS/AP/05-02
ISBN: 92-9189-024-3
PRINTED IN CANADA

OECD PUBLICATIONS, 2, rue André-Pascal, 75775 Paris Cedex 16, France
OECD Code: (96 2005 07 1 P1)
ISBN: 92-64-013601 - n°54407 2005
PRINTED IN FRANCE